Disciplines of Virtue

*Girls' Culture in the Eighteenth
and Nineteenth Centuries*

Lynne Vallone

Yale University Press   New Haven and London

Published with assistance from the Department of English, Texas A & M University.

Designed by Sonia L. Scanlon.
Set in Berkeley type by Rainsford Type
Danbury, Connecticut.
Printed in the United States of America by
Edwards Brothers, Inc., Ann Arbor, Michigan.

Library of Congress Cataloging-in-Publication Data

Vallone, Lynne.
    Disciplines of virtue : girls' culture in the eighteenth and nineteenth centuries / Lynne Vallone.
        p.   cm.
    Includes bibliographical references (p.   ) and index.
        ISBN 0-300-06172-2 (acid-free paper)
    1. Teenage girls in popular culture—United States—History. 2. Teenage girls in popular culture—Britain—History. I. Title.
    HQ798.V34   1995
    305.23'5'0973—dc20   94-40559
                            CIP

A catalogue record for this book is available from the British Library.

10 9 8 7 6 5 4 3 2 1

For Howard

I know they will remember all I said to them, that they will be loving children to you, will do their duty faithfully, fight their bosom enemies bravely, and conquer themselves so beautifully, that when I come back to them I may be fonder and prouder than ever of my little women.

Louisa May Alcott, *Little Women*

Contents

Acknowledgments

I am grateful to the publishers for permission to use revised portions of previously published material: "The Crisis of Education: Eighteenth-Century Novels for Girls," *Children's Literature Association Quarterly* 14.2 (Summer 1989): 63–87. © 1989 Children's Literature Association. Reprinted by permission of the Children's Literature Association. "Laughing With the Boys and Learning With the Girls: Humor in Nineteenth-Century American Juvenile Novels," *Children's Literature Association Quarterly* 15.3 (Fall 1990): 127–130. © 1989 Children's Literature Association. Reprinted by permission of the Children's Literature Association. " 'A humble Spirit under Correction': Tracts, Hymns, and the Ideology of Evangelical Fiction for Children, 1780–1820." Reprinted by permission of *The Lion and the Unicorn.* " 'The True Meaning of Dirt': Putting Good and Bad Girls in Their Place(s)," from *The Girl's Own: Cultural Histories of the Anglo-American Girl, 1830–1915,* edited by Claudia Nelson and Lynne Vallone. Copyright © 1994 by The University of Georgia Press, Athens. By permission of the publisher. "In the Image of Young America: Girls of the New Republic." Reprinted with permission of the Children's Literature Association.

I am very grateful for the personal, professional, and institutional support I have received in the course of the making of this book, and would like to extend my thanks here. The College of Liberal Arts at Texas A&M University awarded me a Summer Research Grant in 1991 that afforded me not only precious time to write, free from teaching responsibilities, but also funded a research trip to the Osborne Collection of Early Children's Books in Toronto,

Canada. Dana Tenny and her staff at the Osborne Collection were always knowledgeable, helpful, and courteous, before, during, and after my stay at Boys and Girls House.

The Department of English at Texas A&M University has proven to be a wonderful environment for scholarship and teaching. My department head, J. Lawrence Mitchell, has been a valued supporter of my work from the beginning. I have many colleagues to thank for their encouragement, kindness, and willingness to read parts of this manuscript: David R. Anderson, Margaret J. M. Ezell, Howard Marchitello, Robert Newman, and Mary Ann O'Farrell. Their comments have proven indispensable. My thanks to Jeffrey N. Cox for his friendship and willingness to help with everything—especially computers. This book has also been immeasurably aided by Pamela R. Matthews's camaraderie and astute readings. Without her unfailing good humor and unflagging support, the writing process would have been a lot less fun.

Through its lecture series, conferences, and colloquia, the Interdisciplinary Group for Historical Literary Study has created an ideal atmosphere for work and play. Always lively, challenging, and perceptive, the fellows and members of the group—especially Jeffrey N. Cox and Larry J. Reynolds—have formed an inspirational community of scholars. I am greatly indebted to the group for the course reductions awarded to me in 1991–94.

I have also been aided in crucial moments by the support of Gillian Adams, Sylvia P. Iskander, Bill Moebius, and Claudia Nelson. Charles Grench has been a thoughtful and conscientious editor.

My debts to my family are perhaps the greatest. Through the years leading up to this book, my parents, John and Phyllis Vallone, have offered much valuable household advice and loving child care. My children, Max and Rosalie, have provided love and laughter, as well as a sense of what's important. My deepest gratitude goes to my husband, Howard Marchitello, for sharing and nuancing every aspect of this book. To my very best reader and very best friend, *i miei più sentiti ringraziamenti.*

Introduction

Pamela, Alice, and Jo

Five little girls, of Five, Four, Three, Two, One:

Rolling on the hearthrug, full of tricks and fun.

Five rosy girls, in years from Ten to Six:

Sitting down to lessons—no more time for tricks.

Five growing girls, from Fifteen to Eleven:

Music, Drawing, Languages, and food enough for seven!

Five winsome girls, from Twenty to Sixteen:

Each young man that calls, I say "Now tell me which

you mean!"

Five dashing girls, the youngest Twenty-one:

But, if nobody proposes, what is there to be done?

Five showy girls—but Thirty is an age

When girls may be engaging, but they somehow

don't engage.

Lewis Carroll, from "A Game of Fives" (1869)

1

An admirer and yet a critic of girls, Lewis Carroll figures the calculus of girl-hood's trajectory in his light verse about the "ages of girls." Unlike the sardonic narrator of *Peter Pan* who announces at the outset that "two is the beginning of the end,"[1] Carroll's fanciful assessment extends girlhood past puberty to "Five dressy girls, of Thirty-one or more" and ultimately to "Five *passé* girls,"[2] identifying the "end" not with the consciousness of growing up—that is, of mortality—but of marriage. Mateless, the girl is held suspended in time, yet she is also increasingly made a figure of fun as she ages. The girl's anxious expectation humorously dismissed by Carroll identifies the point of departure for this book: literary and nonliterary constructions of desirability and mar-riageability. Nina Auerbach notes that "though as verbal and visual artist Car-roll's one true subject was the little girl, his fascination stems not from her littleness but from her potential to grow big."[3] Alice's final growth spurt in *Alice's Adventures in Wonderland* is crossly remarked upon by the Dormouse— "You've no right to grow *here*"—but Alice is able to disarm his complaint by turning it back to him, and by extension, to every childlike figure in the book: "Don't talk nonsense . . . you know you're growing too."[4] The subject of my study is similarly the "growing" girl and her culture's attempts to anticipate, remark, and control that growth. The book does not attempt to cover the entire field of girls' culture; the topic can be broadly or narrowly defined, and its treatment here is necessarily personal and idiosyncratic.[5] I have focused on some significant elements of eighteenth- and nineteenth-century girls' culture found in children's literature, conduct literature, and historical and cultural practices. The ideal of charity and charitable institutions, the domestic science movement, the intersection of class and gender in religious tracts, and literary representations of play are among the topics that help to create the cultural climate of fictional and actual girlhood.

Adolescent girlhood has been represented in literature as a dangerous time for females and for those who care for them: it is in girlhood that the moral values instilled in childhood are tested. The "good" adolescent girl is defined by her virginity—her physical capacity for sexual relations but her mental resistance to these relations before the "proper" moment—and the "bad" girl by her miscalculation of that same moment. The girl's journey from marriage-able to married, maiden to matron, is the focus and fascination of many literary texts of the eighteenth and nineteenth centuries. I will explore this moment of concentrated attention from the wide-angle lens of cultural critique, interro-gating and refocusing our attention on the significance of aestheticized girls' culture. This study investigates girlhood with the evidence supplied not only by eighteenth- and nineteenth-century British and American literature (children's and "adult"), but also by conduct manuals and conduct novels written to guide and reform its youthful readers; religious tracts that inscribe the lower-class girl's expectations within the rigidly enforced boundaries of production and class; institutions of "girlhood gone wrong" including eighteenth-century English asylums for penitent prostitutes and rescue homes in late nineteenth-century America; and social and legal practices such as the dowry system that allowed for the economic transfer of value from the upper-class girl's "jewel" of chastity to her bride-price.

In examining the organization of the rescue home, for example, or the practice of marriage settlements and their ideological bases, I contextualize girls' culture in social, literary, and women's history. Each text has a story to tell about girls, while its authors (upper-class philanthropists, conduct manual experts, social reformers, novelists, legal theoreticians, Evangelicals) are themselves revealed in its telling. My treatment of girls' culture highlights and examines in depth those cultural practices that relate particularly to sexuality and to class, two of the "essential" elements of girlhood that determine the womanhood to follow.

The book is framed by chapters on female institutional reform. Chapter 1 describes eighteenth-century England's Magdalen Hospital for penitent prostitutes and the feminine ideal of charity; chapter 6 discusses the Florence Crittenton Homes for unwed mothers of late nineteenth-century America and their adoption of the domestic science movement's values. In chapter 2, the rhetorical form and function of Hannah Woolley's conduct manual and housekeeping compendium, *The Gentlewomans Companion* (1675), is read in conjunction with Richardson's conduct novel, *Pamela* (vols. 1–4, 1740–41), and its earliest abridgment for children (1756). Chapter 3 discusses the cultural practice of assigning dowry as it is represented in novels (which were avidly read by girls), as well as its legal dimensions and reportage in periodicals and newspapers of the eighteenth century. Chapter 4 examines the institutional organization of England's Sunday school movement and the tracts it produced alongside examples of conduct novels by Hannah More, Mary Brunton, and Jane Austen. Chapter 5 examines nineteenth-century American girls' series books, Louisa May Alcott's *Little Women,* and Mark Twain's *Adventures of Tom Sawyer* and the function of humor and play as a social action both within and without the texts.

This book assumes that the study of girls' culture and girls' reading is crucial to our understanding of femininity, women's history and literature, and ideologies of domesticity, conduct, and class. The history of the novel and the history of "adolescent" or "children's" literature are inextricably linked. In general, however, histories of the development of the novel fail to include children's literature, or refuse to see the implications for the novel of an adolescent (female) readership. Michael McKeon's *Origins of the English Novel, 1600–1740,* for example, while brilliantly discussing the genre's formation, ignores the impact or elides issues of age and gender in his analysis.[6] And yet, the virtually unanimous injunction against novel reading found in conduct literature, periodicals, and didactic fiction for girls and young women from the seventeenth to the twentieth centuries attests to the significance and perceived danger of that readership's literary "hunger." Eighteenth-century female conduct novelists like Mary Brunton, Eliza Haywood, Maria Edgeworth, Fanny Burney, and Charlotte Smith, among others, attempted to address the sociopsychological needs of a female audience by penning books that combined romance, courtship, and desirable behavioral precepts in their plots and characterizations. Samuel Richardson wrote *Pamela* in part for the edification of the "youth of Both Sexes," and Burney linked *Evelina* with the "young ladies and boarding school damsels who read novels."[7]

We find that the warning against novels remained constant; the pathetic "A very recent testimony from a Dying Girl" printed in *The Florence Crittenton League of Compassion: Story of a Great Philanthropy* recounts in a deathbed confession the dangers of novel reading and its attendant vices: "Only a few hours and I shall lie in the silent grave; but in my last moments let me warn one and all; beware of beer; beware of novels; and shun the saloon; these three wrought my downfall. . . . The first step in my downfall was the reading of novels. I reveled in these stories with great delight. They led me to take a second step, which was the theater, then the dance, and then came evil associates, drink and the saloon."[8]

J. Paul Hunter has described the underground system developed by young novel lovers in order to share forbidden reading.[9] The literary "contraband" that I pass along in this study is an eclectic mix of popular fiction such as Hannah More's bestseller, *Coelebs in Search of A Wife*; such literary classics as *Pamela, Little Women,* and *Mansfield Park*; newly canonized works by women like *Evelina*; religious writing like the Cheap Repository Tracts and sermons preached on behalf of penitent prostitutes; "nonliterary" texts like conduct manuals and advice books, forgotten female authors including Mary Brunton; and the representation and actual practice of giving dowry and arranging marriage settlements. In the following chapters I put these texts together in the attempt to offer a context for girls' culture in the eighteenth and nineteenth centuries.

This study offers not only a context for girls' culture in the eighteenth and nineteenth centuries, but is also a book about beloved girl characters. In creating girls' culture and helping to define it, Pamela, Alice, and Jo oversee and inform the chapters that follow. Like all literary and living girls, each of these characters is not only growing, she is also falling—into adulthood and its sexual, commercial, and social concerns. Although Pamela, Alice, and Jo can carry Homeric epithets of their exemplary or endearing qualities—pious Pamela, inquisitive Alice, tomboy Jo—their characters are much greater than these phrases would imply. They, and other literary heroines whose stories follow, have struggled with the complicated requirement for good girlhood that I take as the epigraph for this book: in the words of Father March, "to fight their bosom enemies bravely, and conquer themselves so beautifully."[10] The successful girl internalizes the implicit or explicit ideological messages communicated by her reading, her family, her community, her social class, her sexuality, and finds, ultimately, that happiness and virtue lie within her self-control. Pamela, Alice, and Jo each have moments of doubt, but many occasions of personal triumph: Pamela is constant, Alice is angry, and Jo is independent. And yet, we could revise this equation and arrive at a different but equally accurate and revealing statement: Pamela is independent (in her thoughts), Alice is constant (in her quest to find the garden), Jo is angry (we assume, like her mother, "nearly every day of [her] life" [79]). Each girl must decide how to conquer and then channel her girlish nature—characterized by desire, hunger, anger, ignorance, and aggression—into valuable, beautiful womanly conduct. The means by which this aestheticized conquest can occur, I argue, is communicated by girls' culture. The relationship between feminine conduct and feminine value—for example, charity (chapter 1), physical decorum (chapter 2), silence (chapter 3), Christian meekness (chapter 4), domesticity (chapter 5), and chastity (chapter 6)—is explored by reading complex cultural and textual ideologies manifest in the literature, institutions, and figures of girlhood.

1

The Pleasure of the Act

Charity, Penitence, and Narrative

～～～◯

As [charity] cleaneth the Spirit from the Corruptions of the

World, and from the Filthiness of the Flesh, so it replenisheth

the Soul with the Greatest Satisfaction and Pleasure.

Edward Pelling, *A Practical Discourse Upon Charity* (1693)

Lock'd in each others Arms, by Passion led,

Insensibly she drop'd upon the bed.

I'll say no more, now you may think the rest,

Good the beginning was, the end was best.

Richard Head, *The Miss Display'd* (1675)

Richard Head's *The Miss Display'd, With all her Wheedling Arts and Circumventions, in Which Historical Narration are detected, Her Selfish* Contrivances, *Modest* Pretences, *and Subtil* Strategems, "anatomizes" the story of an Irish prostitute's body in order to warn young male readers against the dangers of her text: "Doubtlesly there are good Women in the World, but they are so few, by reason of the spreading Contagion of their vicious inclinations, that thereby some are induced to believe, that it is onely a supposed goodness, and as imaginary as a Circle in the Firmament. Begging pardon for this digression, I shall leave the good and bad promiscuously one amongst the other; onely pick one out of the flock (a scabbed sheep) whom I shall anatomize, or cut into pieces, for the benefit of such, who will take the pains to read a Lecture on her Carcass."[1] Cornelia, the "heroine" of Head's lecture, possesses an extravagantly beautiful body: "and to compleat her excellency, the rare symmetry of every part of her body was so charming and magnetical, that it was impossible to look on and not be attracted to her."[2] To see her is to want her. And yet, I argue, the most compelling aspect of Cornelia for Head and for all who tell the stories of girls, is not her sexually attractive physical body, but rather the *narration* of her body, the "form" of her fiction.[3] The pleasure Cornelia's body/story affords the narrator is one of participation; we can imagine a kind of prurient interest in the prostitute's physical beauty and sexual adventures, but the greater pleasurable fantasy involves not the fictional body itself, but the body as "historical narrative," that is, as a literal text that can be recovered and understood. This assertion of the truth of her body allows for equal access, for open analysis of it—in the same way that an anatomy lays bare the woman's internal body and opens it up for interpretation—for all "doctors" of social disease.

Richard Head's revealing exegesis of one prostitute's story is the generic equivalent of the criminal biography, popular for its lurid details and descriptions of underworld society and politics. Another significant genre in this vein is the biography of the reclaimed social transgressor: the reformed, the converted, the penitent. The histories of these women, too, have a place in the narratives of pleasure.[4] The prostitute and the penitent are here brought together in the act of charity that renames the "fallen woman" an "unfortunate female."[5] This conflation gives rise to new stories of the pleasure of the act of relinquishment: the penitent resolving (turning away from), the charitable sacrificing (giving up to), the narrator revealing (giving away all). It is exactly this giving (up) of such disparate "possessions" as the prostitute's body (as a means of exchange), and the charitable's income that creates a kind of identity for the prostitute and for the charitable individual that is critical to the telling of their stories and that allows for the communication of the writer's (in this instance, Head's) conception of female sexuality and feminine value.[6] The prostitute becomes the "penitent" who gains both a place in society (however low) and in Heaven; the charitable woman becomes the "virtuous" who also gains a certain social/religious status for her self-sacrifice. The pleasure is not only denial, and may not be denial at all, but the *formation* of identity: the penitent thinking of herself, the charitable thinking of herself, and the narrator—not always male—imagining the Other in relationship to himself or herself.

In contrast to the symmetry and completeness of her body, Cornelia's story is unfinished. Head's narrator informs the reader of all that he knows: when Cornelia leaves England's shores for France in order to increase her language skills (she already knows Greek and Latin), Head's history also ends. The indeterminacy of Cornelia's future allows the narrator of her story the potential for further access to her body/story and greater "play," greater pleasure in the language of her life/story.

In didactic literature for girls—cautionary tales, conduct manuals, novels—there exists a similar desire to tell the story of the "bad girl" as a warning to all who would read her text and either share or avoid her fate. As Amanda Anderson notes, there is a natural affinity between the sexual "error" and narrative: "fallenness is assimilated to narrative itself, identified or equated with a 'downward path.' "[7] The impulse to tell the story of the bad girl, to reveal what is hidden and therefore dangerous about her, is so strong that she becomes a negative emblem, a bad example, and a compulsive addition to texts for girls, the interjection of a (usually) lower-class character into texts for a middle-class readership. The ideological urge to compare the bad with the good, to punish or transform the bad into the good, is both class- and gender-based; differentiation is necessary in order to preserve social order, and to uphold moral values. This urge is prevalent not only in fictional constructions, but in historical institutions as well.[8] This first chapter focuses on the idea of the bad girl (here the prostitute) and the ideal of charity and demonstrates how these two ideological "obsessions" coalesce in considerations of the figure of the eighteenth- and nineteenth-century girl as both fictional construct and as reader of an "adolescent" literature.

My understanding of the charity girl's dual nature—as both giver and recipient—reflects the ideological designs of femininity in the literary and cultural history of eighteenth- and nineteenth-century England. That is, I describe the ways in which middle-class English society attempted to formulate the *idea* of the prostitute (how she was to be interpreted, contained, and controlled) through the establishment of charitable institutions for penitent "fallen" young women that were based upon the conduct manual *ideal* of the domestic (charitable) female. The paradigmatic white middle-class lady-in-training prescribed in conduct books and brought to life in conduct novels, gives money, goods, and time to the poor, and in return receives reciprocal personal value. This value can best be described as both moral and aesthetic; by behaving according to a certain set of norms (extending home duties to include caring for the poor) delineated through conduct manuals, sermons, periodicals, and novels, the girl becomes valuable as a member of an ideologically "superior class" who will recreate those conduct-manual values in subsequent generations. Her value has an aesthetic appeal as charitable actions increase the "beauty" of her nature and highlight the picturesque and didactic aspects of the innocent sacrificing for her social "inferiors."[9]

Before turning to my examination of specific texts and institutions concerned with ideologies of femininity and behavior, I would like to define my use of related terms that are key to my discussion below. "Charity," of course, has both common and religious meanings that have evolved from the Latin *caritas* which is, generally, the Christian ideal of love. My use of "Charity" refers specifically to the Pauline sense of the word as the greatest Christian grace, characterized in part by its negatives: "Charity suffereth long, and is kind; charity envieth not, charity vaunteth not itself, is not puffed up. Doth not behave itself unseemly, seeketh not her own, is not easily provoked, thinketh no evil" (1 Corinthians 4–5). I will concentrate, however, on "charity," an extrapolation from *caritas* denoting benevolence to the poor, almsgiving, and other measures for the relief of the needy.[10] My use of the term "philanthropy," by contrast, is the most general of the three, as it denotes the practical assistance of charity, which comes from humankind's love and concern for itself, not necessarily originating in the Christian sense of following the example of God's (Christ's) love for humanity. In other words, "philanthropy" contains "charity."

Frances Power Cobbe's *Essays on the Pursuits of Women* (1836) distinguishes between the roles of men and women in philanthropic pursuits. She understands these differences to be analogous to the complementary relationships men and women have to jurisprudence: feminine virtue governs the laws of the heart and soul, and masculine ethics establishes social and moral laws.

Cobbe imagines the best figure of a female philanthropist by combining her body (which both houses these internal laws and undertakes charitable work) with the social "body" of laws created by men: "We want her sense of the law of love to complete man's sense of the law of justice . . . we want her influence, inspiring virtue by gentle promptings from within to complete man's external legislation of morality. And, then, we want woman's practical service. We want her genius for detail, her tenderness for age and suffering, her comprehension of the wants of childhood to complete man's gigantic charities."[11]

Thus, man's laws are "seen" (as text, read in action) and woman's laws are "felt" (in sympathy, in Christian love).[12] The indeterminate and "universal" nature of "masculine" philanthropy—"man's" love of "mankind"—is distinct from the charity promoted as necessarily forming part of virtuous woman's conduct. In the following pages, as in the above discussion of *The Miss Display'd,* I will discuss stories told about "bad" girls (especially former prostitutes) in sermons, pamphlets, reports, conduct manuals, and apocryphal lore of seventeenth-, eighteenth-, and nineteenth-century England. My focus here is on the penitent prostitute and her relationship to the charitable institution. I suggest, ultimately, that the "girls of charity"—recipient and the giver—are joined not only in the gestures of outstretched hands, filled and empty, but in the societal scrutiny that is turned upon them both. The pursuit of "pleasure" defines the particular behavior of each: the storytellers (of sermons or of the novels for middle-class girls I discuss in subsequent chapters) create female characters whose sexuality can be regulated and contained; the penitents rapturously pray for a return to virtue, and the charitable girls are rewarded on earth with personal and "material" satisfaction. Or so says the cultural and literary ideology that constructs an ideal of female behavior that quickly dissolves into the norm.

On May 7, 1811, the Reverend Melville Horne preached a sermon celebrating the fourth anniversary of the founding of the London Female Penitentiary. Designed to become an inexpensive advertisement of sorts for the Penitentiary (copies sold for one shilling), this sermon, like others of its genre, first encourages its readers to sympathize with the Penitentiary's aims and its inmates, and then persuades them to donate money for the expansion of its efforts. The goal of the London Female Penitentiary was "to afford an Asylum to females who, having deviated from the paths of virtue, are desirous of being restored by religious instruction, and the formation of moral and religious habits, to a respectable station in society."[13] The sermon's topic is forgiveness toward prostitutes in particular, and the virtue of Charity in general. Horne takes as his text Luke's description of the penitent prostitute who, in bathing Christ's feet with her tears and wiping them with her hair, reveals her great love and great sorrow: "And, behold a woman in the city, who was a sinner, when she knew that Jesus sat at meat in the Pharisee's house, brought an alabaster box of ointment, and stood at his feet behind him weeping, and began to wash his feet with tears, and did wipe them with the hairs of her head, and kissed his feet, and anointed them with the ointment" (Luke 7:36–50).

In his discussion of this tableau, Horne compares the prostitute with the prodigal son and indicates that polite society's response to those fallen women now residing in London ought to be as forgiving and as loving as that of the biblical father who celebrated his penitent son's return. By naming her "prodigal," Horne emphasizes the woman's place in the narrative as main character, de-emphasizing, by turn, the greater biblical message of the scene that exposes both the Pharisee Simon's pride in his "little sins" as well as his "little love." In the creation of a heroine for this text (Luke's and Horne's own), then, Horne satisfies the narratological desire—arising, in part, from the fear of the unknown—that accompanies a woman seemingly without a known or knowable story (her story cannot literally be known, and as prostitute she has been sexually "known," but her story of sinfulness cannot be known—understood—by the virtuous) by filling her story's gaps with the history of her childhood, fall, and redemption. It seems obvious that Horne becomes involved in the literary story he tells about the biblical character: she is a sinner, but one who has fallen *from* grace and privilege; presumably she can, therefore, be recalled *to* grace.[14] Like the prodigal son, the woman completes a circular movement back to the goodness she has forsaken, a movement not without importance, as she is returned, and restored to society, to culture.[15] Although a wretched sinner in the eyes of society (Simon stands for all "Pharisees"), she is less "other" than she would have been if born to begging and misery. We see this appeal to identification over and over in any plea for charitable assistance: the charitable person must recognize himself or herself (or someone he or she loves) in the fallen other.

The story of the penitent prostitute offered a familiar narrative to readers: degeneration and the promise of redemption spiced with sexual transgression. It is precisely the conflated story of a dichotomized female sexuality that defines the attraction of institutions such as the London Female Penitentiary and sermons like Horne's, for the enjoyment of the dramatic and suspenseful narrative of both unlicensed and domestic female sexuality housed in one body is both irresistible and socially sanctioned. "As close to fiction as to life," the penitent and her story conflate into a single fascinating object to observe.[16] The ideology of charity compels persons, if not morally requiring them, to read this text and give. Of course, the perceived moral distance between the righteous and penitent also enables sacrifice on the part of the "upright" in the name of the "fallen" in order to maintain that separation. This relationship is most easily facilitated when, in the case of the prostitute, the girl is seduced or kidnapped, or in some manner changed from essentially good (good or good-enough class, good conduct, good education) to temporarily debased.[17] The charitable person finds it easier to give, so the theory goes, when the needful persons's identity seems to be mistaken, or shaken from an essential innocence.[18] Through charity the "true" identity—one of reassuring sameness and worth as opposed to threatening difference and worthlessness—can be restored to the penitent.

In Horne's sermon, the narratological desire is satisfied when he recasts the unnamed biblical "woman of the city" in the mold of the familiar myth of the depraved London prostitute:[19] "She had forgotten the good instructions of her youth, and cast off the fear of her God; renounced the modesty of her sex, and braved the censures of the world. At first weak, she soon became vicious. Corrupted, she learned to be a corrupter. The scorn of her own sex, the pernicious Syren lured to ruin every youth void of understanding, who came within the influence of her sorceries. Having, perhaps, brought the grey heads of her own Parents with sorrow to the grave, she had become a terror to every father and mother of her neighbourhood" (6). She also contains the seeds of repentance, however. As suggested above, the sinner must come from goodness, as it is assumed to be easier to return to childhood's innocence than to forge virtue as an unreclaimed adult. The anonymous author of *Remedies for the Wrongs of Women* (1844) asserts in the petition presented before Parliament urging the enactment of strict laws to punish those who directly promote the "illicit" sexual relations in "infants" (people under 21 years of age), as well as any person connected with keeping a brothel where "infants" are housed for wrongful intercourse, "it has been usual to regard these unfortunate beings as *the daughters of crime,* whereas they are generally *the children of misfortune.* . . . Poverty and the want of female occupation, coupled with a defective system of moral and religious education, for which the poor sufferers themselves are not to blame, appear to be, so far as they contribute to their own ruin, the chief cause of their misfortune."[20]

Described by Horne as an inebriate as well as a prostitute, our tearful "Mary Magdalene" (Horne later asserts that Gospel history has considered her to be that famous penitent harlot) suffers the "stings of remorse" which will lead to her repentance.[21] (The exorcism of the seven devils which Luke mentions in the eighth chapter also aids her redemption.) Horne substantiates with "facts" his story of Mary Magdalene's life and background: "This Mary of Magdala, for so we will call her, appears to have been a woman of some rank, education, and fortune; otherwise, she would hardly have been mentioned with the wife of Herod's steward [in Luke 8:2], as ministering to the Lord of her substance, or as coming with spices to embalm his body" (8). These facts also indicate the special viciousness of her prostitution because she clearly, then, did not resort to selling sexual acts as a means of survival, but "volunteered" them (9). While we do not know how Mary Magdalene was first introduced to a life of prostitution, Horne seems to forget here his earlier sympathy for the girl seduced or kidnapped from her respectable station in life. Horne's passionate and dramatic imaginings, however, describe her as once beautiful, made monstrous only by the seven devils who come to inhabit her body: "That once alluring eye now rolled in terrific phrensy; that graceful person, distorted by hideous epilepsy, had lost its power to please" (9). The sensual aesthetic of the alabaster box which the "woman from the city" brings to Simon's house to anoint Christ, signifies her past sins of consensual appetite: a decorative "toy" in the service of bodily pleasure, "the ornament of her formerly luxurious toilet" (10). Within Simon's house, however, the box signifies penitence, abasement, and domestic, rather than sexual, servitude.

At this moment Mary's relationship to her body is yet again renamed by Horne—from self-conscious beauty, to demonic possession and distortion, to housewifely distraction: "She enters modest and silent, with her hair loose and neglected, her countenance downcast, and suffused with burning blushes. With a timid eye she enquires for her Lord, and, while every countenance is fixed on her with astonishment and abhorrence, she steals with slow steps along, till she stands behind her Saviour" (10). With her body (tears and tresses) and for forgiveness of her body (her passions, her "ill-treatment" of her body) she cleanses the body of Christ. This retelling of the biblical story highlights the moment of self-abnegation of the body that the penitent prostitute must effect in order to appear truly repentant; her use of her body and its products to honor Christ, is, at the same time, the most eroticized moment as well. This paradox marks a change from a temporal, earth(l)y obsession with the body and its appetite to a heavenly "aphysical" disregard for the body. Mary Magdalen's prostration/prostitution before Christ is so affective precisely in its relationship to bodies. In addition to its erotic elements, Horne's dramatic story that traces the prostitute from beauty to ugliness, from straight-backed pride to stooped submission, from wealth to poverty, has the elements of tragedy although, of course, the ending, in a religious sense, is the most successful of all: the happy return to the Father.

At this moment in Horne's text, the prostitute as forgiven prodigal is effectively paired with recent inmates of the London Female Penitentiary whom Horne is attempting to benefit with his sermon. Horne tells some success stories as examples: "The Daughter of a respectable character was in the Penitentiary 18 months. Her Father was reconciled; and, dying while she was in the house, left her £1500, and a Legacy of £100 to the Institution" (22), and "Two have been reconciled to their Husbands in consequence of having been received into the Penitentiary" (23).[22] These brief tales reveal the monetary pleasures of London's major charities: the pleasure of this repetitious institutional act of regeneration, *for* the needy penitents, but also *as a result of* the needy penitents. This is the pecuniary value of forgiveness, as opposed to the biblical understanding of its spiritual value.

The relationship between the penitent prostitute and the literary heroine is further demonstrated at the close of Horne's sermon where he fantasizes the "gothic" exclamation of one of the four hundred prostitutes who had been turned away from the penitentiary for lack of room (hence the plea for greater funds to expand the facility): "O Sir, when the door of the Penitentiary was shut against me, the cup of salvation seemed snatched from my feverish lips. My feet were rooted to the spot; my limbs trembled. The night seemed to assume a tenfold blackness, and despair froze my heart. No tear could flow; no groan found utterance. As I recovered from my stupor, I retired with slow reluctance. Then I cried, now hath a father's curse blasted me indeed, and my mother's broken heart is required of me. As these gates, so are those of heaven for ever closed against me" (30).

At this point, Horne's need to write himself into the text also reveals his desire to control the prostitute's story—from the literary character he summons to an "actual" person he creates in the fictional narrative of his sermon. The imagined heroine later hears of a sermon to be preached for the penitentiary (Horne places himself in the text not only as the speaker of that sermon, but as the "sir" to whom the girl has made her plea), which, we assume, will offer her some hope of assistance. As we have seen, Horne has clearly convinced himself of the penitent's need through his own rhetorical strategy of constructing his sermon's heroine in the image of the "literary" Mary of Magdala superimposed upon a London prostitute.

We might ask, then, whose body is in the text? Helena Michie's discussion of D. G. Rosetti's poem about a sleeping prostitute, "Jenny," asserts that "from the beginning of the poem a slow process of metaphorization distances both reader and speaker from [Jenny's] body, first by use of conventional tropes and finally by the transfiguration of Jenny herself into a sign."[23] I would argue that in the sermons preached in support of charities for fallen women, however, these same conventional tropes and objectifications bring the reader *closer* to the prostitute's body/story (as in Head's narrative of Cornelia, the sexual woman's body *is* her story) rather than separating them. Yet it is accurate to say that the sermons are body-less in that the penitent prostitute—the conflated figure of biblical character, daughter, sister, and siren—is quite literally *every-body*.[24]

Women have historically participated in philanthropy primarily in their two circumstances of relative power over property, enabled in both cases by death—their husbands' or their own. In the earliest recorded history of philanthropy in England (from the fifteenth century), however, the significantly greater amounts were donated by men. The explanations for this phenomenon are, of course, apparent enough: a woman had little control over real property or her donations were subsumed under her husband's name.[25] Yet later economic and social conditions, especially during the nineteenth century, enabled women to spend more time in relieving the wants of the poor and offered them greater opportunities to wield their feminine influence outside of the home. The anonymous author of "Charity as a Portion of the Public Vocation of Women" (1859) strongly advocated charity work as the proper venue for female energy: "Women have it in their power to give that which is invaluable in the cause—leisure, thought, and sympathy. In charity there will ever be found a congenial sphere for the fruition of the unemployed energies of women."[26] This is not to say that one day women were awakened by a cry in the streets which alerted them to the fulfilling possibilities of charity work; as an ideological construct, charity work and almsgiving had traditionally been considered part of women's domestic duty—here for the benefit of the "world's family" (or at least those religiously and politically sanctioned peoples such as the "deserving" English poor, the heathen, and the enslaved) rather than one's own nuclear family and neighborhood.[27] As W. K. Jordan notes in *Philanthropy in England, 1480–1660,* the doctrine of "good works" was a central tenet in the Protestant faith upon which "the whole great edifice of Protestant charity must be securely and eternally built."[28]

Popular ideologies of femininity promulgated by both men and women in conduct books, sermons, and periodicals stressed that the woman, with her difference from man expressed both as saintly and childlike, was especially suited to perform charitable works as an extension of the domestic ideology that kept her arts in the home. Her skills in needlework, food preparation, and children's education were brought together to help clothe, feed, and educate the poor. The charitable activities of women included visiting the poor and sick, making them clothes and linens, donating money to relief societies, educating children in Sunday schools, working in "rescue" homes for prostitutes and "fallen" women, and conducting missionary work by distributing bibles and religious tracts.

The original asylum for penitent prostitutes in London was the Magdalen Hospital (or Magdalen House), established in 1758 (admitting eight penitents) and incorporated in 1769.[29] Its successes helped to spawn other similar projects, among them the London Female Penitentiary (1807) for female criminals, the British Female Penitent Refuge (1829), the London Society for the Protection of Young Females (1835), the London Female Mission (1836), and the Westminster Penitent Female Asylum (1837).[30] *Metropolitan Charities* (1844) attempted to classify comprehensively various London charities (including, for example, dispensaries, almshouses, colleges, annuity funds, and penitentiaries) to aid benevolent persons in choosing among the various charitable institutions for donations. "Voluntary funding," as Ann Jessie Van Sant argues, helped create the "socially conservative" nature of institutions like the Magdalen Hospital: voluntary funding "implied that the relief of distress should be a moral obligation, to be voluntarily assumed, rather than a legal provision on which the distressed could depend—in marked contrast to the Poor Law, which, however illiberally administered, potentially redefined the status of the needy, making them dependent not on a system of reciprocal obligations but on the law."[31]

The institution "flourished," however, under these conditions and the Magdalen Hospital was, by its own statistics, quite successful in the reformation of young prostitutes throughout the years it operated: from 1758 to January 4, 1802, out of the 3,437 admissions to the hospital, 2,230 girls left under the category "Reconciled to friends, or placed in service." Some girls (those admitted were between 16 and 20 years of age) were lost to death (66), mental disorders or other illnesses (99), self-discharge (499), or discharge resulting from "improper behaviour" (476).[32]

The 1802 "By-Laws and Regulations of the Magdalen Hospital" painstakingly outlined the rigidly organized and programmatic nature of the institution. For example, the penitent underwent a 15-step process for admission into the house. The training she received in the house, it was believed, would "rehabilitate" her for mainstream society and allow her to earn and keep the social value attributed to "honest" domestic labor.[33] Admission to the facility was by "petition" only[34]; step six of the required application process reduced each petitioner to a number that served to identify both the applicant and any recommendations of support written on her behalf. The petitioners were called by their numbers which served to protect them, for if the petitioner was not admitted, her identity would not be revealed. Every petitioner was physically examined (those who were pregnant or diseased were disqualified) and questioned by the governing board,[35] which was allowed to ask "only such questions as are likely to enable them to judge whether the petitioners are proper objects to be received into the Hospital."[36] The approval of two thirds of the all-male board was necessary for admission to the institution. If not admitted, the applicant could reapply at any time, but once admitted, could never seek a second admission, even if she had fallen into her previous means of livelihood.[37] The attendants of the house—physician, chaplain, matron, doorkeeper, and so on—were measured against certain profiles to determine eligibility for employment. The physician was required to be a married man (or widower) not under 30 years of age, and the matron a single woman between the ages of 35 and 50. The physical plant had been carefully planned so as to minimize the exposure the girls would have to the staff of the house: the "lodge" was set near the road and separated from the wards (where the girls resided) by a "large court." No one but the chaplain, the matron, and her assistant were allowed to go into the wards.[38] We see in these rules the correlation made between the regulation of the prostitute's body (through physical exams, uniform clothing, and controlled sleep patterns) and the body of prostitutes—how, as a group, they were housed, negotiated, contained.[39]

Within the Magdalen House (or any rescue home) the penitent prostitute remained public. Although access to the penitent was restricted—her name might be changed and she could not have "private" relationships—her institutional incarceration alone carried the weight of knowledge by association. Her social standing was openly understood and obvious, yet within the institution the penitent's right to privacy was seemingly protected. In *Advice to the Magdalens* (1776), William Dodd sternly admonished the girls to leave their curiosity about their housemates aside: "Reproaches for past irregularities are forbidden; no enquiry into names or family is permitted; but all possible discouragement given to the making any discovery, which the parties themselves do not approve."[40] "Tell your story to no one," was posted on each ward's wall in the second Magdalen House.[41] However, the separation of the penitents, the hymns and prayers that were chosen for them to recite or sing, the regulation of their bodies and speech and movement all served to create a "theater of pathos,"[42] and to remind the inmates and the donors (or society in general), of their stories, their names. No distinction was needed, really, for they all told the same story and all shared the same name: Magdalen.

The Magdalen Hospital was organized according to the principle of a kind of "liberal" containment: great precautions were taken in order that the girls were generally hidden—yet revealed when necessary for political (usually fundraising) reasons—and corresponding avenues were instituted that enabled the girls to be "known" (again the play on the understanding of "know") and heard. It was important that the girls be sheltered from prying eyes (or at least from penniless or uncharitable voyeurs), but it was more important that those who might come into contact with the prostitutes be protected from the "assault" of their powerful, tempting bodies, while at the same time moved to pity by their perhaps even more tempting pathetic stories.[43] Reverend Horne is an example of one who "succumbed" to narrate the prostitute's story by creating a storyline for the prostitute heroine and then insinuating his narrator-self into its ending, making his presence necessary for closure. Given this urge to mingle with the penitent prostitute, the males associated with the running of the charity had to be "safe" and domesticated men. The Magdalens were thus segregated from the public sphere by incarceration in the institution as well as integration within society's imagination. "Integration" was of course necessary in order to publicize the success of the charity, to solicit and gain funds, and to quiet naysayers who were shocked by what was perceived to be institutional support for indecent living.[44]

The prostitute's place in society was also endlessly scrutinized. Mayhew's catalogue of the prostitute in *London Labour and the London Poor (Those Who Will Not Work)* (1861–62) "examined" the prostitute's body in order to "display" it: "It will be necessary that we should take as comprehensive a view of the subject as possible, collecting a large and multifarious body of facts, and examining the matter from almost every conceivable point of view."[45] This publicity and examination were effected through the institution of chapel services that were open to the public, but which partially hid the penitents behind a screen and revealed their presence through their singing. In my research on the Magdalen charities I have found conflicting evidence as to the organization of the penitents in the chapel services. Within other remarks about the success of the Magdalen House, Fielding comments, "Nay, the *public* are themselves, in some measure, judges, by seeing their decent and commendable deportment in the *Chapel,* which has dispelled the doubts, and dissipated the scruples of many hesitating objectors to this design."[46] William Dodd's *Advice to the Magdalens* instructs the penitents on their public appearance in the chapel: "And it is thought advisable, that worthy people, desirous of seeing this good work, should be admitted to the Chapel, let that be another forcible motive to particular humility in behaviour. The humble, meek and downcast look becomes those who are in a state of penitence, and will ever recommend; the bold and dauntless stare will give but mean ideas of reformation; though, indeed, such as have any sense at all of their past shame, will find little courage to animate the wandering eye."[47] Sarah Green's description of actual visits to chapel services quoted below, however, indicates that the prostitutes remained behind a screen and made their presence (and their penitence) known through their voices. An 1848 essay on the Magdalen Hospital in the *Quarterly Review* shares this description of the veiled penitents: "The poor women are packed together, as ungainly lumber, in galleries carefully screened from the gaze of the more honoured congregation below."[48] Perhaps the theoretical model set forth by Dodd and Fielding was later altered in actual practice; one of the rules of the Magdalen Hospital—the manager of the chapel could confiscate tickets from anyone deemed "improper"—suggests that the effect of the prostitutes' presence on visitors to the chapel may have been difficult to control. The effect is the same in either case, I would argue. Bentham's *Panopticon* describes visitors to the prison's chapel who witness masked prisoners appearing as if players in a theatrical. In *Imagining the Penitentiary*, John Bender comments that "in this chapel, the prisoners become histrionic objects arranged to create a moral impact on a public audience."[49] The organizers of the Magdalen chapel had a similar moral impact in mind when they either overtly displayed the prostitute (behind the screen of shame, as Dodd suggests) or partially hid her (behind the physical screen from which her voice can be heard). As Van Sant comments, "The distance created by the artificiality of the presentation (as aesthetic distance) coincides with—even represents—the social distance between contributor and philanthropic object."[50]

Green's *Mental Improvement for a Young Lady, on her Entrance into the World; Addressed to a Favourite Niece* (published anonymously in 1793), written for her sixteen-year-old niece, Charlotte, frankly discusses the Magdalen chapel in the letter "On Chastity":

> You have often, when a few years younger than you are now, accompanied me to the Magdalen Chapel, and, while you admired the singing, have very sensibly asked me about the institution of the charity, and what the women were who sang, and why they were concealed from public view by blinds? I then evaded the question, which, I suppose, has since been resolved to you; if not, I now send it to you.
>
> They are poor unhappy women, who, weary of a life of guilt, are desirous of entering on a new course, and, by sincere penitence, washing out the stains of their former transgressions. It is a most glorious institution, and reflects immortal honour on the unfortunate man who was the founder of it! They are called Magdalens from the penitent Mary, who had been a famous courtezan in the court of Herod, and who, repenting of her former crimes, cast herself at the feet of our Saviour, bathing them with her tears, and wiping them with her hair. She obtained forgiveness, and let us hope these poor unhappy Magdalens do the same; but, I have been told, they too often return to their former course of life: This certainly must be from their not meeting with sufficient charity and encouragement from the rigidly virtuous of their own sex! See the fatal consequences of the loss of virtue and reputation![51]

The fact that the aunt could address the subject of prostitution in conjunction with a lesson on chastity reveals the dangers she felt might threaten her niece at her entrance into the world. Armed with knowledge (and a constructed image) of the unchaste, the girl is better able to absorb the lessons of chastity: "the fatal consequences of the loss of virtue and reputation."[52] The penultimate lesson in Green's sermon on the Magdalen charity, however, concerns the limitations of charitable organizations like the Magdalen Hospital within a morally bankrupt society. The virtue of Charity may be biblically greater than faith and hope, but Sarah Green indicated that charity (being a part of Charity) was often wanting—in this case, by a particularly gendered intolerance: "rigidly virtuous" women unable to act in an adequately charitable manner toward their fallen sisters.

The myriad sermons and religious texts that preach the subject of philanthropy in a broad sense generally do not consider the biblical ideal of Charity as one of the duties particular to women (as are, for example, childrearing, religious instruction, domestic management), and the disposal of property (large sums of money, land, bequests) is generally not considered a female right. Conduct manual writers, however, call "charity"— that narrowed aspect of philanthropy which involves the giving of the self and/or minor financial support, a feminine imperative—"the great duty of alms-giving"[53] that is crucial to the social and moral development of the Christian girl. The final pages of this chapter will consider the means by which certain female behaviors, ratified into conduct manual code, construct different kinds of *value* —-moral, aesthetic, and "actual"—against which eighteenth-and nineteenth-century girl readers were formed. In the same way, the prostitute in charity is forcibly identified with her "stainless" sisters, so that the young prostitute becomes the penitent. This movement better contains the potential danger of the unrestrained (in language and culture) female body.[54]

Rather than explore or document further Frances Power Cobbe's division between masculine, juridical charity and feminine, emotional charity, I focus on the role of the girl of charity—both as giver and recipient.[55] The pleasures of the charitable act "are ravishing and transporting; they sensibly affect the heart, and penetrate to the very inmost recesses of the soul."[56] The pleasurable act of giving is also self-interested as it creates a "surplus value" for the good (charitable) girls that can be purchased on the marriage market by the worthy suitor. Of course, that value is fictional, and abstract. The value that the poor girl receives when participating in the charitable enterprise, by contrast, seems quantifiable: she receives food and clothing, domestic training to help her gain employment, as well as shelter, tracts, a Bible—all worth a certain ascribable market value.

In *Letters on the Improvement of the Mind* (1773), Hester Chapone writes to her young niece that the monies set aside for charitable purposes ought not to be considered one's property any longer—the "right" of the poor to these funds is great enough to transfer their ownership: "I think it an admirable method to appropriate such a portion of your income, as you judge proper to bestow in charity, to be sacredly kept for that purpose and no longer considered as your own. By which means, you will avoid the temptation of giving less than you ought, through selfishness, or more than you ought; through good-nature or weakness."[57] Chapone thus argues for a kind of regulation of money earmarked for charitable giving to avoid the excesses of rigid economy or wasteful giving.[58] Moderate giving can supply the wants of moderate need: all those who ask are, by their abasement, worthy of some assistance. The author of *The Polite Lady* (1760) admits to a difference in desert between those persons needing charity that accords to their culpability in their "wretched condition," yet also warns his girl readers that "to excuse ourselves from performing acts of charity by such frivolous pretexts [as judging desert], is perhaps in itself a more heinous crime than any that can be justly laid to the charge of the unhappy beggars."[59] In "On Economy," Chapone does not hesitate to distinguish among objects of charity: "In general, charity is more useful, when it is appropriated to animate the industry of the young, to procure some ease and comforts to old age, and to support in sickness those whose daily labour is their only maintenance in health."[60] One means of promoting honest labor in the able-bodied young was "rescue work," the rescuing of prostitutes from the streets, putting them in asylums created for their rehabilitation, and teaching them domestic arts, which after leaving the institution could be used to earn a living as household help. In his defense of the London Female Penitentiary, Blair describes the economics of work that is not labor, but spiritual growth: "The penitents are constantly employed in household business, or some art in which they have been instructed,—and a *sixth part only* of the produce of their earnings is allowed to them. This portion is not, however, immediately put into their hands; and, in disposing of it, they are encouraged to lay out a little in works of charity and mercy. By this method, they are gradually taught to be industrious and frugal; while at the same time, they learn to be kind, humane, and benevolent to their fellow-creatures, especially to those 'who sit in darkness and the shadow of death.' "[61]

In this way, those working girls who were the antithesis of conduct manual girlhood, those whose spent sexuality rendered them penniless in the conduct manual "department store" of values and on the marriage market, could gain value within that same paradigm by giving up their previous means of subsistence and choosing incarceration with other former prostitutes or mistresses. The penitent also "chooses" religious and domestic training in payment for food and shelter (and a certain moral "relief," one assumes). The successful conduct-manual or conduct-novel heroine, by contrast, brims with value to spend and yet retains or gains even greater wealth through the act of giving (to the family, to the composition of the drawing room, to the worthy suitor, and to the poor), through passivity or decorous behavior.[62] The *object* of charity, however, when she is a decidedly "bad girl"—a prostitute, seduced country girl, or abandoned mistress—who has lost the value of chastity (what Milton calls the "serious doctrine of Virginity") is emptied of all conduct-book and novelistic value.[63] This negative balance is transformed into positive value only when the penitent enters into a symbiotic relationship with the giver and through actual production or labor. The 1817 report of the Guardian Society explains this process: "While indeed the common street-walker should be driven from all places of honest resort; yet, with a truly English spirit, and what is more, with truly Christian sympathy, the moment she appears possessed of a broken and contrite spirit, *that* moment all hostility should cease. We no more would call her an abandoned woman, but an unfortunate female."[64] Her value is held suspended in transition by a semantic distinction that upholds what is understood to be the pleasure of the acts of giving and receiving charity. The prostitute needs to be desexualized in this movement from unreclaimed girl of the streets to honest domestic worker. By contrast, the charitable girl *gains* in her sexual attractiveness through her growth in Christian virtue. The charitable girl—the good girl—must be sexual in order to fulfill her duties as wife and mother; the prostitute—penitent or unregenerate—must be stripped of sexuality to contain her undutiful nature. In the conduct novel for girls, we see our heroines negotiate sexual desire according to their understanding of duty. Only after a successful containment of desire within duty can the character attain happiness.

Chapter 2 examines adolescent literature's charitable girl in this position of enjoying one aspect of the luxurious pleasures of selflessness. The assimilation and reflection of the middle-class ideal of feminine behavior (selflessness being an important part of that ideal), increased a girl's value in an increasingly capitalistic market. Richardson's *Pamela* is the fictional progenitor of a girl raised by her virtue/value to material or worldly success. Needing the flawed, the frail, the faulty young woman as contrast and ballast, the Pamelian trope of success—with virtue comes (domestic) happiness—is built on the backs of the penitents. Pamela asks B, "And what is left me but words?"[65] Pamela's success depends upon words, and she is a fitting point of departure for my discussions of stories of girls and their cultural contexts. Reflecting upon Pamela's corpus—her physical body as well as the body of her text (and they become the same thing as Pamela pads her body with her letters)—reminds us of Head's narrative of the prostitute Cornelia's body. And these two stories are similar: narratives of the bodies of the virtuous girl and the sinful girl recall the desire to identify (with) each. We read the narratives of both good and bad girls—in novels, sermons, tracts, hymns—with pleasure.

2

"The Matter of Letters"

Conduct, Anatomy, and Pamela

⁓

Teach me, dear sir, continued I, and pressed his dear hand to my lips, teach me some other language, if there be any, that abounds with more grateful terms; that I may not thus be choked with meanings, for which I can find no utterance.
Samuel Richardson, *Pamela; or, Virtue Rewarded* (1740)

In cutting up all manner of small Birds, it is proper to say, Thigh them; as thigh that Woodcock, thigh that Pidgeon; but as to others say; Mince that Plover, Wing that Quail, and Wing that Partridg, Allay that Pheasant, Untach that Curlew, Unjoint that Bittern, Disfigure that Peacock, Display that Crane, Dismember that Hern, Unbrace that Mallard, Frust that Chicken, Spoil that Hen, Sauce that Capon, Lift that

Swan, Rear that Goose, Tire that Egg.

Hannah Woolley, *The Gentlewomans Companion* (1675)

As we have seen, the Magdalen charity of the eighteenth century kept its "eye" on the penitent prostitute, regulating her behavior, clothing, food, and spiritual and sexual life within the relatively closed world of the institution. We turn now to consider another kind of overt surveillance of the female: conduct literature that both visualizes and enforces manners and morals for young women. The "good girls" (or at least not actively "bad" girls) who were the audience for such literature exist outside of the institution, yet at the same time they are held "captive" by a persistent Eye that both sets standards for girls and then evaluates ("anatomizes") them as objects within a prescribed visual field.

Drawing upon Mikhail Bahktin's formulation of the body as a site of conflict, Peter Stallybrass discusses the formation of the female body and "trace[s] the connections between politeness and politics."[1] He argues that in Renaissance England "the surveillance of women concentrated upon three specific areas: the mouth, chastity, the threshold of the house. These three areas were frequently collapsed into each other. . . . Silence, the closed mouth, is made a sign of chastity. And silence and chastity are, in turn, homologous to woman's enclosure within the house."[2] My concern with the female body in this chapter is similarly centered upon the surveyors and those under surveillance, but I will focus my attention upon both the speaking subject (in *Pamela*) and the Eye/I of conduct discourse where the Eye never blinks but to deny the autonomy of the I.

In didactic literature for girls, the "matter of letters" (both language and correspondence) within the discourse of conduct and the language of anatomy that describes and enacts the delimitation of female experience can become, I suggest, the language of abridgment.

Conduct Anatomized

Advice-givers of today and ages past have felt with some conviction that the conduct of young men and young women was a subject worthy of notice, and thus the conduct manual that codified behavior—domestic and social—

was a genre published consistently from the Middle Ages to the nineteenth century.[3] Although publications were generally concerned with the duties and behavior of aristocratic young men, occasionally these works would append some pages considering, by contrast, the duties of young women.[4] Girls and women were shut out of the political, commercial, and religious arenas, yet they were viewed as the rightful cornerstones of rational, domestic English society, and, as such, needed to be closely guided in order to maintain (or shore up) that internal structure. Many of the seventeenth- and eighteenth-century conduct manuals for women served as the only textbooks of female education available—textbooks of conduct—in the absence of other serious theoretical or curricular discussions. John Locke's influential *Some Thoughts Concerning Education* (1693), was popular for its inclusive, humanistic understanding of the (upper-class male) child's psychology, physiology, and social roles. Locke treats female education cursorily, however, in a few corollary letters. A classical (masculine) education was considered unseemly, unfeminine, and dangerous to the female mind—if the idea was conceived of at all—and many parents and educators sought an "alternative" education for girls that was in fact a simple reiteration of the moral and social rules of the day, a kind of on-the-job training, in effect, in the ways of chastity, sobriety, piety, and domesticity.

Hannah Woolley's *Gentlewomans Companion* is a compendium of directions for right female conduct that describes in particular the domestic and social roles of young gentlewomen, and also touches upon the duties of servants in a large household (for example, "Instructions for all Nursery-Maids in Noble Families" or "To Scullery-Maids in great Houses"). The text functions, as the title page proclaims, as "an exact Rule for the Female Sex in General." The specific kinds of guidance offered varies from a description of the duties children owe to their parents, to an alphabetized listing of key recipes in the art of cookery; from an admonition against patching the face, to "Choice and Experimental Obseryaions in Physick and Chyrurgery, such which rarely fail'd any who made trial thereof"; from a set of rules guiding a girl in matters of the heart, to a group of sample letters on all occasions (some with sample replies) for the reader to copy. Woolley's manual, which attempts to codify female behavior exhaustively, will operate as my prooftext of the discourse of conduct, and "guide" to the discussion of the ways in which that discourse functions in girls' fiction, using *Pamela* as the example.

Although Woolley's disquisition on the grammar of carving small birds creates to our modern ears a kind of humorous sing-song verse, it is a powerful example of the discourse in feminine conduct: a distilled moment of command.[5] The imperious direction implicit in "Allay that Pheasant, Untach that Curlew" indicates not only the exacting mistress ordering her servant to perform a particular duty, but also the imperative voice found in conduct manuals, as well as in didactic literature generally. In each command to carve is the suggestion of a specific "victim" or even carcass awaiting the knife. One is invited to imagine a hand selecting and discarding, identifying and focusing upon *that* particular object to dismember rather than another, just as Woolley's counsel identifies a specific "object" and proceeds to inscribe it within a set code of desirable behavior befitting that object: "Advice to the Female younger Sort" or "Of young Gentlewomens fit hours and times for their recreations and Pleasures, and how to govern themselves therein." But it is the language of "anatomy" in this selection rather than command that is in fact most emblematic of the ways in which the figure of the young woman (here the gentlewoman) is accommodated in discourse.[6] Whether the discourse be called guide or instruction or direction or suggestion or rule, it creates within other ideologies of seventeenth-century patriarchal culture a body of behavior—sanctioned or transgressive—performed by a gendered body and then proceeds to dissect it to reveal its "textuality," its implicit argument. That in this discourse the autonomy of the young woman is violated is indeed partly a function of the "nosiness" of conduct literature, but I would also suggest that conduct literature for girls—of which Woolley's is just one seventeenth-century example out of hundreds of European manuals published during three centuries—maintains a certain level of aggression by wielding elements such as the language of command, anatomization, and control against its subjects. "Dismember that Her[n]" is perhaps not too far off the mark.[7] We are reminded at this juncture of Richard Head's contemporaneous *The Miss Display'd* wherein he performs an anatomy of the prostitute's story/text, and finds her both captivating and corrupt.

Woolley's "Universal Companion" of female conduct combines directions about such areas of female duty as cookery and "surgery" that were often addressed in other, specialized volumes—Woolley's own *Ladies Directory* (a cookbook published in 1670) and the Countess of Kent's *A Choice Manuall, or Rare and Select Secrets in Physick and Chyrurgery* (1653) for example.[8] In her "Epistle Dedicatory" addressed to "all Young Ladies, Gentlewomen, and all Maidens whatever," Woolley boasts, "many excellent Authors there be who have wrote excellent well of some particular Subjects herein treated of. But as there is not one of them hath written upon all of them; so there are some things treated of in this Book, that I have not met with in any Language, but are the Product of my Thirty years Observations and Experience." Yet Woolley also distinguishes herself from the generally repressive ideologies of conduct manual authors (male and female) in her feminist thought which appears periodically, depending upon the subject. For example, Woolley begins her lengthy manual by invoking the common rant against the present status of female education, but then lays the blame for that miserable state of affairs at the feet of men overshadowed by their "towring conceits:"

> Most in this depraved later Age think a Woman learned and wise enough if she can distinguish her Husbands Bed from anothers. Certainly Mans Soul cannot boast of a more sublime Original than ours; they had equally their efflux from the same eternal Immensity, and therefore capable of the same improvement by good Education. Vain man is apt to think we were meerly intended for the Worlds propagation, and to keep its humane inhabitants sweet and clean; but, by their leaves, had we the same Literature, he would find our brains as fruitful as our bodies. Hence I am induced to believe, we are debarred from the knowledg of humane learning, lest our pregnant Wits should rival the towring conceits of our insulting Lords and Masters. (1–2)

There is greater variation in the conduct literature and educational treatises written particularly for or about boys, however, than exists in similar seventeenth-century literature for girls. For example, John Milton's *Of Education* (1644) treats the actual organization of a private school, and Locke's essay combines curricular with social and political concerns, whereas (early) manuals for girls are obsessively concerned with the education of the domestic and social female. Woolley's discussion anatomizes the domestic social body into separate "actions:" general deportment ("Good instructions for a Young Gentlewoman, for the age of Six to Sixteen"); gesture ("Of the Government of the Eye"); occasion ("Rules to be observed in walking with persons of honour"); courtship ("Of the guiding of a Ladies love and fancy"); example ("The Gentlewomans Mirrour, or Patterns for the imitation of such famous Women who have been eminent in Piety and Learning"); conjugal relations ("Of Marriage, and the duty of a Wife to her Husband"); command ("Of Womens Behaviour to their Servants, and what is to be required of them in the House, or what

"The Matter of Letters"

30

thereunto appertains"); and composition ("Writing Letters"). This table of contents enacts the anatomization of that domestic social body by separating and carefully carving it, like the small birds, into "pieces" of merit (consumable and sanctioned) or disgrace (disgusting and transgressive). Thus, in each identified or named portion of the body, the good is celebrated and the bad excised.

Woolley's discussion of gait and gesture is a good example of this kind of synechdochical scrutiny: taking a particular behavior and splitting it apart from the "body" and then using it as an example of the entire being. Thus the seemly or unseemly gesture becomes the visual representation of both the girl's exterior (body) and interior (soul)—what can be seen and what is inferred: "It is an easie matter to gather the disposition of our heart, by the dimension of our Gait. A light carriage most commonly discovers a loose inclination; as jetting and strutting, shew haughtiness and self-conceit. Were your bodies transparent, you could not more perspicuously display your levity than by wanton Gesticulations" (37). The girl's degree of obedience to her parents or competence in the kitchen could be similarly analyzed. Once rhetorically anatomized, the girl is to put herself back together, having realized that bodily "organization" alone will impress reason: "These unstaid dimensions, argue unsetled dispositions. Such as these, discretion cannot prize, nor sound judgement praise. Vulgar opinion, whose applause seldom receives life from desert, may admire what is new; but discretion only that which is neat" (38).

In the same way, the regulation of the eye is executed in Woolley's chapter "Of the Government of the Eye." As nature has no desires but those of necessity and survival (which, properly defined, are imperatives and not desires at all), the "natural Eye" is the standard upon which all Eyes should be turned and against which evaluated: "They are the Casements of the Soul, the Windows of Reason: As they are the inlets of Understanding, so they are the outlets or discoverers of many inward corruptions" (39). Desiring Eyes—the "wanton Eye," "unclean Eye," "ambitious Eye," and "covetous Eye"—are exposed and vilified.[9]

My double focus on the "eye" of conduct discourse—the eye of the omnipotent author who sees and anatomizes the girl reader, and the eye/I of the objectified girl herself—can be further illuminated by consideration of a third eye: the "attentive eye" artists train upon their subjects. Svetlana Alpers describes the Dutch artists and the microscopists (such as Leeuwenhoek) as similarly—to each other and also to the conduct writers—visualizing their objects of fascination as both parts and wholes: "First and second, the double cutting edge of the world seen microscopically is that it both multiplies and divides. It multiplies when it dwells on the innumerable small elements within a larger body. . . . It divides when it enables us to see an enlargement of a small part of a larger body or surface. . . . Third, it treats everything as a visible surface either by slicing across or through to make a section . . . or by opening something up to expose the innards to reveal how it is made."[10] So, too, does the attentive eye of conduct discourse multiply, divide, and dissect in order better to visualize, understand, and communicate the essential Girl.

Yet the Girl—actual or fictional—and her eye/I are not as easily observed as a Leeuwenhoek animalcule, or appreciated as a Vermeer still life. For example, Pamela can control neither her desire to "scribble" nor her wandering eye. In one early instance of her "clear-sightedness," Pamela reveals her warm feelings for B and her admiration for his "handsome" actions after his mother's death: "I always thought my master a fine gentleman, as every body says he is: but he gave these good things to us both with such a graciousness, as I thought he looked like an angel" (11). Woolley, however, would admonish such fanciful (and dangerous) gazing: "Send not forth a tempting Eye to take another; nor entertain a tempting look darting from another. Take not, nor be taken. To become a prey to others, will enslave you, to make a prey of others will transport you. Look them upward, where the more you look, you shall like; the longer you live, you shall love" (41). This warning is an astonishingly accurate profile of Pamela's history, its dangers, and its rewards. Pamela certainly looks upward—upstairs, that is, toward a higher station than her birth should allow. Through the exchange of illicit glances Pamela is both enslaved and transported, the inheritor of a uniquely Pamelian moment of class mobility—so Richardson intended. Much later, trapped at the Bedfordshire estate, Pamela contemplates drowning herself, but finally rejects suicide—professing of her obedience to God's providential designs, a conduct imperative Woolley of course had advocated. By this (in)action Pamela reveals both her impatience with her uncomprehending eye and her greatest earthly hopes:

What art thou about to do, wretched Pamela? How knowest thou, though the prospect be all dark to thy short-sighted eye, what God may do for thee, even when all human means fail? . . . And who knows, but that the very presence I so much dread of my angry and designing master, (for he has had me in his power before, and yet I have escaped,) may be better for me, than these persecuting emissaries of his, who, for his money, are true to their wicked trust, and are hardened by that, and a long habit of wickedness, against compunction of heart? God *can* touch his heart in an instant; and if this should *not* be done, I can *then* but put an end to my life by some other means, if I am so resolved. (181)

Woolley would enjoin Pamela to silence, again focusing upon those parts— eye and mouth—the girl should be able to control in order to "dam up" effectively those parts she might not: "The Index of your hearts you carry in your eyes and tongues; for shame learn silence in the one, and secrecy in the other. Give not the power to an insulting Lover to triumph over your weakness; and which is worse, to work on the opportunity of your lightness. Rather dam up those portals which betray you to your enemy; and prevent his entry by your vigilancy" (96). Pamela (a telling girl) cannot help but communicate.[11]

Woolley gives stern advice to active Eyes in love: "The means to prevent this malady, which like a spreading Canker disperseth it self in all Societies, is to abate your esteem for any earthly Object. Do you admire the comeliness of any Creature? remove your Eye from thence, and bestow it on the contemplation of the superexcellency of your Creator" (40). Indeed, Pamela accepts this advice, albeit in "contemplation" of a different creator than Woolley intended young ladies to gaze upon: while Pamela's purity creates B anew, so B's "legal" relationship to Pamela re-forms (creates) her a lady. As Pamela says, maid no longer, "In short, he says every thing that may embolden me to look up, with pleasure, upon the generous author of my happiness" (373).

At the conclusion of *The Gentlewomans Companion*, Woolley discusses a kind of self-creation—letter writing—yet offers patterns for imitation. For Woolley, letters are not a means for self-expression, but rather another forum or proving ground testing obedience to a code or system. Half a century after Woolley, Richardson interrupted writing one epistolary project—a volume of letters in the form of a complete secretary—for another. He composed *Pamela; or, Virtue Rewarded* from an anecdote he remembered hearing many years earlier about a beautiful servant girl whose virtue was sorely tried yet who was ultimately rewarded for her constancy by marriage to her wealthy abuser/suitor.[12]

That Richardson had a target audience in mind and the practical means of securing that audience's attention is indisputable.[13] His knowledge of popular books (even the disparaged romances) and the printing and bookselling trade stood him in good stead when writing his own fiction. Although Richardson professed to be writing "a Story, which shall catch young and airy Minds, and when Passions run high in them, to shew how they may be directed to laudable Meanings and Purposes, in order to decry such Novels and Romances, as have a Tendency to inflame and corrupt," *Pamela* was a controversial book.[14] It is beyond the scope of this chapter to discuss in detail the barrage of "anti-Pamelas" printed after the novel's publication in 1740, but the following brief comments will sketch the context of its reception. The most notorious of the "anti-Pamelas," of course, is Henry Fielding's *Shamela*, in which the heroine, a crafty bawd, dupes Mr. Booby, her suitor, into marrying her.

The anonymous *Pamela Censured* (1741) is an extended invective against Richardson's novel, designed, so the author states, to influence Richardson's subsequent editions.[15] This pamphleteer is particularly angered by what he perceives to be Richardson's transgressions of literary and social boundaries. This blurring of generic boundaries provokes the author to describe Richardson as a kind of hybrid, a literary monster: "HALF-EDITOR, HALF-AUTHOR of *Pamela*" (9). *Pamela Censured* also decries Richardson's novel as sexually stimulating and therefore unsuitable for its young audience: "Here the lovely Nymph is underss'd [sic] in her Bed Chamber, without Reserve, and doing a Hundred little Actions, which every one's Fancy must help him to form who reads this Passage, and in the midst of all this, the Squire is introduced: and however she and Mrs. *Jervis* may endeavor to keep down the *Under Petticoat*, yet few youths but would secretly wish to be in the Squire's Place, and naturally conclude they would not let the Nymph escape so easily" (41). The letter from a "stay'd sober Gentleman" that caused the pamphleteer to reflect upon *Pamela* cautions that female readers may resort to masturbation as a result of the unrelieved sexual tensions produced by reading the novel ("she privately may seek Remedies which may drive her to the most unnatural excesses," 24). Lennard Davis notes that Chandler and Kelly's *Pamela's Conduct in High Life* (1741) responds to *Pamela Censured* with an ad hominem attack directed at the author's perversity: "He is unfair in his quotations and gives us such an idea of his own vicious inclination, that it would not (I fear) wrong him to think the shrieks of a woman in labour would excite his passions, and the agonies of a dying woman enflame his blood and stimulate him to commit rape."[16]

Richardson believed that *Pamela* (and his other novels as well), carefully crafted to wed narrative to conduct manual principles—the regulation of servant girls and masters, duties to parents and husbands, education, letter writing, piety, and chastity—offered young readers a safe alternative to other literary productions that had not their moral interests at heart. This marriage was so successful that Richardson, at the behest of his admiring readers and in response to those who misread his moral aims, published (anonymously at first) *A Collection of the Moral and Instructive Sentiments, Maxims, Cautions, and Reflexions, Contained in the Histories of* Pamela, Clarissa, *and* Sir Charles Grandison (1755). *Pamela* is anatomized into alphabetized headings, subheadings, and pithy moral sentiments creating a veritable abecedarian of Pamelian (and Clarissian and Grandisonian) conduct.[17] The character Pamela can also be understood to be composed of a series of smaller units—her Eye, as we have seen, and the letters she writes. Pamela, as pen, scripts her self in narrow rule. While Mr. B as letter is a significant character, Pamela is greatest as the super-compressed "P"—a letter, in letters.[18] Pamela demonstrates the perfect congruence between the two areas most important in composition, according to Hannah Woolley: "Matter and Form" (218). Matter, of course, is what you communicate ("Of Intelligence or Advice" or "Of Friend-chastisement," for example) and Form is its "shape" ("Forms of thanks for Courtesies received," subscription and superscription). The beauties of P are numerous: she, like the penmanship Woolley urges, is "curious" and "delights the sight [of the reader]" (229) so that all who see P love her (or learn to do so): the ladies of B's neighborhood remark upon her figure "See that shape! I never saw such a face and shape in my life; why, she must be better descended than you have told me!" (49). B's love is also inflamed by the beauties of her correspondence: "I have seen more of your letters than you imagine . . . and am quite overcome with your charming manner of writing, so free, so easy, and many of your sentiments so much above your years, and your sex; and all put together, makes me, as I tell you, love you to extravagance" (82–83). P is shapely body, composed mind, and Matter well-worded.

Pamela Epitomized

No; let us have *Pamela* as *Pamela* wrote it; in her own words, without Amputation or Addition.

William Webster[19]

Documented reflections on *Pamela* have shown that modern female readers are not immune to Pamela's "affective" story. The responses to *Pamela* in the journal entries written by Florian Stuber's composition class were overwhelmingly positive: heartfelt, warm, thoughtful. For example: "I see Pamela, not only as a character in the eighteenth century, but as a girl today, growing up and having to face problems with sexuality, puberty, love, trust and family loyalty"[20]; "Pamela portrays a character that is timeless. A majority of women have lived what Pamela is experiencing. Pamela is the character of the innocence I have lost. I hope that Pamela can remain strong, and I wish for her to maintain the little girl that once survived in myself."[21]

We know that contemporary readers both sighed and scowled at *Pamela*; it is interesting to learn that some modern readers find Pamela to be a model, a true conduct model as Richardson created her: "I think of Pamela as an example. Now when I have to make an important decision about myself or others, I ask myself, 'What would Pamela do?.' "[22] Stuber calls this "inspirational" aspect of *Pamela*'s effect on young readers the "generative Richardsonian moment, for it is that moment of generational change that provides the opportunity for action in *Clarissa* and *Sir Charles Grandison* as well as in *Pamela*."[23]

Pamela's effect on young female readers was designed to be significant, as we have seen, and the novel clearly has continued to establish and confront issues of female acculturation (growth, sexuality, autonomy) in modern times. The first abridged version of Richardson's novels, entitled *The Paths of Virtue Delineated; or, the History in Miniature of the Celebrated Pamela, Clarissa Harlowe and Sir Charles Grandison, Familiarised and adapted to the Capacities of Youth,* appeared in 1756.[24] Newbery and Carnan's 1769 abridgment of *Pamela* for children was very popular: it appeared in at least thirteen editions in the United States and was cited in Elizabeth Newbery's *Catalogue of Instructive and Amusing Publications for Young Minds* in 1800.[25] Another abridgment appeared in 1813—*Beauties of Richardson: being the history in Miniature . . .*

The 1756 *The Paths of Virtue* was reviewed in both the *Critical Review* and the *Monthly Review*. The *Critical Review* praised Richardson's work in general but had little to say about the abilities of the abridger to represent Richardson's novels: "The character of the books, with an abridgement of which we are here presented, is already so well known, that it would be needless for us to say anything upon that head, nor is it properly our province. The author must certainly have secured by them the esteem of every friend to virtue and religion: and we are glad to find them now reduced to such a size as may fit them for every hand; for certainly few books of entertainment are so well adapted to the instructions of youth." The reviewer quotes a brief selection from the abridgment of *Clarissa* "whereby the reader will become better acquainted with the talents of our abridger, nor will they, we imagine, displease him."[26] Generally hostile to Richardson, however, the *Monthly Review* somewhat sourly considers the abridgment, ultimately directing the reader to an attack on Richardson appearing elsewhere in the same issue. The review excerpts some of the "Epitomizer's" prefatory remarks: " 'It consists,' says he, 'of miniatures taken with as much care as possible, from those large pictures of human life; [the histories of Pamela, &c.] 'and it is hoped, that none will be so unjust as to imagine, that this is done with a design to injure the beautiful originals. In draughts so small, much must be left out, to make room for the more distinguished figures. And even some of the noble and admired touches omitted, from the impossibility of representing them in so small a compass.' "[27]

Although *Pamela* had been written "to Divert and Entertain, and at the same time to Instruct, and Improve the Minds of the Youth of both Sexes," the abridgment radically alters the text for the youngest novel readers. The most striking change in the abridged form of *Pamela* is that the formal epistolary structure of the original has been dispensed with entirely. It is particularly significant, then, that the abridgment of *Pamela* violates her "formal" characteristics by rewriting the story in flat prose (nonepistolary), silencing her voice (third-person narrative), and denying her body, thus separating form from matter. This abridging for younger female readers functions as a refined usage of the conduct discourse of anatomy discussed above; in the abridgment, Pamela functions not as speaking subject, but as the spoken object. In a shift entirely consistent with the process of anatomization, the abridgment is a translation of the visualization—an operation crucial to both anatomy and in conduct discourse. In its transformation of the text from epistle to narrative, the abridged *Pamela* displays the production—and privileging—of the emblematic over the "embodied," fulfilling the conduct literature imperative of visual coherence that Richardson's Pamela, as evidenced by those suspicious of her motives and methods, achieves with some effort. The "visually coherent" girl, as opposed to the mysterious or unknowable girl that the conduct books deny and denigrate, is easily conceptualized and labelled "modest," "virtuous," "chaste." In this way, the language of anatomy that we have seen used to some effect in the conduct manual is reproduced in the children's text as well. In the abridgment the text is dissected (or amputated) for didactic reasons—to create an automatically acceptable exemplar—whereas conduct discourse separates the domestic social body/text into parts for examination and evaluation. In either case, excision and dismemberment serves the reader's moral training. The child's version of *Pamela* is broken into seven short chapters that cover

Pamela's adventures only until her marriage. Each chapter is headed by a brief summary of events; the morals, however, are reprinted in full. An editor's postscript admonishing parents to be sure to foster virtue in their children's hearts from a very early age has been added to the story's conclusion. This addendum does not appear in any edition of the original and was obviously included for pedagogical effect.

The politics of *Pamela*'s abridgment functions by way of what might again be referred to as the language of anatomy: the mechanisms of inclusion and exclusion of narrative detail, the imagined (or, perhaps, fantasized) audience's influence on the didactic imperative of the original, and the tensions created when a novel that aspires to a certain moral didacticism becomes a pedagogical paradigm for an educational program for (especially female) children. The abridgment of *Pamela* is a form of cultural appropriation of the text that creates a gendered social critique. Thus, the most significant "excision" in this version of *Pamela* is its epistolary form, as I have suggested above. Of course, in the years that had passed before *Pamela* was abridged for the first time in 1756, the novel as a genre had continued to change and develop, and the epistolary novel, while popular to the end of the century, was joined by other novelistic forms of characterization. But the removal of the novel's authority and power from a children's book has ideological implications far beyond that of generic convention.

"Writing to the moment," Richardson's phrase for his epistolary style, is writing at its most intense, while emotions run the strongest, where the intended audience is multilayered, including both the recipient of the letter and the readers of the novel.[28] This complexity of design and characterization is lost when the story is flattened to a third-person narration of the most "significant" aspects of Pamela's life. Linda S. Kauffman's discussion of "amorous epistolary discourse" uses *Clarissa* as a Richardsonian example, yet her general remarks on the significance and function of the epistolary form can also be applied to the first part of *Pamela*: "The heroine's discourse is meant as a performance to be spoken, a letter to be read; she utters her desire in the absence of the beloved. The narrative consists of events reported by the heroine to the lover; it is oblique and elliptical because we frequently see only the repercussions of events that, like the love affair itself, are never narrated. Other acts of communication are enacted rather than reported in the narrative: the heroine's writing reenacts seduction, confession, persuasion, and these constitute what 'happens' in the text. She writes in the mode of amorous discourse, transforming herself in the process from victim to artist."[29] Thus, the absence of the epistolary style in *Pamela*'s abridgment truncates her "transformation" so that she attains not artistry in self-creation, but a kind of static symbolic and iconographic state considered fit for a moral children's book (and conduct discourse as well). This is not to deny the considerable power Pamela can yet wield as an emblem of virtue—like Clarissa, much of her character resonates because she is a literary paragon of morality. However, Pamela's code of right conduct, which for all its seeming rigidity actually undergoes severe testing and questioning in the novel (deciding to stay on at B Hall, wondering at her rights to certain presents, considering suicide), is reduced to "highlights" in the juvenile version. The weight of characterization falls hard upon Homeric epithets that stress Pamela's victimization: "lovely maid," "distressed beauty," "artless sufferer," "injured beauty." Pamela loses her "voice" and thus her autonomy and capacity for self-knowledge. It is in these moments of Pamela's "epitomization" that we see the conduct discourse of scrutiny operating on another level; just as Woolley's manual synechdochically represents young women as Eye, or Gesture, or Gait that is presumed faulty (and therefore in need of the guidance the manual provides), the epithetical descriptions of Pamela the Younger reduce her to little more than an easily visualized marker of female behavior or status.

The loss of the epistolary form also relieves the narrative of much of the burden of uncertainty in Pamela's story. Pamela's letter writing (like Clarissa's) is fraught with and enlivened by the fear of discovery. The threat of danger is lost when epistolarity is abandoned. The *reader* knows that Pamela's virtue is rewarded from the very first, of course, but that sense of immediacy and danger critical to *Pamela*'s relationship to the world and to language is thus abandoned, banishing a disquietingly unstable present tense in favor of the more comforting third-person past-tense narrative.[30] Pamela loses her Eye/I in the abridgment of her story and becomes, in her external consistency, the conduct manual ideal that Woolley proposes. Pamela's fantasies are omitted and so we lose our ability to identify with her. This is a weakness in the abridgment, certainly, as its power as a didactic tool is either lessened or increased as a result of its audience's reaction to it. If we do not love Pamela—love to be (like) her—we cannot learn her story's lessons.

The abridgment's first summer-house incident, for example, succinctly and hurriedly renders Mr. B's motives and actions and Pamela's reactions, yet includes very little of Pamela's passionate and moving arguments against B's indecencies:

> But one day being at work in the summer-house, at the further end of the garden, her master, who had all along pretended to be kind to her, from his regard to the request of his dying mother, and was too fearful of her honour to trust her in the same house with his sister's nephew, shewed himself in his true colours; for, following her thither, he rudely entered the summer-house, and would have behaved in a manner very unbecoming a gentleman, had she not got loose and escaped: But he suddenly held her back, and shut the door, when, losing all the respect she had entertained for him, she told him she would not stay. You won't, hussey! cryed he, enraged. Do you know whom you speak to? Yes, Sir, I do, she returned, bursting into tears; but well may I forget I am your servant, when you forget what belongs to a master: Yet, I shall be so bold as to say, that though poor, I am honest, and were you a prince, I would not be otherwise.[31]

I quote a long passage to demonstrate not only the general nature of the abridgment, but also its syntactical and grammatical style: breathlessly piling on generalization after generalization, subordinating nothing, but stringing together independent clauses so that the effect is a kind of free fall that bumps and hits selective plot moments to arrive hurriedly at the crucial moral maxim Pamela throws in B's face. Pamela's declaration that she would keep her honor even if her ravisher were royalty is indeed a slap to B, for the suggestion, even if Pamela denies its importance, is that B's manhood is less than princely. The truncated dialogue at the end of the summer-house passage quoted above is a direct transcription of the original version from letter 11, but much of their dialogue prior to this point has been omitted.

This choice of detail is critical not only for the heavily weighted effect of Pamela's moral sentiment asserted at the end of an episode, but also the omission from the dialogue and description that allows for this emphasis. In the original version, Pamela is handled quite roughly by B for an undetermined length of time, and her response to his sexual advances is ambiguous: "I struggled and trembled, and was so benumbed with terror, that I sunk down, not in a fit, and yet not myself; and I found myself in his arms, quite void of strength; and he kissed me two or three times, with frightful eagerness.—At last I burst from him, and was getting out of the summer-house; but he held me back, and shut the door" (16). It is the indeterminacy of the dash after "frightful eagerness" and before "At last," as well as Pamela's state of "not myself," which would seem to give the "censor" pause. We might not assume, with Fielding and others, that Pamela is *enjoying* herself, but her reaction, although morally correct at the finish, allows for the dreamlike state she falls into as a result of B's sexual advances and her own somatic response: she becomes another (aroused) body—"not herself"; she is unaware of how much time elapses or how free Mr. B actually becomes.[32]

Pamela's licentious nature, so sharply disapproved of by Povey, Fielding, and others, is largely excised in the juvenile edition for obvious reasons, removing those provocative descriptions of Pamela's undress, the particulars of Mr. B's intentions, the double entendres ("I wish I had thee quick another way"), and the suggestions of Mrs. Jewke's "perverse" interest in kissing the beautiful young captive.[33] Pamela's reaction to the closet incident, where Mr. B rushes upon her and Mrs. Jervis in bed and is foiled in his attempts to rape Pamela only by Mrs. Jervis's fortitude, Pamela's fainting, and his own "cowardice," is described in the original novel in suggestive detail: "I found his hand in my bosom; and when my fright let me know it, I was ready to die; and I sighed and screamed, and fainted away. And still he had his arms about my neck; and Mrs. Jervis was about my feet, and upon my coat. And all in a cold dewy sweat was I" (60). The episode is summarized thus in the abridged version: "Pamela was almost undressed, and Mrs. Jervis was in bed when hearing a rustling noise in the closet, *Pamela* cried, God protect us! [In the original, a more curious Pamela cries "Heaven protect us! but before I say my prayers, I must look into this closet" (59)] and went towards it, and was greatly frightened to find her master, in a silk and silver morning gown, who wanted to behave in a very unbecoming manner to her. . . . Mr. B, little regarding what she said, took such liberties as extremely terrified the innocent and modest virgin, who sighed, screamed, and fainted away" (26–27).

There are details of the novel which elsewhere remain for the young audience's pleasure, however. Pamela's ruminations over the new clothes she will need to rejoin her parents "properly," and the efforts she undergoes to secure them, are described in minute detail—presumably a "safe" and appropriate means for the diversion of fashion-conscious female readers. Descriptions of monsters also abound. No gruesome detail of Richardson's original is spared in the description of Mrs. Jewkes or Colbrand so that they, even in their emblematic form, are dehumanized and delightfully scary. Mrs. Jewkes is described as "about 40 years old; her person was squat and pursy; her face was flat, broad, and red; her nose flat and crooked, and her large eyebrows hung over a pair of dead, spiteful, grey, goggling eyes; her voice was hoarse and manly, and she was as thick as she was long" (34).

The editorial observations on the characters and scenes that appear at the end of *Pamela* are reprinted in full in the juvenile edition. At this point the pedagogical purpose of Pamela's moral virtues is delineated forcefully as an example for young readers to follow. Here Richardson's first part of *Pamela* ends, but the abridged version contains an additional editorial paragraph directed toward the parents who may have read the story aloud to their children, and who have most certainly purchased the book. The added text reminds parents that they have the serious responsibility for the careful upbringing of their children in the paths of virtue, and warns them of the heartache which could (and probably would) ensue if these admonitions are ignored:

> The editor has but one word more to add to the observations above-meantioned; and that is, that all parents ought to be most particularly attentive to proper cultivation of the minds and understandings of their beloved offspring; for it is a certain fact, that the tempers and dispositions of children may be modulated either to vice or virtue, with equal ease. Man, from his cradle, is an imitative creature; whatever objects, therefore, are set before the eyes of children, or whatever precepts are laid open to their minds, be they good or bad, are equally soon impressed upon them. A child will rejoice in having an opportunity of drowning a puppy or a kitten and will behold it in the agonies of a cruel exultation; but be it remembered, that this principle does not end here: the youth will be led on from one cruelty to another, and even at last, perhaps, entertain designs against some nobler victims, who may not[,] like a *Pamela,* have the virtuous courage to defend itself. Let their little hearts, therefore, be rather formed upon a more enlarged plan; let them be taught to rejoice in defending the life of a fly, or in giving a sparrow its liberty, and the consequences will be habituated to a more general principles, and they will be ready upon all occasions to punish vice, and to protect innocence, although even at the hazard of their lives. (166–168)[34]

This extra passage to parents suggests rather obviously that the abridged version of *Pamela* functions as an educational text for children rather than an entertaining novel—a charge that has been leveled at the complete *Pamela* as well. Richardson's *Pamela,* as we have seen, includes much of the conduct manual milieu in which it was created, while at the same time it expands the generic conventions of the romance. The creation of a female character who possesses both an authoritative voice and authentic emotion heralds the "rise" of the conduct novel in the latter half of the eighteenth century, which contains both conduct discourse as I have described it above and the conventions of the novel of courtship.[35] In the attempt to modify *Pamela* further to serve readers younger than the eager adolescent novel readers Richardson was baiting with his moralistic cum romantic narrative, however, much of Richardson's complex social vision is lost. What remains are the moral maxims and sentiments insufficiently fleshed out by the succinct telling of the novel's plot, ultimately reducing *Pamela* the Younger to an educational program ideologically based in a prioritization of matter over form.[36]

The second part of *Pamela* concludes where this discussion began, with the question of female education and conduct. Pamela, who by novel's end has the care of six children (her four sons; a daughter; and B's illegitimate child, Miss Goodwin) becomes interested in theories of education and makes Locke's *Thoughts Concerning Education* the subject of numerous letters to her husband.[37] As part of her educational program for very young children, Pamela spins tales or fables of her own creation. After the young children leave the room, Pamela complies with Miss Goodwin's request for a *"Woman's* Story," and tells the history of four girls: Coquetilla, Prudiana, Profusiana, and Prudentia. Each girl, not surprisingly, lives up to her name and is miserable or happy accordingly. Miss Goodwin listens attentively and makes appropriate and judicious comments on each character's story, but when Pamela finishes the tale of Prudentia, she cannot conceal her emotion: " 'O Madam! Madam! said the dear Creature, smothering me with her rapturous Kisses, *Prudentia* is YOU!—is YOU indeed!—It *can* be nobody else!—Oh teach me, good GOD! to follow *your* Example, and I shall be a *second Prudentia*—Indeed I shall!' "[38] Pamela, who was rewarded for her successes as a conduct mistress, now functions as an advisor to a girl *without* a story—girls similar, presumably, to her readers. (Miss Goodwin, we are told by "the editor," marries at eighteen "a young Gentleman of fine Parts, and great Sobriety and Virtue: And that both she and her Spouse . . . emulated the great and good Examples set them by Mr. and Mrs. B.").[39] Pamela had maintained her honor and virtue in the face of fantastic circumstances unlikely to enter the lives of her readers, or Miss Goodwin herself, whose interesting history happened before she was born (the story of the illicit romance between her mother and B). Now fully embodied as a matron whose adventuresome adolescence can be told as a children's tale only when safely behind her, and firmly secure in the past tense rather than "to the moment," Pamela assumes her place on the nursery chair with unquestionable authority as a maternal educator and conduct book paragon.

3

The Value of Virtue

Dowry, Marriage Settlements,

and the Conduct Novel

Who can find a virtuous woman? for her price is

far above rubies.

Proverbs 31:10

'Tis the custom of som (and 'tis a common custome) to choose

wives by the weight, that is by their wealth.

James Howell, 1645

We leave Pamela rocking on the "nursery chair" surrounded by her children like some dainty version of Perrault's tale-spinner Mother Goose, her position as maternal educator firmly established. If Pamela's narrative had continued beyond this point, surely her greatest educational challenge would have been to raise her daughters to survive adolescence with their family values, reputations, and hymens intact. An exaggerated version of this struggle for virtue, of course, has been Pamela's own story, the trials of which she would not want to see repeated in her daughters' lives. Pamela need not worry, however, as she demonstrates the skills necessary to craft their happy endings. Just as her own ability to withstand B's pressures was, in part, a judgment upon the moral education she had received from *her* parents, Pamela, too, must enable her daughters to negotiate successfully the difficult and often lonely passage from child to woman, from maiden to matron. This chapter briefly discusses maternal education (or its absence) in the social and moral "preparedness" of the heroine in literature for adolescent girls. Then, in order to concretize and historicize the "value of virtue," I will turn to a consideration of the actual practice of dowry and marriage settlements. I conclude with a reading of two conduct novels written about and read by girls, Richardson's *Sir Charles Grandison* (1753–54) and Burney's *Evelina* (1778), in which the fictionalized enactment of marriage contracts illuminates the relationship between the intended husband and his bride. The worthy suitor indicates his intention to end courtship by the bestowing of his name, property, and bloodline through marriage, and the heroine, by signing the marriage articles—the difficulties of which she communicates through her body—signals her acceptance of the change in her status from the privately beloved to the publicly claimed.

I

Mitzi Myers notes that literature for children in the eighteenth century can be understood as transmitting social and cultural values from "surrogate mothers" to "daughters."[1] In their literary works for girls these women writers often confronted the need for maternal education by defining it and then offering idealized characterizations of it in their narratives. In Sarah Fielding's *The Governess: or, Little Female Academy* (1749), for example, there are two maternal teachers: Mrs. Teachum, the headmistress of a female boarding school, and Miss Jenny Peace, the eldest student. It is fourteen-year-old Jenny, however, who embodies the "true" maternal influence in the school, as her abilities to instruct and guide have come from the example of her good mother (now dead), whereas Mrs. Teachum is the "mouthpiece" of her (deceased) husband's teachings.[2] Mrs. Teachum's weaknesses as a moral guide are clearly demonstrated by her disciplinary tactics: after a physical brawl between the girls over the rights to a particularly luscious apple, Mrs. Teachum responds by imposing an unnamed "severe Punishment" on each pupil, and forcing them to make up with each other. The punishment and false promises of friendship, however, fail to reconcile the girls, as "a Grudge and Ill-will [remained] in their Bosoms" (6). Jenny, however, educates each combatant to the wrongs she has committed by demonstrating the "reasonableness" of personal "gain" through peaceful submission to others: "But don't you know, Miss *Sukey,* it would have shewn much more Spirit to have yielded the Apple to another, than to have fought about it? Then, indeed, you would have proved your Sense; for you would have shewn, that you had too much Understanding to fight about a Trifle. Then your Cloathes had been whole, your Hair not torn from your Head, your Mistress had not been angry, nor had your Fruit been taken away from you" (7).

The difference between the (reasonable) maternal and (inadequate) paternal educational legacies is emblematic of the female appropriation of writing for and about the moral and intellectual education of young women.[3] Jenny is empowered as a maternal educator and nurturer through the good education she has received from her mother; the continuity of that education is then demonstrated through her influence on the boarding-school girls.[4] Jenny Peace must leave the school at book's end (a conclusion that is entirely consistent with the eventual separation that occurs between the child and the mother in adolescence) to be reunited with a kind aunt. She does not depart, however, before having wrought her gentle influence upon every student in turn, instilling in each the maternal legacy she herself had been given. Indeed, Jenny becomes a powerful symbol of conduct-book values for Mrs. Teachum's pupils: "If any Girl was found to harbour in her Breast a rising Passion, which it was difficult to conquer, the Name and Story of Miss *Jenny Peace* soon gained her Attention, and left her without any other Desire than to emulate Miss *Jenny's* Virtues" (125).

The acceptance and practice of the "reasonable submission" Jenny advocates will prepare the girls for their later roles as marriageable daughters. Good maternal education will successfully prepare its "graduates" to participate in the competitive marriage market: submission will lead to the bride's later reluctance to confront adult sexuality (addressed later through the metaphor and practice of marriage settlements).

Jenny Peace—like all conduct novel heroines—must leave the private sphere of childhood and enter the public realm of adulthood only to return to private, domestic space. In this case, she returns not as a wife (like Burney's Evelina) but as a surrogate daughter to her aunt. This ultimate return to "mother" rather than husband in *The Governess* marks one difference between the conduct novel and fiction for younger girls, the latter which addresses an audience in preparation for mature sexuality and familial and social responsibility.

Many of the young girls requiring guidance in Mrs. Teachum's school are either motherless or inadequately mothered. The adolescent characters of Mary Wollstonecraft's *Original Stories from Real Life* (1788) are also sorely in need of maternal influence. Mary, fourteen, and Caroline, twelve, are sent to the care of the exacting Mrs. Mason who, like Mrs. Teachum, has lost both a child and a husband, yet is willing to undertake the job of surrogate mother and teacher of the girls. Through stories and examples from "real life," Mrs. Mason teaches the girls—whose faults are typically female and adolescent: ignorance, vanity, and a "turn for ridicule"—the benefits of charity submission, industry, humility, and devotion. As a mother figure, Mrs. Mason is exalted; her maternal influence and wisdom extend beyond her young charges to other "child-like" persons including the poor, the servile, and the suffering, who also profit from her attentions.

Just as the girls begin to "visibly improve," they are summoned by their father to spend the winter in London. Mrs. Mason travels with them to help them settle in and to impart a few last lessons appropriate for urban living and purchasing: to shop carefully, to live frugally in order to be generous to the poor, and to pay all debts on time. She leaves Mary and Caroline with a useful conduct book they have created together by this narrative of fault and correction: *Original Stories* itself.[5] Before the book ends, Mary and Caroline are able to demonstrate, through charitable actions (or shame for uncharitable ones), their new adherence to conduct book values.

In both *Original Stories* and *The Governess* the students of Mrs. Mason and Jenny Peace have learned their lessons well and are ready to enter the world armed with a good education. That Mrs. Mason's girls (and presumably some of Jenny's as well) travel from a retired life in the country to the city is not incidental. This movement from rural (private) to urban (public) is symbolic of the limitations of the maternal education, which ends before the female characters' entry into the social and sexual sphere where they must be assimilated without the mother-figure. This moment of autonomy is the most dangerous time of a young woman's life: she is on her own between her roles as dutiful daughter and obedient wife.

Within the paradigm of good maternal education, the adolescent is conducted to the brink of adult sexuality empowered with the virtues of modesty, chastity, and piety. However, the novel for younger girls does not bridge this gap from the presexual to the sexual. It is the province of the conduct novel to represent and demarcate "healthy" female sexual experience from virgin to bride.[6] As we have seen in the first chapter, the charitable or virtuous girl has value to spend as she chooses. Mary Poovey, among other critics, has commented upon "the power of what moralists called '[the girl's] Negative:' the right to resist or even reject the proposal of a suitor."[7] A conduct novel heroine must learn the market—as commodity and merchant—so that she can first create herself as desirable raw material for the worthy to choose, and then bestow that value upon him (and her eventual children). In this way, the maternally organized system of education, whether absent or present, is fundamental to the girl's value and is completed by a patriarchically determined—and terminal—education based on sexual desire and social and legal convention.

II

I have possessions ample enough for us both; and you deserve to share them with me; and you shall do it, with as little reserve, as if you had brought me what the world reckons an equivalent.

Samuel Richardson, *Pamela*

In its attempts to delineate and codify virtue, conduct discourse epitomizes the virtuous (see chapter 2), and transforms virtue from an interior goodness to formal, exterior characteristics. Virtue also has economic consequences through the transfer of property: only the "marriageable" (chaste) girl can be chosen as bride. " 'The Chastity of Women,' said Dr. Johnson . . . 'is of the utmost importance, as all the property depends upon it.' "[8] That is, her virtue (and property its sign) is transferred from the good girl to the husband through the bride's portion. She is rewarded, in turn, by the marriage settlements that establish her rights to property after "coverture" in the event of her husband's predecease.[9]

At common law, the widow has the right to "dower": generally the widow receives one-third of her husband's property seised either at the time of the engagement or held at the time of his death. Dower was considered "inconvenient" for wealthy men, however, as it could function as a "clog to alienation," in Blackstone's words[10]; that is, it was difficult to control property (whether by selling or granting it) once the widow had life-tenancy rights to it. Dower, therefore, fell into disuse by the eighteenth century in favor of jointure. If a woman agreed to a jointure (a settlement for her widowhood) at the time of her marriage, her dower was effectively barred. Jointure amounts were not related to the husband's property, but often tied to the size of the dowry: "By the later seventeenth century the amount specified for jointure in relation to the size of the bride's dowry was tending to become standardized at about £100 of jointure for each £1,000 of dowry. Thus in 1677 Lord Herbert agreed to a jointure of £730 a year for his wife Anne Ramsey, daughter of a substantial London merchant, whose dowry was £8,000."[11] There is debate over whether the move toward jointure in early modern England increased or lessened women's property rights. Blackstone, for his part, favored jointure.[12]

In her erudite study *Married Women's Separate Property in England, 1660–1833,* to which I am greatly indebted, Susan Staves succinctly describes the impetus behind marriage settlements and the parties who actually contracted them: "In general, eighteenth-century marriage settlements often had three important objects: to entail land on the groom and his male descendants so that it could not be sold away from the family, to bar dower for the bride and give her a jointure instead, and to arrange portions for daughters and younger sons born of the marriage. Although it is sometimes said that only the very privileged married with settlements, in fact, settlements were common among substantial country freeholders and among city business or professional people."[13]

In light of these laws and practices, Pamela's poverty would seem to make her unmarriageable and, in fact, B laments society's insistence on the institution of marriage and Pamela's seeming unfitness for it: "But what can I do? Consider the pride of my condition. I cannot endure the thought of marriage, even with a person of equal or superior degree to myself; and have declined several proposals of that kind: How then, with the distance between us in the world's judgment, can I think of making you my wife?" (223). The answer, of course, is that in order to embrace Pamela legally, B must desire her virtue. In this case, Pamela's "real" (actual and excessive) virtue rectifies the imbalance caused by her lack of real property. In the courtship plots of *Sir Charles Grandison* and especially Frances Burney's *Evelina,* the virtuous heroine is chosen in spite of her relatively limited resources or without knowledge of her wealth, respectively.[14]

The economically poor heroine can be chosen because of the gendered systems of exchange operative in conduct literature: the matriarchal/feminine economy of virtue, and the patriarchal/masculine economy of money. The preadolescent girl functions within the world of the former: she must prove her value through familial bonds of sisterhood and daughterhood (even if only metaphorical ones, as in the case of Jenny's pupils). The girl then must enter the larger commercial sphere of the marriage market, where the value of her virtue can be exchanged into currency. If marriageable, she leaves the matriarchal or private family for the public patriarchal arena where courtship and marriage are conducted and arranged. Reverend Villars, while neither mother nor father to Evelina, "maternally" nurtures, educates, and prays for his foster daughter without leaving his private space.

Although it might seem that these systems are antithetical, or that without the influx of real property in marriage the patriarchal system would surely crash for the expense of all these worthy yet poor wives, in literary texts the two economies are reconciled through the force of a coherent social vision that prizes an aristocracy of feminine manners—chaste and "aesthetic" behavior— as much as the wealthy estate. (The theory is rarely put into practice, though: many "economically disadvantaged" heroines turn out to be secretly wealthy.)[15] The at times competing interests among free trade, patriarchy, and class endogamy coalesce within the ideological struggle over the true value of marriage. Erica Harth discusses the "changing value of married love" as it is represented by the conflict surrounding Hardwicke's Marriage Act of 1753, and argues that "the proponents of each side display remarkable internal consistency. Either you regulate the flow of wealth through regulation of love and marriage, or you leave both wealth and love to circulate 'freely.' The language of land was also the language of the benevolent paternalism that regulated the world of guilds and mercantilism."[16] The two systems of value can be exchanged into like currencies by means of an ideological equation where (x)virtue $= (y)$money. In actual marriages, however, the economics of pervasive and public patriarchy felt through social, religious, and legal rules and customs, overshadowed any other imagined system. This is not to argue that many nontraditional marriages did not take place, only that the powerful norm did not support them.[17]

Although to be chosen by the worthy suitor—to deserve such attention and approbation—is the greatest reward for literary heroines, it is within the negotiation of dowry and marriage contracts that the "value of virtue" is finally solidified. That virtue has material and cultural value is clearly demonstrated in conduct manual discourse, as well as in the discourse of penitence for sexual "crimes." The heroine's material (economic) value—her inheritance, dowry, jointure, income, and earning capacity (if working class)—is inevitably influenced by her cultural (social) value as a modest, charitable, pious, and chaste girl.

Pamela and B can marry only after each recognizes the worth of the other: B must choose Pamela and she must validate that choice through her substitution of virtue for the "world's equivalent." Pamela is ashamed of her poverty only in response to B's preference, because sex—not money—is the contested issue in their relationship up to the moment of marriage. At that instant, the question of equitable exchange of goods and services shifts from the sexual (B's offer of "corrupt" articles to ensure Pamela's submission to his desire) to the contractual. Pamela reveals her substantial knowledge of contracts when she frets that she is an empty-handed bride, unlike other women B might have married: "I am thinking, sir, said I, of another mortifying thing too; that were you to marry a lady of birth and fortune answerable to your own, all the eve to the day would be taken up in reading, signing, and sealing of settlements, and portion, and such like: But now the poor Pamela brings you nothing at all" (354).

In describing the requisite components to make a binding contract, William Blackstone discusses the need for the reading, signing, and sealing of the deed.[18] In addition to these formal characteristics, of course, is the necessary component to any legal contract: sufficient *consideration*. Consideration is the mutual interest that binds two parties in a contract, the equal inducement to make the promise. Without proper consideration, there can be no enforceable contract: "unless the promisee has either conferred a benefit on the promisor, or incurred a detriment, as the inducement to the promise," the contract is void.[19] Marriage uses *good* consideration (as opposed to *valuable* consideration) in the making of a general civil contract: "a *good* consideration is such as that of blood, or of natural love and affection . . . being founded on motives of generosity, prudence, and natural duty."[20] B learns to appreciate the good consideration that Pamela brings to their marriage, and denounces any other kind as avaricious and unbecoming: "I want not to be employed in settlements. Those are for such to regard, who make convenience and fortune the *prime* considerations . . . for, as to my own opinion, you bring me what is infinitely more valuable, an experienced truth, a well-tried virtue, and a wit and behaviour more than equal to the station you will be placed in" (355, my emphasis).[21] Pamela and B's companionate marriage is one literary response to the problem of assigning and rewarding the value of virtue. But Richardson intended Pamela to function as a fictional anomaly, the better to serve as a moral exemplar to his (her) readers. The following discussion interrogates the function of a crucial stage in the conduct novel heroine's life: the negotiation of marriage settlements. This period is critical as it signals the end of courtship (the heroine's virtue has been proven), but occurs before marriage while the bride maintains a legal identity. Within this negotiation, the fictional and historical questions concerning the value of the bride's virtue are answered.

Marriage settlements involved not one-way but mutual endowment. Generally, the dowry or bride portion was a gift of property or money given to the bride, usually by her father (but conceivably by other family members, depending upon circumstances). Its terms had probably been determined in her parents' or brother's marriage settlements; in turn she gave it to her husband upon marriage. Modern use distinguishes "dower" from "dowry": as discussed briefly above, dower is the common-law right of a widow to life-interest in one-third of her husband's property seised in fee during coverture.[22] I will refer to the bride's portion at marriage as her "dowry."[23]

The assumptions about dowry that Pamela laments allude to the monetary relationship between the bride and groom that is generally established before the sexual union takes place. The historian Lloyd Bonfield describes the prevailing custom of the bride's portion: "Regardless of whether the bride was an heiress, she was required to make a contribution toward enlarging her prospective husband's estate. This contribution, the bride's portion, might take the form of land or cash; if it was the latter, the marriage settlement often required the purchase of estates which were to descend with the patrimony. In the main, this process favoured the 'great magnates'; as landowners with more substantial rent rolls could offer more generous jointures, they commanded the brides with the largest portions."[24]

The history of upper-class dowry awards in the eighteenth century cannot be separated from the legal device of the so-called "strict settlement" that wealthy families used to protect their social status through the protection of their land. Eighteenth-century landed society "required" large dowries in order to increase their property holdings, while at the same time holding the family's wealth secure for future generations. The arrangement of the wife's income in the event of her husband's predecease—her dower or her jointure—therefore, was critical to the heir's prospects.[25]

The theoretical center of the debate over dower versus jointure is the distinction between public and private. Believed to be a common-law *right* of all widows (but adulterous ones),[26] dower blurred the distinction between the private action of marriage between two consenting adults and the public action of property transfer that affects future generations of citizens. Of course, marriage has always functioned as a regulated social act as well as a legal action. Laws of custom and of the state have controlled who may marry (age, gender, relational degree), when, and where. The passage of Hardwicke's Marriage Act of 1753, the most significant of the legal checks on marriage, was an attempt to prevent the "Fleet Marriages" (clandestine marriages performed within the "rules" of the Fleet Prison) reportedly common in the eighteenth century. It held, in part, that parental consent was necessary for all daughters under 21 years of age, and that all engaged couples must post banns three weeks in advance of the wedding ceremony (time of day and location were also regulated) to signal their intention to marry and to give dissenters opportunities to object.[27] The rights in conflict relating to marriage were the right to control land (selling, improving, and giving) versus the right of the state to protect its citizens and its moral code, and regulate the transfer of land and property.[28]

The Dower Act of 1833 (and the substitution of jointure made in some marriages before this time) privatized the legal relation between the husband and wife, and retained all rights for the husband. The Dower Act "allowed legal intellectuals to feel that they had corrected an error but preserved for individual women no socially enforced rights; an individual woman got nothing but what her own husband privately elected to bestow."[29] A husband could choose to award "pin money" to his wife for her sole use during the marriage. A "relatively new social phenomenon in the late Restoration and early eighteenth century," pin money allowed the wife a minor personal fund, generally an annual sum that enabled her to buy personal goods that belonged to her absolutely.[30] In this way, pin money functioned as separate property under coverture.

Interpretations differ as to the primary motivators in the creation of marriage settlements. Conventional thought indicates that fathers were in charge of the arrangements.[31] In *The Patriarch's Wife: Literary Evidence and the History of the Family,* however, Margaret J. M. Ezell questions this assumption, as families were quite often fatherless: "In his study of the Court of Orphans, Charles Carleton suggests that at least one child in three in Tudor and Stuart England lost his or her father before reaching maturity."[32] Ezell determines that widows were often the negotiators of their children's marriages.[33] Regardless of the gender of the primary marriage conductor, however, the positions of the bride and groom remain fixed and immutable.

The dowry's actual value, of course, varied according to each family's wealth, inclination, and size. Determining the amount of the dowry was a matter of family politics wherein the daughter often had little authority: "Since provisions were an item of family expenditure which might painlessly be diminished, there was a danger that some fathers might heed the advice of Lord Delamar, and seek to economize at the expense of their 'excess children': 'To provide convenient matches for your daughters if you can, is without doubt your Duty, as also to give them good portions, but not such as will make your eldest sonne uneasy, for that is to give them more than comes to their share.' "[34] A bride was therefore often a minor player in the production of marriage, needing the "protection" of her father (or her future husband in some cases) to insure her standard of living.[35]

The clandestine epistolary element of Lady Mary and Edward Wortley Montague's courtship (1710–1712), as Mona Scheuermann points out, is fairly obsessed with matters of property, dowry, settlement, and estate. Their maneuverings represent a fascinating example of real-life, take-your-gloves-off marriage negotiations where the prospective groom and in-laws press for financial advantage while the interested bride protests, yet must stand and watch. Wortley importunes, "If £60,000 should be added to the estate of your family (as I hear it will) the giving of £20,000 or £25,000 out of it for portions is a very trifle. . . . For what you now cost is certainly more than the interest of 2 very large portions. If your father and brother joyn in this it may easily be done and surely a brother cant take it ill to hear such a thing mention'd."[36] Lady Mary's parents opposed the match in part because Wortley refused to "burden his estate" by entailing it on his eventual heir. Her parents rather accepted the improbably named Honorable Clotworthy Sheffington as son-in-law, whose treatment of Lady Mary would be more considerate, allowing her generous pin money (£500 a year) and a per annum sum (£1,200) if he should predecease her.[37]

Unlike the heroines discussed below, Lady Mary has a few choice words for her beau about his peculiar pecuniary lovemaking and dilly-dallying. While denying any mercenary interest in him, she throws his rival's "charms" in Wortley's face: "I think there cannot be a greater proof of the contrary than treating with you, where I am to depend entirely on your generosity, at the same time that I have settle'd on me £300 per Annum pin money and a considerable jointure in another place, not to reckon that I may have by his temper what command of his Estate I please; and with you I have nothing to pretend to."[38]

They do elope and marry; Lady Mary Wortley Montague becomes an actual epistolary heroine in her own right. Within literary treatments of courtship and marriage, however, the marriage settlement generally highlights the ethical behavior and moral worth of the affianced couple (especially the bride) rather than "petty" machinations of the parents (*Clarissa* is an exception). Indeed, in terms of the groom's role, in the novel of sentiment the contractual element of property transfer within marriage—rather than undermining the man's emotional commitment—serves to strengthen and enlarge his role as protector.

I would like to return briefly to the didactic *Pamela:* Pamela's "published" virtue obviates the need for a public (or actual) dowry. B's intentions toward Pamela must undergo great change before he can marry—and they do: from the desire to ravish (her body) to the desire to lavish (his property). B's new "verbal" position styles him not only a savvy grammarian and linguist of moral conduct, but also a worthy suitor in the conduct novel tradition. In fact, one of the measures of B's intentions throughout the book is the degree to which he indicates his willingness to provide for Pamela. The parodic settlements he attempts to coerce Pamela to sign are indeed generous (in a fit of passion B doubles the usual property settlement: "If the terms I have offered are not sufficient, I will augment them to two-thirds of my estate" [202]). But they also corrupt the premise of good contracts: sufficient consideration. Pamela's future products—illegitimate children— are not legally recognizable as heirs and thus the contract fails because the provisions for a mistress and illegitimate offspring offer "illegal consideration" and are against "public interest." B can afford to ignore marriage settlements because Pamela's legitimate children represent a kind of "legal tender" in the transmission of heirs that is to B's benefit in the transfer of property and continuation of his name.

While the courtship plots of many eighteenth- and nineteenth-century conduct novels drew much of their interest from issues of dowry and suitors' intentions (matrimonial and economic intentions essentially function similarly), it is my hope that this focus on the technical legal aspects of actual property transfer in marriage has not obscured our perception of the lively interest people took in the conflation of love and money—or private life made public—that dowries represented. Capitalizing on the ever-popular fascination with the mating rituals of the wealthy, periodicals such as the *Gentleman's Magazine* (1731–1914), and newspapers such as *The Daily Post-Boy* and the *London Chronicle* reported dowry amounts in their wedding announcements. Cannon notes that "one of the crucial ingredients in the success of Edward Cave's *Gentleman's Magazine* was the monthly column of marriages, which gave the amount of dowry, real or invented, and any piquant garnishings that could be provided" (73).[39] A sampling of the *Gentleman's Magazine* for 1753 (the first year after *Sir Charles Grandison*'s publication) and 1778 (*Evelina*) reveals some interesting statistics about dowry amounts as well as gossipy tidbits thought worthy of publication.

The marriage announcements, located in "The Historical Chronicle" section each month, were generally very short. A typical example from 1753 would indicate the date of the wedding, the groom's name and address, the bride's name and address, the names of "significant" relatives, and, frequently, the amount of dowry presented at the time of the marriage. The fictional Harriet Byron's announcement, for example, would read something like "Nov 16 Sir Charles Grandison, Bart., of Grosvenor-street and Hampshire;—— to Miss Byron of Northamptonshire, £13,000."[40] There were also variations on this model: at times, social class was aggressively broached when a groom's occupation was mentioned (for example, from March 1753, "Mr. Mason, an eminent brewer" was married); sometimes the bride's name was omitted in favor of establishing her "lineage" through father or first husband.[41]

Information of interest to the "enquiring" reader included namedropping ("Frederick Stanton, Esq.; nearly related to the E. of Stamford" [September 1753]), explanations of behavior (the notice for Mary Worgan's May 1753 marriage indicated that while she had been "lately chosen organist of St. Dunstan in the East; since her marriage she has resigned"), and curious facts about the wedded couple (nonagenarians marrying after a twenty-seven-year courtship [November 1778] and the marriage between "John Ford, aged 19, 5 feet 6 inches high to Biddy Carr, aged 23, 3 feet 3 inches high" [April 1766]).

It is important to note that in only 41 of 170 published marriages for the twelve months of 1753 were dowries reported at all (in three cases, per annum incomes were given). In other words, in only approximately 25 percent of all marriage announcements were dowries included. The amounts ranged from £2,000 to £150,000, with the mean dowry at £16,000 and the median at £10,000 (without the £150,000 "spike," however, the mean would have been £12,700).

My second sample from 25 years later reveals a different picture. One hundred and ninety marriages were reported in 1778, but only one dowry amount was published: in November 1778, Daniel Wilson married Miss Egerton, only daughter of Samuel Egerton, MP, with a £500,000 fortune. The frequency of dowries reported seems to drop off to almost nothing by the mid-1760s, so that, for example, the Earl of Strathmore's marriage to Miss Bowes was reported without a £ sign: the bride was denoted "the richest heiress in England" (144). Edward Cave (or "Sylvanus Urban"), the founder of the magazine, died early in 1754, and it may be supposed that the magazine's character changed under different editorship; another reasonable supposition is that the publication of dowry amounts increasingly was considered ill-bred, and that only the largest dowries were exposed to the public's delighted consumption at all.[42]

III

[T]he female Bodies are more tender and *moister* than the *Male*: and so Mens Bodies being harder and drier, they are more slow in ripening; and Womens Bodies, because they are softer and moister, are more quickly ripe; like as it is to be seen in Plants and fruits, whereof that which is more soft and moist is sooner ripe, than that which is hard and dry.

Henry Swinburne, *Treatise of Spousals* (1686)

Any estate in lands, or any pecuniary provision, given to an intended wife before marriage, bars dower, *provided* she will join in the conveyance, if she be of full age; and if she join in it with her father or guardian, if she be under age.

Blackstone, *Commentaries on the Laws of England* (emphasis mine)

Henry Swinburne's theory of wetness explains to his satisfaction gender distinctions accountable for the difference in the legal capacity to contract marriage: boys were capable at fourteen years of age; girls, twelve years of age. (This theory seems to make some literary sense when we consider how many heroines dissolve into tears during the course of their courtships). In fact, Ann Kibbie argues that the tensions between the sexual and economic identified by Steven Marcus in *The Other Victorians* may be mitigated "through a perfectly organized, natural circulation of liquid wealth."[43] This "liquidity of sentimental economy" operative in the narrative of virtue as well as of (sexual) exchange, links economics and sexuality through not only tears but also, in Fanny Hill's terms, through the "dissolvent" that is "the body's sexual fluids."[44] In the conduct novel, a genre that clearly unites economics and sexuality through the timely union of appropriate lovers (in terms of wealth, virtue, and general attractiveness) and the creation of a new family with a combined economic base, the heroine's moist body—her ability to cry in joy, sympathy, and charming frustration—provides another signal of her virtue and her value. (Her moist sexual attractiveness, however, is just as important). It is not only the case, as in *Pamela,* that domestic value creates market value, as Nancy Armstrong argues in *Desire and Domestic Fiction,* but that market value in conjunction with domestic value helps to define the valuable girl, and in so doing, requires a further relinquishment of power and autonomy that marks the movement from maiden to matron, from valuable (potential) to purchased (spent).

Every marriage "begins" with the private moment of the proposal. These "spousals"—the mutual promise to contract marriage at a future date—were regulated and, like marriages themselves, could be considered valid or invalid. In fact, a legitimate spousal functioned as a contract in the seventeenth century, and held the two parties as good as married under the law (that is, one could not legally contract spousals with another, or engage in sexual intercourse with another without committing adultery). The contraction of spousals could be a family event, especially in the case of "infants" when parental involvement was especially common.[45] In the legal contraction of spousals, as in the proposal to marry, both parties must consent to the future marriage, must signal his or her intention. The worthy suitor indicates his generous intention by pledging his faithfulness to the maiden, giving his "word"; by contrast, the beloved may proclaim her assent through silence or inarticulateness or through the body's "signs": fainting and blushing. Like the visible blush, the inaudible consent is a sign of femininity and the "woman's embodiment of modesty and sensitivity."[46] There is little difference between Pamela, who asks "what is left me but words" and then "loses" language in marriage (she admits to the loss of descriptive power after her thoughts are overwhelmed by gratitude) and the epistolary brides Evelina, Harriet, and Clarissa, who are each silenced once engaged (or in anticipation of an engagement). Dorothea E. von Mücke's interesting study *Virtue and the Veil of Illusion: Generic Innovation and the Pedagogical Project in Eighteenth-Century Literature* discusses Clarissa's refusal to act in contradiction to parental authority, and her attendant inability to compromise "the integrity of her heart."[47] Clarissa's paradox is played out in terms of the legal issues considered in this chapter: Clarissa's independence ("that I should be made sole") is feared by her repressive family, and, in order to control her body and her property, they would force her to sign the marriage settlements. Although Clarissa is willing to give up the property bequeathed to her by her grandfather, her intention is to avoid a direct refusal of her parents' wishes in favor of an indirect refusal by the "substitution" of "gestural language" for the "symbolic order of written transactions"[48]: "I resolve then, upon the whole, to stand this one trial of Wednesday next—or, perhaps I should say, of Tuesday evening, if my father hold his purpose of endeavoring, in person, to make me *read,* or *hear* read, and then *sign,* the settlements. That must be the greatest trial of all."[49] Von Mücke reads Clarissa's intentions in thwarting her parents' desires for her marriage as resulting from her fears about her inability to withstand intact a confrontation with the father and his law. Her signature on the marriage contract "would annihilate her heart."[50] Clarissa's only solution is to refuse through a loss of bodily agency: " 'If I can prevail upon them by my prayers (perhaps I shall fall into fits; for the very first appearance of my father, after having been so long banished from his presence, will greatly affect me) if, I say, I can prevail upon them by my prayers to lay aside their views; or to suspend the day.' She expects this interruption in the chain of writing to arise from her physical reaction to the sight of her father. Her fits would affirm his parental authority as a reaction of love and awe at his sight while rendering her incapable of signing."[51] Harriet Byron's inability to sign proceeds not from fear, but marks her modesty; she is ashamed to be thought "too" aware of the legal arrangements of marriage, Grandison's wealth and generosity to her, and their impending sexual union, lest she be considered "forward," "knowing," or "grasping." She must literally sign herself into Grandison's hands, and what embarrasses her is the knowledge and awareness of this voluntary act of relinquishment and public avowal of sexual maturity.[52] By signing the articles, the heroine makes what is private, public.[53]

Richardson's *Sir Charles Grandison* (1753–54) unites many of the legal, moral, and fictive concerns discussed thus far in this chapter and therefore will introduce my analysis of the literary treatment of marriage negotiations. The arrangement of Harriet Byron's dowry and marriage settlements, and, in particular, her reaction to them, reaffirms the worth of both Harriet and Grandison and the appropriateness of their marriage.

Like *Pamela* and *Evelina* (to the extent that Orville does not know Evelina's financial status), *Sir Charles Grandison* offers an unequal marriage in terms of fortune, but deems it appropriate and equivalent on the basis of the merit of each partner. An only child and an orphan, Harriet comes from a good family, but her fortune is limited because her father's estate had been entailed upon male issue and therefore legally devolved upon distant relatives at Mr. Byron's death, depriving Harriet of a large inheritance. The letter written by Harriet's guardian, Mr. Deane, to Sir Charles informing him of the particulars of Harriet's portion is such a fund of information regarding inheritance, jointure, estate income, and the role of the groom that I will quote liberally from it:

> It has always been my notion, that a young gentleman, in such a case, should, the moment he offers himself, if his own proposals are acceptable, be spared the *indelicacy* of asking questions as to fortune. We know, Sir, yours is great: But as your spirit is princely, you ought to have something worthy of your own fortune with a wife. But here, alas! we must fail, I doubt; at least, in hand.
>
> Mr. Byron was one of the best of men; his Lady a most excellent woman: There never was a happier pair. Both had reason to boast of their ancestry. His estate was upwards of Four thousand pounds a year; but it was entailed, and, in failure of male heirs, was to descend to a second branch of the family . . . Mr. Byron died a young man, and left his Lady *ensient*; but grief for losing him, occasioned first her miscarriage, and then her death; and the estate followed the name. Hence, be pleased to know, that Miss Byron's fortune, in her own right, is no more than between Thirteen and Fourteen thousand pounds. It is chiefly in the funds. It has been called £15,000 but is not much more than thirteen. Her grandmother's jointure is between 4 and £500 a year. We none of

us wish to see my god-daughter in possession of it: She herself least of all. . . . She [Mrs. Shirley, the grandmother] therefore can do but little towards the increase of her child's fortune. But Shirley-manor is a fine old seat, Sir!—And there is timber upon the estate, which wants but ten years growth, and will be felled to good account. Mr. Selby [Harriet's uncle by marriage] is well in the world. He proposes, as a token of his love, to add £3,000 in hand to his niece's fortune; and by his will, something very considerable, farther expectant on his Lady's death; who being Miss Byron's aunt, by the father's side, intends by her will to do very handsomely for her.—By the way, my dear Sir, be assured, that what I write is absolutely unknown to Miss Byron.

There *is* a man who loves her as he loves himself [Mr. Deane]. This man has laid by a sum of money every year for the advancing her in marriage, beginning with the fifth year of her life, when it was seen what a hopeful child she was: This has been put at accumulated interest; and it amounts, in sixteen years, or thereabouts, to very near £8,000. This man, Sir, will make up the Eight thousand Ten, to be paid on the day of marriage: And I hope, without promising for what this man will do further at his death, that you will accept of this Five or Six-and-Twenty thousand Pounds, as the chearfullest given and best-bestowed money that ever was laid out. . . . [54]

As to settlements in return, I would have acted the lawyer, but the *honest* lawyer with you, Sir, and made demands of you; but Mr. and Mrs. Selby, and Mrs. Shirley, unanimously declare, that you shall not be prescribed to in this case. Were you not Sir Charles Grandison? was the question. . . . Most other men ought to be spurred; but *this* must be held in. But, however, I acquiesced; and the more easily, because I expect that the deeds shall pass through my hands; and I will take care that you shall not, in order to give a proof of Love where it is not wanted, exert an inadequate generosity.[55]

Mr. Deane's letter touches upon many of the vagaries and intangibles that can affect the marriage portion and, by extension, the social and commercial "worth" of the bride. He describes one arm of the strict settlement that can reapportion land within the larger family in order to preserve the land for male heirs (and thus keep it in the family, for if Harriet had inherited her father's property, it would have become Grandison wealth after her marriage). That the size of Harriet's fortune had clearly been bandied about in social circles ("It has been called £15,000 but is not much more than thirteen") and that she is the object of the affections of both the virtuous and the avaricious even before she leaves Selby-house to visit London, attests to the public nature of a heroine's financial attractions. The widowed grandmother Mrs. Shirley's jointure is mentioned as a potential source for the increase of Harriet's fortune, but an income that would, in its possession, reflect badly upon the bride. As we also see in the above letter, Harriet's conduct as a child of even five years of age has direct consequences for her future financial prospects. Her "hopeful" behavior, once wedded to a "hopeful" (interest-bearing) investment, nets Harriet eight thousand pounds.

It is also critical to her heroism that Harriet's ignorance of the marriage articles, which Mr. Deane emphatically asserts, is evidence of Harriet's "purity" of mind. Like her awareness of sexual matters, her knowledge must be tentative and attenuated. Grandison refrains from consulting Harriet on the particulars of her settlements "for tenderness." He implies that her good sense would have made her a worthy partner in a discussion of this topic, but his regard for her delicacy stops him: "Our Equipages, my dearest life, are all in great forwardness. In tenderness to you, I have forborne to consult you upon some parts of them, as my regard for your judgment would otherwise have obliged me to do. The Settlements are all ready" (6:175). Although it is not made clear from Grandison's letter from which part of the settlement his "tenderness" protects Harriet's delicacy, one can conjecture that he means to spare her any discussion of the transferral of his property after his death. It is interesting to note how this "consideration" manages to exclude Harriet from her financial prospects in marriage—an action entirely consistent with the feminine values promoted in conduct manuals and conduct novels. The heroine's understanding of (and conscious participation in) the negotiation of marriage settlements would render her immodest.[56]

Consistent with this ideology of distance from knowledge and "consciousness," Harriet Byron's relation to her marriage articles is described not in her own letter, but in a letter written by Grandison's sister, Lady G. Although a large group of curious parties are invited to hear the articles read, one of the most significant parties to the contract, the bride, begs to be excused. Once summoned for the actual signing of the settlements, Harriet is unable to put pen to paper:

Mr. Deane, Sir Charles, Lord and Lady W.[,] Mrs. Shirley, Mr. and Mrs. Selby, Lucy, Lord L. and I, withdrew, to read, and see signed, the Marriage-articles, soon after tea. . . . When they were ready to sign, the dear Harriet was sent for in. She would not come before. She begged, she prayed, she might not. The first line of each clause, and the last, for form sake, were run over, by Mr. Deane, as fast as he could read. How the dear creature trembled when she came in, and all the time of the shortened reading! But when the pen was given her, to write her name, she dropt it twice, on the parchment. Sir Charles saw her emotion with great concern; and held her up, as she stood. My dearest life, said he, take time, take time—Do not hurry; putting the pen each time, with reverence, in her fingers. She tried to write, but twice her pen would not touch the parchment, so as to mark it. She sat down. Take time, take time, my Love, repeated he. She soon made another effort, his arm round her waist—She then signed them; but Sir Charles held her hand, and the parchments in them, when she delivered them.—"As your act and deed, my dearest Love?" said Sir Charles.—"Yes, indeed," said the dear creature, and made him a courtesy; hardly knowing what she did. (6: 216)

Harriet's reluctance to sign (like the reluctance to name the day of marriage—a "pathology" from which both Pamela and Evelina suffer) indicates her modesty and appropriateness as a wife.[57] The signing of the marriage articles literally and figuratively formalizes the bride's acquiescence to her husband. Yet her virtue and modesty disallow her from eagerly announcing her desire. The signing of the marriage contract communicates publicly (in literature) the desire to co-mingle property as well as body, and therefore this event must be delicately narrated in order to underscore the heroine's behavior in a manner consistent with her other virtues.

At the moment of signing Harriet is literally stabilized (by Grandison as he supports her body, as well through the social stability conferred by the married state), whereas the unknown and aliased Evelina Anville, although virtuous, is at first a kind of threat to the rigid London and Bristol beau monde. Sir Clement Willoughby, finding himself pleasantly in lust with Evelina, avidly pursues the beautiful but mysteriously circumstanced teenager, yet when he is questioned by Lord Orville concerning his intentions toward her, Willoughby quickly renounces any desire to marry an unknown quantity with a "worthless" dowry:

" 'My intentions,' cried he, 'I will frankly own, are hardly known to myself. I think Miss Anville the loveliest of her sex, and, were I a *marrying* man, she, of all the women I have seen, I would fix upon for a wife: but I believe that not even the philosophy of your Lordship would recommend to me a connection of that sort, with a girl of obscure birth, whose only dowry is her beauty, and who is evidently in a state of dependency.' "[58] Orville's desire for Evelina, which is nearly as inappropriate as B's for Pamela, is sanctioned through his intention to provide for her absolutely—to supply her dowry.[59] Hughes cites an historical precedent for this kind of leniency in the case of another kind of "inappropriate" marriage: "Pope Benedict XII viewed as sufficient grounds for allowing the marriage, contracted within the forbidden degree of consanguinity, between the Genoese patrician Tropa Cattanco and his poor, but aristocratic bride Salvagia Lercari the fact that the groom had constituted his wife's dowry."[60] In fact, once properly affianced, Orville admits that he had been "imprudent" in declaring his intentions toward Evelina before accounting for her seemingly awkward familial circumstances: "[H]e frankly owned, that he had fully intended making more minute enquiries into my family and connections, and particularly concerning *those* people he saw with me at Marybone, before he acknowledged his prepossession in my favour: but the suddenness of my intended journey, and the uncertainty of seeing me again, put him quite off his guard, and 'divesting him of prudence, left him nothing but love' " (389).[61] Mrs. Selwyn is so concerned that Orville might act like a typical young man and change his mind about Evelina upon reconsideration of his economically rash decision to marry a disinherited heiress, that she satirically counsels Evelina to hasten Orville to the altar: " 'Now, my dear,' continued she, 'I advise you by all means to marry him directly; nothing can be more precarious than our success with Sir John; and the young men of this age are not to be trusted with too much deliberation, where their interests are concerned' " (369).

Circumstances are such in this dramatic affair that Evelina, while she confesses her love for Orville, does not formally consent to be married to him. Always an "occasional" speaker, as John Richetti notes, Evelina's "deference to the discourse of others" is unfailingly correct.[62] In this scene, Evelina's silence allows for the "greater discovery" of Orville's love to be amplified, and the articulation of her own desire to be suppressed, thus reinforcing her powerlessness and emphasizing her modesty in the face of male desire, despite her reciprocated affection.[63] Orville realizes Evelina's failure to accept him when he asks Evelina for "one hour's conversation" to "confirm my happiness" (353). But the astounding news of the counterfeit Miss Belmont and Sir John's penitence interrupts the usual progression of an impending marriage, and, with Mrs. Selwyn acting as conveyancer, the management of Evelina's personal life and the transferral of property occurs without her. The highly efficient Mrs. Selwyn convenes all necessary *male* parties in arranging Evelina's affairs, and responds to Evelina's shock at being informed that she was to be married in the following week by reassuring her of her uselessness in the business of marriage: "As to consulting *you,* my dear, it was out of all question, because, you know, young ladies hearts and hands are always to be given with reluctance" (377). As Mrs. Selwyn ironically intimates, in literature for girls the virtuous heroine's response to the creation of marriage articles functions as another indicator of her worth; the management of the articles is a moral activity as well as an economic one.

The valuable legacy of Caroline Evelyn, Evelina's mother, is to be found in Evelina's face and figure, as the worthy Orville recognizes and the inappropriate Willoughby does not. Once confronted with the sight and sound (through the recitation of a letter Caroline had written just prior to her death) of his wronged wife, Sir John Belmont also acknowledges Evelina's worth, and owns her (both emotionally and legally) as his daughter and heiress. The "gift" of his name and his money are considered to be equivalent—the name having real value: "Sir John will give you, immediately, £30,000; all settlements, and so forth, will be made for you in the name of Evelina Belmont" (378). Acting the modest young heroine, Evelina waives her right to participate in the marriage settlements by informing Orville: "I assured him, I was almost ignorant even of the word [settlements]" (380). Orville, in fact, is so comfortable with his rights over Evelina, that he gives away, in effect, one-half of Evelina's portion: "For I learnt, by Mr. Macartney, that this noblest of men had insisted the so-long-supposed Miss Belmont should be considered *indeed* as my sister, and as the co-heiress of my father! though not in *law,* in *justice,* he says, she ought ever to be treated as the daughter of Sir John Belmont" (387).[64]

Two observers of "bridal behavior"—Mrs. Selwyn ("young ladies hearts and hands are always to be given with reluctance") and Charlotte G. ("[Harriet] made him a courtesy [after signing the articles]; hardly knowing what she did")—thus note reluctance and unconsciousness in the face of public admission of adult sexuality (marriage and settlements). I have argued that these behaviors are in response to male expectation and intention. This is not to say that the virtuous brides do not intend marriage: in fact, both Evelina and Harriet are notable heroines for "loving (the man) first," which is a potential difficulty for both of them as their hearts are in danger of breaking and their love in danger of exposure. The problem of their first love, however, emphasizes the fact that only male intention is finally significant (will he choose me or not?). Conventionally, the female response to male attention ought to be primarily reactive and unconscious if the maternal education—or its equivalent—has been successfully imparted and internalized. *The Governess* describes in detail the unfavorable results of inadequate mothering, as well as the positive behavioral and personality changes that can be wrought by the maternal surrogate. Both Harriet and Evelina are essentially orphans who were fortunate in the kind nurturing and education offered by friends or relatives. Yet, by virtue of the maternal surrogates' care, Harriet and Evelina are protected from the detrimental lack of maternal education as it is demonstrated in *The Governess*, *Original Stories*, and countless other eighteenth-century books for children and conduct novels for adolescents like Eliza Haywood's *History of Miss Betsy Thoughtless* (1751) and Elizabeth Inchbald's *Simple Story* (1791).

The sharply contrasting masculine and feminine modes of behavior demonstrated in the conduct novel and in domestic ideology delimit female submission to social convention—that is, to male desire—as a private action, whereas the male intention that constructs social custom and ideology is construed as public. These two gendered means of virtue come together in the marriage settlement (both historically and fictionally) and result in the production of the sign of virtue, modesty, education, and consent: a public and conscious renunciation of adult sexuality on the part of the woman, and its commodification through the settlement.

In the above discussion I have argued that in girls' culture, as it was constructed through both legal practice and through the genre of the conduct novel, domestic value and market value reflect each other. Chapter 4 considers how feminine value—and the value of childhood—shifts again in the late-eighteenth and early nineteenth-century novel, in part, through the influence of the Evangelical reformers of the age. Fanny Price of Jane Austen's *Mansfield Park* embodies a Pamelian domestic value (modest, submissive, *private*) wedded to a kind of Evangelical spirituality that culminates in a desirable stability of both class and sexuality.

4

The Happiness of Virtue

Evangelicalism, Class, and Gender

*Virtue and Happiness are not attained by chance, nor by a
cold and languid approbation; they must be fought with ardour,
attended to with diligence, and every assistance must be
eagerly embraced that may enable you to obtain them.*
Hester Chapone, *Letters on the Improvement of
the Mind* (1773)

*Being from the lowest order of people they have not been
taught to associate happiness with virtue.*
Rev. Thomas Stevenson (1814)

After Jenny Peace has reconciled her eight quarrelling schoolfellows to each other, she reminds them of the theory of "rational happiness" underlying her method of peacekeeping: "nothing can shew so much Sense, as thus to own yourselves in Fault: For could any-thing have been so foolish, as to spend all your Time in Misery, rather than at once to make use of the Power you have of making yourselves happy?" (10). Jenny's rhetoric is indeed persuasive: imbued with an understanding of the symbiotic relationship between happiness and virtue, each girl is able to regulate her behavior successfully so that "all Quarrels and Contentions were banished from [Mrs. Teachum's] House" (125). The present chapter considers the ideal of domestic "happiness" for upper- and lower-class girls as it is constructed by female reformers and novelists writing about and for a young female audience. Unlike Pamela, Evelina, and Harriet (yet similar to the penitent prostitutes), the Christian girl heroines of Hannah More, Mary Brunton, and Jane Austen are "blind" to any desires beyond ideologically conservative values of domestic happiness. Building upon the conduct manual edifice, these stories add an aggressively religious form to that structure. The chapter also discusses "home economics": private homes and public bodies. While the private home functioned as a social and literary ideal, created in response to various social and political revolutions, the female body—the "home" for future generations (and site of economic exchange)—remained public and "open" through the promotion of ideologies of conduct, religion, family, and patriotic sentiment.[1] Certainly the Evangelicals (and conduct-manual writers as well) had variable interests in female (or lower-class—the two function similarly) "privacy." On the one hand, their religious doctrine was dedicated to the eradication of a private self, while on the other hand, they were committed to the construction and sanctification (perhaps largely compensatory) of the private space of the home. This chapter will explore the contrast between the Christian girl heroine's accessible "transparency" and the quest to establish an insular, private home.

I

The reformers of the political and domestic "manners" of the lower classes focused on the idea(l) of the Home as a means to regeneration and contentment. In *The Making of the English Working Class*, E. P. Thompson identifies the response of the upper classes to the laboring classes' struggle for political reform as a "counter-revolution" founded on the belief in "the necessity of putting the house of the poor in order."[2] In addition, the Evangelical movement was steadfastly and single-mindedly conducting a "domestic revolution" which focused on "feminine" issues: religion, home, and family.[3] The religious fervor of the times spilled over into concerns with educational reform, especially that working-class children be taught to know their God and to read His book. It was hoped that parents would be sufficiently inspired by the good example of their newly literate (and perhaps considerate) children and thus learn to read the Bible and embrace its tenets of humility, submissiveness, and patience, even in the face of social, economic, and political inequality.[4]

Within these coordinating and often cooperating revolutions, a figure of significant interest to the participants was the child, in particular the lower-class child. In the texts of reform, the child is imagined in varying ways, and it is thus not a single image of the child, but rather a multiplicity of images that are produced within this literature.[5] However, these competing images of the child or of childishness—whatever their particular descriptions—are necessarily the projection of the adult reformer's perception of a lack in the child and fear *of* the child: the child is, in effect, a potential revolutionary, or, conversely, once provided with appropriate (Evangelical) reformative education and guidance, a well-mannered and content subject.[6] Evangelical fiction attempts to organize experience from a consistent, coherent vantage point—here combining the soteriological imperative with political and social conservatism. The movement from the ideals of the Evangelical collective mind to the conception of the child, in this case, is further complicated by insistent ideological demands placed on this literature: writing appropriately for the newly literate, the poor, the faithless, the female.

Anna Laetitia Barbauld's *Hymns in Prose for Children* (1781) was written for the young child—in fact for the "pastoral" children of privilege as a *class*—in a form that celebrated harmony and beauty, whereas Hannah More's *Cheap Repository Tracts* (1795–98) were written for the older "industrial" child stripped down to the essentials of social class, gender, and region.[7] As this child is rooted in specificity, so, too, is the method of the tract which posited an exemplary child—such as Pamela (or sometimes a bad example)—as a map for behavior. In this way form is wedded to function in a simple and direct causal relationship not "muddied" by metaphor.[8] The writers of Evangelical and other religious children's fiction were influenced in their construction of the perceived child by the inheritance of Locke's image of the tabula rasa, the often negative response to Rousseau's "hereticism," and the beginnings of a backlash against literary didacticism that culminated in the Romantic celebration of the child as Wordsworth's "father of the man." Thus the religious writers for children—most of them female—were not only participants in the creation of a specific child in response to their specific literary output, but also inheritors of a masculinist ideological understanding of the child.

Although confined by Evangelical conservatism, and not "feminist" in any contemporary understanding of that term, Hannah More's gender concerns in the *Tracts* bespeak a notable difference from a privileging of male experience by acknowledging the potential of positive feminine self-knowledge and action. We see in More's prose and in her philanthropic pursuits an emphasis on the "material" child, rather than the "spiritual" child celebrated in Barbauld's writings. More is concerned with the state of her readers's souls as well as their bodies and homes and focuses on the child's value on earth rather than eventual reward in Heaven.[9] To demonstrate this value, More's exemplary heroines (and heroes) are materially rewarded for choosing goodness. In fact, the pedagogical method of the Sunday school system was based upon rewards for attendance, good behavior, and diligence (as opposed to intelligence), a system not original to the movement, but adopted from current educational practices. Thus More (and the Evangelical movement) "provided" for the child (fulfilled its perceived need) both literarily and literally. An example of this caretaking office is the system of approbation which More and her sister Patty established within their women's clubs for those girls who were about to be married. Every year at the annual club day, each affianced girl who could produce her minister's written testimonial to her good character was given a Bible and a pair of white stockings knitted by the Mores themselves. This bride portion emblematizes Hannah More's assessment of the girl's needs; the Bible operated as a kind of day-book of wifely instruction and the stockings were a personal gift from metaphoric mother to daughter, clothing both the naked spirit and the naked body with a no-nonsense, maternal warmth.[10]

In her Evangelical novel for children, *The History of the Fairchild Family* (volume 1, 1818), Mary Martha Sherwood's generic manipulations not only replicate aspects of both the *Hymns* and *Tracts* but, most significant, those of the domestic novel. In this way, *The Fairchild Family* further domesticates Evangelical literature for children, reflecting some of the concerns of the emergent genre found in literature for adults. Michael McKeon's discussion of the "epistemological crises" associated with the instabilities of social and generic categories can illuminate Sherwood's *Fairchild Family*—not to demonstrate

Evangelicalism's failure or narrative incoherence, however, but as a reflection of Evangelicalism's tendency toward deinstitutionalization and sublimation within general reform movements (the social result) and diffusion within the domestic novel (the literary result) of the early- and mid-nineteenth century.[11] We are reminded of Dickens's *Bleak House* and his satiric condemnation of Mrs. Jellyby's obsessive "telescopic philanthropy" for the natives of Borrioboola-Gha undertaken at the expense of her household. Like Charles Dickens, the Evangelical writers believed reform was to begin in the home through the construction of an ideal child. As I discuss below, there is very little distinction made between child and marriageable woman: the ideal child as she was conceived by Evangelical writers embodies, of course, the very same values as the Christian wife. This generic overlap also produced an amalgamated recipient child: a child of privilege taught mostly by example, yet situated within fully described domesticity, as opposed the *Tracts*, which revealed the lower-class child as literally alone in the world, as servant of another's household, or alienated member of an unhealthy family.

In their literary responses to the perceived spiritual needs of the nation's youngest citizens, More and Barbauld employed different rhetorical and generic strategies in reaching their target audience. Barbauld used analogy in her *Hymns in Prose for Children* written for the children of the upper and middle classes, while Hannah More employed example to persuade the *Cheap Repository Tracts'* lower-class readers.[12] These rhetorical strategies also reflect a certain class bias that can be described as the metaphoric versus the representational, spiritual incentive versus material incentive, and the aesthetic versus the economic. Written for the same objective—to instill a love of God and His World—the *Hymns* "preach" to the children of privilege to love God: as we respect and are awed by the beauty of nature so should we be thankful to and praise the God who is the creator of nature. More's *Tracts,* by contrast, teach by incentive and example. (In the course of the narrative, the economic well-being of the faithful is elevated, and the godless are further degraded or debased.) Within the pastoral world of the *Hymns,* to praise God, rather than the struggle for survival, is the only imperative.

Barbauld's *Hymns in Prose for Children* was very successful: the book was highly praised and went into multiple editions both in England and America. (*Hymns* was still in print 55 years after Barbauld's death.) Intended to be memorized and recited by the very young, the *Hymns* stress the importance of *identification*—that the child see sin in himself or herself and God's handiwork in the world. The *Hymns* describe events and scenes from the middle- to upper-class child's life and specifically relate them to the duty of loving and praising God. The nature of the relationship between God and child is explained through analogies emphasizing protection and authority and the loyalty which then results: God is as the shepherd, the parent and the sovereign (Hymn 3) who therefore requires fealty, love, and obedience; God is also the supreme governor of the world as a king is of his country, magistrates are of a town, and a father of his family. Unlike More's *Tracts,* which demonstrate right conduct of the individual for her own (often economic) gain through pointed example, the *Hymns* stress the duties owed a benevolent God who both creates and protects his creation. Material need and desire never enter the world of the *Hymns.* Childhood is pleasant; the world is ranked and organized in a coherent and meaningful way; night passes safely in restful sleep: "You may sleep, for he never sleeps: you may close your eyes in safety, for his eye is always open to protect you. When the darkness is passed away, and the beams of the morning-sun strike through your eye-lids, begin the day with praising God, who hath taken care of you through the night."[13] Within this class dynamic, God can be represented to the "pastoral" child through analogy in a manner that the "industrial," urban child would have difficulty comprehending, since his or her relationship to the world is more often characterized by danger and insecurity. Labor is understood in the *Hymns* to be part of a unified and attractive life in the service of God and family, by tending, as it were, a new Eden (Hymn 8): "See where stands the cottage of the labourer, covered with warm thatch; the mother is spinning at the door; the young children sport before her on the grass; the elder ones learn to labour, and are obedient; the father worketh to provide them food: either he tilleth the ground, or he gathereth in the corn, or shaketh his ripe apples from the tree: his children run to meet him when he cometh home, and his wife prepareth the wholesome meal" (53–54). The laborer's children are described in the same manner as the young animals of springtime "sporting about their mothers in innocence and joy." In this utopian world, class divisions are unrepresented: the metaphor of family extends from God "down" to the household servants, creating an idyllic familial harmony.

Barbauld's *Hymns* celebrate a pastoral verdure that More's tracts never do, notwithstanding More's Shepherd of Salisbury Plain: in Barbauld's pasture children enjoy the sight of lambs frolicking with their mothers, while More's laboring child gathers the wisps of wool left in the brambles to card and spin and knit homely stockings. Both Barbauld's and More's attitudes politicize childhood by reflecting and maintaining certain hierarchies of class and gender. In Barbauld's writing, God is metaphorized as father and king. In More's work, a class bias influences her program of promoting literacy among the poor—a program complicated by a progressive "maternal agenda" of redressing societal ills. Each writer ultimately looks toward and attempts to determine the child's future as a citizen and a potential political force. As an "institution," the *Cheap Repository Tracts,* like the Sunday school movement itself, was ideologically motivated in its political conservatism: reinforcing the status quo while reforming the morals of the poor. Indeed, the Evangelical writing for lower-class children was narrowly prescribed and highly systematic, describing the movement of lower-class children from a godless and unhappy state to a pious and prosperous one (this a relative term), usually through the intercession of some authority, whether it be a person of rank, an "official" of the Sunday school movement, or one of the "saintly poor."

Below I focus on More's tracts written for girls that feature female characters. In these tracts the political conservatism of propertied Church of England Evangelicals concerned with the morals and behavior of the poor in general was condensed to scrutinize the conduct of the lower-class girl. Thus "feminine" virtues or foibles to be emulated or avoided are featured in this literature. Here we see the Evangelicals' imagined child change his clothes, and, like Virginia Woolf's Orlando, become a girl. Upon the figure of the girl (especially the lower-class girl) the imperatives of right feminine conduct and class conduct converge, intensifying the ideological focus on behavior. The dual concerns of sexuality and production do not clash, however, as they sometimes do for fictional girl heroines, for the lower-class girl kept effectively in her place through the Evangelical ontology of separate on earth but one in the eyes of God. (In the case of Pamela, her "work" is to convince B that her social value—that which is "above" labor—lies exactly in the melding of her debased class with her elevated morality.) The *Tract* heroines need to behave properly in order to produce adequately—all within the sphere of (working-class) contentment. Hannah More's religious tracts function as a gendered discourse, and inform the conduct-manual discourse and conduct literature popular in the eighteenth century (like Hannah Woolley's work discussed in chapter 2).[14] More was certainly not a feminist: she refused to read Mary Wollstonecraft's *Vindication of the Rights of Woman,* crying, "Rights of Women! We will be hearing of the Rights of Children next!"[15] Her female-centered *Tracts,* nevertheless, focus our attention on contemporary understandings of the powerful nature and influence that the conduct of women and girls had on their individual lives as well as to society as a whole.[16]

Mitzi Myers's revisionist work on the Georgian period, for example, credits the didactic work of writers like More and Anna Laetitia Barbauld with confronting society head-on to "advance social betterment."[17] "More's Repository illustrates how woman's educative and caretaking role fed into new strains of social fiction," Myers observes, "and her work exemplifies how women could translate female ideology's didactic imperative into an authoritative voice capable of documenting and interpreting historical realities."[18] More believed, as did all Evangelicals, in the separation of the male and female spheres, and in the importance of maintaining that separation. In the three tracts included in her *Complete Works* that feature women or girls as the main characters, not surprisingly, the good girl is rewarded (either materially or spiritually or both) and the bad or foolish girl is punished. In my reading of the *Tracts* as a gendered discourse, I will focus on "Betty Brown," the most complex and, for our purposes, the most interesting of these representative texts.

Betty is an emblematic conduct-book heroine (like Evelina) and a precursor of the Victorian girl-heroine (young Esther Summerson in *Bleak House,* for example): an orphan without any name, save the generic "Betty Brown," which is meant to denote gender and social class rather than lineage. "Well-looking" and the possessor of a "natural" goodness, Betty represents, therefore, good "raw material" for the Evangelical industrial machine that hopes to produce sober, pious, and dependable domestic workers. More creates a character who has all of the ingredients for success within the working-class stratum and then proceeds to enable her achievement while making what is coincidental or natural in Betty's life and story seem determined and logical. Thus, Betty's obedience to an unknown woman of the upper class directly results in her material and personal success.

Betty Brown makes her home on the streets of London with no means to support herself save begging. An ambitious girl, she decides to help herself to a higher standard of living. Mrs. Sponge, a moneylender and inveterate con artist, quickly notices Betty's charms and naivete, and sets her up as an orange seller, loaning her five shillings. The bargain, however, maintains that Betty pay interest on the loan every day, as well as purchase food and lodgings. Betty, understandably, finds it difficult to get ahead on her rounds until she meets a gentlewoman who takes an interest in Betty's life story. She strongly advises Betty to leave Mrs. Sponge—Betty has paid seven pounds and ten shillings on the five-shilling loan over a year's time—to adopt honest business practices, to give up drink, and to think of her immortal soul. The lady enhances the scenario she describes by offering Betty a gown and a hat on the "easy condition she should go to church."[19] Betty "obeys" and is ultimately rewarded by greater capitalist fruit in the forms of a sausage shop and a tract hero husband.[20]

As an orphaned beggar with no one to protect or provide for her, Betty faces the very real temptations of intemperance, dishonesty, and indolence, as each results in one kind of pleasure or another. The dangers of the sexual marketplace within which Betty's beauty and virginity (not to mention her own sexual desires) place her, are elided in the *Tracts*; no men appear in the story except for the mention of Betty's eventual husband. Given the harsh realities of living in poverty in London, where succumbing to seduction or actively seeking it was often a means of survival, this is perhaps surprising.[21]

Prostitution and poverty were common bedfellows in the eighteenth century (as they remain today), and a popular literary "obsession" whether in the form of entertaining fiction or sober sermons (see chapter 1). But for More, the detailing of passion did not belong in religious tracts for children; she believed that knowledge of certain behaviors offered greater danger than ignorance of them. When editing the *Tracts,* More was strict in her standards of acceptable material: "Of six ballads offered by her old friend William Mason, three were firmly rejected by Miss More on the ground that there was too much love and politics in them."[22] In this way we see the ideological Evangelical program at work promoting one kind of literature for an idealized child audience.

Betty does not rise dramatically above her apparent birth-station (as she might have, if she was a heroine in a Dickens tale, for instance) but is rewarded in what is considered, by the Evangelicals and wealthy classes, to be a just and prudent manner. It is clear that the lady (as the spokesperson for the Evangelical societies and for "charity" in general) also expects Betty to take responsibility for her own life, and sheds no tears over the inequalities of their situations: "It is not by giving to the importunate shillings and half crowns, and turning them adrift to wait for the next accidental relief, that much good is done. It saves trouble, indeed, but that trouble being the most valuable part of charity, ought not to be spared; at least by those who have leisure as well as affluence. It is one of the greatest acts of kindness to the poor to mend their economy, and to give them right views of laying out their little money to advantage" (249). Like the charitable institutions for penitent prostitutes, the religious tracts of the late-eighteenth and early-nineteenth centuries focused upon female conduct in so far as the ideal of charity expressed in each case conformed to the same belief in training girls for self-sufficiency and independence within the laboring class. As "instruments of charity," the tracts and the female reformers who wrote, promoted, and distributed them extend the ideologies of houses of reform beyond their walls. (I will return to the open institution and the inculcation of "home values" within and without the institution in chapter 6).

Through "industry and piety" (and help from the benevolent lady), Betty Brown's life is changed from beggary and misery to contentment and financial success. A simple girl with simple wants (after becoming an orange-girl she is "as proud and as happy as if she had been set up in the first shop in Covent Garden" [248], Betty Brown's desires are fulfilled beyond her hopes. What more, her creator might have asked, could she have wanted? My hypothetical interrogative increases our awareness of the Evangelical "political unconscious" that imagines the readers' desires satisfied with the narratological equivalent of a promised good night's rest after a pleasantly tiring day. As Myers notes about the strategic value of late-eighteenth-century female educators' fiction, "displacing Cinderella love plots with plots about the learning process, they recuperate virtue rewarded."[23] Betty's story of very real rewards for honesty, sobriety, and piety might have seemed a fairy tale to the working-class children who read it, but it was written as a clear example to follow, as an educative tool forged to create and impress a literate and ethical working class. The Evangelical reformers understood this practical literature to be the first step toward their goal of acquainting poor children intimately with their Creator and imbuing them with a sense of responsibility toward moral rules and godly laws, as well as king and country.[24] Both Anna Laetitia Barbauld and Hannah More attempted through their writing to raise the morals of their child readers by revealing Scriptural injunctions and exhorting their readers—gently in the case of Barbauld, and rather aggressively in More's—to respect God, themselves, and their neighbors. Barbauld and More—albeit with differences in literary genre and audience—articulated a program of social reform dedicated to the *spiritual* equality of believers in a materially heterogeneous world.

Sherwood's *History of the Fairchild Family,* by contrast, bridges the gap between tract and popular domestic novels for children (such as Catherine Sinclair's *Holiday House* [1839] and Charlotte Yonge's *The Daisy Chain* [1856]) and mediates both the ideological texts of the Evangelical and reform movements and the attendant changes in narrative form and content visible in adult fiction of the period (Jane Austen's novels come to mind). *The Fairchild Family* puts into detailed practice the methods of the tracts: in narrative form, the reader learns the ending of the story, that is, how the child "gets good." Each chapter ends with an occasional prayer and a hymn sung by the Fairchild children (to be learned by "any little children"). In this way each lesson couples the tract message with the poetry of the hymn at the same time that the lesson is embellished through a rudimentary plot and generally unsophisticated prose.

The story of the Fairchild family creates an appealing domestic idyll. We are introduced to a family whose lives are recounted in an episodic narrative inscribed within a pastoral world of order and self-sufficiency. The family lives far from town in a comfortable house surrounded by a garden. There are only two loyal servants (the Fairchilds are middle-class gentry) who take care of the heavy work, and the children are educated at home by their parents. The three young children have jobs to perform as well; everyone knows his or her duties and tries to perform them admirably and honorably, though not always successfully. Therein lies the plot of the book: to show how the children fail in their duties toward each other, their parents, and God and to emphasize how best to avoid and overcome the sinfulness to which all humans—but especially children—are subject.

Emphasis in *The Fairchild Family* is placed not on the individual child as an example or object of reform as articulated in the *Tracts,* but on the nuclear family as a unit and the relationships among family members.[25] The fantasized "incomplete child" of the Evangelical reformers is perceived in the novel as a member of the healthy family (or operating as the catalyst to the creation of a healthy family). It is within this insular space that the domestic novel negotiates experience and doubt by positing a normative worldview of appropriate behavior and desires. The domestic novel fixates on the home as the site of meaningful exchange. We also see this movement in the quest to establish a home in *Mansfield Park* (discussed below), as well as in *Bleak House* and *Jane Eyre,* to name only three examples. *The Fairchild Family*'s intermediary position as an ideological fiction in relation to this genre is exemplified in its relationship to death, where death outside the family is reviled, yet celebrated when experienced within the family.

It is within this context of transgressive, external death that the infamous scene of the hanging corpse occurs. The three children have fought over a doll, and during the fracas Emily shouts to Lucy, "I hate you with all my heart, you ill-natured girl!" to which Lucy responds, "And I hate you too; that I do!"[26] The punishment for the enactment of childish hatred is a visit to the corpse of a man who had been hanged years before for killing his brother.[27] The narrative relates the transgressive violence of the family fight as the action violates "natural" bonds of love and duty. The bonds of familial love are emblematically used in Evangelical fiction to represent the relationship between God the father and his earthly children, a relationship mediated by the fraternal Christ. (The secular novel rejects this model, of course, but perhaps not completely. The happy home, or happy school, in the case of *The Governess,* becomes the substitute for the religious model of unity and strength.) To kill one's brother or sister is to kill Christ within oneself and forfeit all hope of salvation. The Fairchild children learn their lesson and then willingly pray for "new hearts" that will help them to conquer the "natural" hatred that exists in every person's (every child's) breast.

The episode of the hanging corpse is also important to the consideration of the children's domestic novel and the novel for girls as it exposes (hyperbolically) the degree to which feminine passion, here read "anger," is to be feared and avoided as a disruption of domestic tranquillity. Although the example of sibling hatred is fraternal, it does not seem coincidental that the children who are found most guilty of anger are the two girls. Henry's sins tend to be those of disobedience and pride, whereas the girls are guilty of willfulness. Conquering anger and aggression is certainly a religious tenet and functions as such here, but it is also a conduct-book imperative for girls. Mrs. Fairchild has so internalized these lessons that, as a morally superlative mother, she is considered too delicate to witness the unpleasant sights that her daughters must withstand. Mrs. Fairchild's delicacy and saintliness also prefigures the female moral advisors found in later domestic fiction by Elizabeth Gaskell (Margaret Legh in *Mary Barton*) and Charlotte Brontë (Helen Burns in *Jane Eyre*). Mary Wollstonecraft's Mrs. Mason, by contrast, is hardly squeamish in the face of a crisis—physical or moral. Lucy and Emily will travel toward piety and fragility as they grow into Christian wives and mothers, a condition that represses the general barbarity of the child, creating, ultimately, characters of feminine exaltedness.

Emily Fairchild demonstrates the deleterious effects of deceit and disobedience by stealing forbidden plums and failing to confess her fault until after she has caught a dangerous fever from wearing damp clothing. Her illness was a direct result of her attempt to cover up the plums' accusatory stain by washing out her pinafore. Obeying her parents' rules about sweets would have avoided this confrontation between God's will and the child's and avoided as well a threat to Emily's life. The Evangelical understanding of this incident is not that internal error can be allegorized through the body, but that there is no such thing as privacy or inner thoughts or secret sin. After regaining her health, Emily realizes that she is never alone: as a vigilant parent, God will watch her and as God's child she will be chastened or punished by him. Certainly a primary tenet of almost any moral tale holds that disparity between the inner and outer self cannot be tolerated.[28] Inner thoughts that disagree with exterior actions (guilt coupled with a calm countenance, for example), would allow for a kind of embodied privacy threatening to the world of guidance for girls, thus the communication of interior purity relies upon easily interpreted corporeal signs such as blushing, fainting, and stillness or silence: the body cannot lie. When the inner self becomes all in all, no real privacy exists for the characters or the reader. A purified mind (and therefore a unified one), such writers as Fielding, Sherwood, More, and Austen would agree, is a requirement for virtue and happiness.

The new domestic Evangelical works for middle- to upper-middle-class children, such as *The History of the Fairchild Family,* are certainly ambitious, and as extended strings of tractlike episodes, strain against and indeed transform the tract through absorption in the cares and concerns of domesticity. It is this new emphasis on familial, "asocial" privacy that speaks most intimately to the development of the domestic novel, a movement away from the public atmosphere of reformative hymns sung in unison and didactic tracts distributed by the thousands.[29] This current ideology of private space, however—represented in part by the estate or family seat in the domestic novel—simultaneously "chafes" against the *lack* of privacy we have seen operative in literary and extraliterary Evangelical ideologies of female conduct. That is, the "home" daughter or wife in the works of Austen, Charlotte Yonge, and the Brontës, for example, although firmly ensconced in private space, is also "publicly" scrutinized within and without the text, whether by patriarchy generally, or by an authorial censor steeped in the theory of the equivalence of transparency and goodness.

Although the Evangelical movement did not cease its operation suddenly in the early part of the century—the Evangelical Alliance was formed in London in 1846—with passing years and the deaths of some of its founders, it waned as a national obsession.[30] In 1833 Hannah More and William Wilberforce died and a bill emancipating slaves was made into law. The Sunday Schools as educational institutions ceased to be controlled by religious societies and were gradually absorbed into national educational reform. (They remained as institutions of more strictly religious instruction). The domestic novels for children and those adult novels that resonate with the ideological influence of the Evangelical movement also marked the fading political importance of Evangelicalism. The concurrent rise of a reactionary *social* isolationism meant, on the one hand, to establish a national politics and, on the other, to delimit private domestic boundaries which become the new literary (novelistic) fascination.

II

A good wife is the temperate zone, where alone love delights to inhabit, and free both from the frosts of peevish virginity, and scorching heats of rageing lust, injoys a perpetual spring; She is the perfection of a man, or a lost rib restored to a compleat and perpetuate humane nature; a true coppy of our Mother Eve before she dialogu'd with the Serpent.

Susanna Jefferson, "A Bargain for Bachelors, or: the Best Wife for a Penny" (1675)

In the introduction to *The Ideology of Conduct,* Nancy Armstrong and Leonard Tennenhouse describe one of the ideological effects of the conduct book as the creation of a new system of determining female value which had a calculated effect on the dynamics of class structure: "These modern conduct books proffer an educational program on the grounds that it will make these women desirable to men of superior quality, in fact more desirable than women who have only their own rank and fortune to recommend them. . . . In becoming the other side of a new sexual coin, the aristocratic woman in turn represented surface instead of depth, embodied material rather than moral values, and displayed idle sensuality where there should be constant vigilance and tireless concern for the well-being of others."[31]

In their fiction, Hannah More, Mary Brunton, and Jane Austen also participate in constructing a feminine ideal informed by a conduct-book and religious ideology that concentrates on the behavior and education of their girl characters. Armstrong notes that by the early nineteenth century this feminine ideal represented by the conduct books "passed into common sense," which accounts for Austen's ability to bypass descriptions of the detail and tedium of domestic life. *Pamela* and the plethora of conduct literature elevated the rules governing sexual politics to the status of the norm, the expected, and the exemplary.[32]

The configuration of a hegemonic female value—in the novel witnessed first in *Pamela* and clearly delineated through conduct novels—combines with the literary component of Evangelicalism's program for moral reform and results in the creation of Evangelical conduct novels for girls. Hannah More's *Coelebs in Search of a Wife* (1809) is perhaps the most significant example of this genre. Mary Brunton is a lesser-known Evangelical conduct novelist whose works— which include aspects of melodrama and romantic comedy—promote the regulating influence of religion and the necessity of religious conversion in achieving contentment and a good marriage. The Evangelical inheritance Jane Austen reveals in her novel of female education and religious feeling, *Mansfield Park,* focuses on a new type of heroine within the novel of manners: the Christian girl.[33] These examples of the novel written expressly for girls (in the case of *Coelebs*), novels read by girls, and novels featuring girl heroines, further refine the female ideology of value: the domestic ideal. In these novels, the moral mettle of the young heroine is certainly evaluated and rewarded, but the reward is placed within a strictly domestic system that requires near seclusion from society to acquire meaning. As Armstrong notes, "It is a woman's participation in public spectacle that injures her, for as an object of display, she always loses value as a subject."[34] This "looking to home" represented in fiction has political overtones as well. The conservative English reaction to the French Revolution emphasized the "otherness" of France and an isolationist national identity; the growing middle class and capitalist economics threatened the older agrarian tradition and values; and the Napoleonic wars, which rearranged the European continent and nearly threatened English soil, only further drove England to seek the safety of enclosure.[35] The assessment of value, therefore, lies within the boundaries of privacy; this sanctuary grows so small as to include ultimately only a room or rooms within a household. Fanny's schoolroom, for example, is where her moral vision is challenged, yet survives the temptations of unalloyed pleasure found in the figure of Edmund. At the beginning of the nineteenth century the feminine ideal was emphatically religious, domestic, and *private.* The adolescent girl who is "out," therefore, moves from the relatively public sphere of courtship and the negotiation of marriage settlements to the intensely private world—gained through marriage—of her own household.[36] Briefly, the private home—often called "the estate" for the upper classes and the "house of the poor" for the lower—contrasts with the ideologies of both Richardson's *Pamela* and eighteenth-century charity where "home" is recreated in the community. That is, B and Pamela will function as instructive examples of the new "old-fashioned" family for their neighborhood: as Sir Simon Darnford says to Pamela after she escapes from Lady Davers and Jackey, "We husbands hereabouts . . . are resolved to turn over a new leaf with our wives, and *your* lord and master shall shew us the way" (426). As we have seen, houses of reform such as the Magdalen Hospital represent a similar "expansion" of the caretaking family that embraces the "deserving unfortunate."

Always a pragmatic visionary, Hannah More appropriated the romance novel and transformed it—much as she had the bawdy broadsides and ballads for her *Tracts*—into material for her Evangelical program of moral reform. *Coelebs in Search of a Wife* is all about love, but a rational, governable, *private* love that leads to a reasonable marriage. *Mansfield Park* resembles *Coelebs* in that Austen's heroine maintains a strict understanding of love as private, especially when losing that control threatens her own happiness. Heroines Evelina and Harriet Byron, however, are notable here for the relative publicity and early revelation of their feelings. Evelina uncovers her love for Orville to Villars and her friend Maria Mirvan, and her feelings for him are suspected and made much of by the Branghtons and Mrs. Selwyn. Harriet's partiality, of course, is of concern to the self-interested Grandison sisters, who desire Harriet as a family member, as well as to Harriet's cadre of anxious relations and gang of suitors. More, like conduct-book writers before her, was concerned with the effects of reading fiction and poetry on a girl's morals and manners. From the genre's beginning as romance, novels were so popular among female readers that they were considered to be dangerous and in need of regulation.[37] In her *Strictures on the Modern System of Female Education* (1779), More writes: "Novels, which chiefly used to be dangerous in one respect, are now become mischievous in a thousand. They are continually shifting their ground and enlarging their sphere, and are daily becoming vehicles of wider mischief."[38] Whether *Coelebs* functions as a novel at all is subject to some debate. Mary Hopkins considers it to be like "a series of essays modeled on those of *The Spectator* and *The Rambler*," and More herself, in the preface, acknowledges that "the Novel reader will reject it as dull. The religious may throw it aside as frivolous."[39] Like the longer domestic Evangelical narrative (such as *The Fairchild Family*), *Coelebs* contains features of both the conduct novel and religious tract. The preface of *Coelebs* admits to love, but, in comparison with the kind offered in titillating romances, love is a rational, sober, and dutiful emotion: "Love itself appears in these pages, not as an ungovernable impulse, but as a sentiment arising out of qualities calculated to inspire attachment in persons under the dominion of reason and religion, brought together by the ordinary course of occurrences, in a private family party" (ix).

Coelebs is the narrative of a journey of discovery: Charles is set upon a quest by his parents to learn for himself the effects of different treatments of female education upon marriageable daughters.[40] The duty children owe to their parents in decisions of marriage is not coincidental in *Coelebs*: Charles is a *son* fulfilling parental desires by examining the daughters of his parents' peers. Charles spends as much time describing the mothers as he does the girls, assuming that a girl reproduces her mother. Charles's mission is simply to find a girl educated for Christian marriage and then to marry her.

This task is not destined to be easily fulfilled, for Charles has many requirements for an appropriate wife. Rather typically, he takes Eve as portrayed by Milton to be his feminine ideal. Through Charles, More parries the remarks she feels are sure to be directed against this choice of the perfect domestic woman. Milton's "household good" is not, in Charles's mind, "drudgery or servility," but an economics of domesticity that represents "the most appropriate branch of female knowledge" (2). In fact, without domestic knowledge, Charles affirms, the wife "may inspire admiration abroad" but "will never excite esteem, nor of course durable affection, at home, and will bring neither credit nor comfort to her ill-starred partner" (3).[41]

This strong statement outlining the duty of woman to man only increases in emphasis as Charles discusses (albeit guardedly) a woman's conjugal duty to her husband. Milton has "presumed to intimate that conjugal obedience 'is woman's highest honour and her praise' " (4). On this point Charles rather emphatically invokes the apostle Paul who "is still more uncivilly explicit than Milton" and relates that submission to the husband's wishes (which includes sexual desires) does not imply "degradation" but rather, fulfills part of the female duty to "promote good works in her husband" (4). More considers this duty to be a form of power that "raises her condition, and restores her to all the dignity of equality; it makes her not only the associate but the inspirer of his virtues" (5).[42] Thus, the novel wrestles with the question of female autonomy within marriage, giving service to the view that a woman's power of moral influence is so great that wifely submission can be said to "inspire" what is good in a husband.

Eve is admired especially for her domestic management skills: she never protests when Adam unexpectedly brings an angel to dinner, and she voluntarily leaves at the absolutely most appropriate moment in their conversation (as Charles says, so that she will not hear Raphael's account of her "birth," beauty, and Adam's love, which thereby secures her humility).[43] Finally, Charles believes it is Eve herself (as opposed to Milton) who credits Adam's "manly grace" and "wisdom" superior to her own beauty and intellect.

Neither a sophisticated literary critic nor a feminist, Charles takes his task of finding a wife very seriously. He searches for a good companion—one who will share his religion, keep his home, and teach his children—who will therefore deserve his love. Charles's thoughts on such a deserving wife have been instilled in him by his mother—now dead—and his father. His mother's main requirement for her son's mate was that she be consistent and "proportionate:" "In character, as in architecture, proportion is beauty" (14). She gives him a quick overview of her opinion on current practices of female education; like conduct-book authors and commentators on female education, Charles's mother disapproves of feminine "accomplishments" that fail to regulate conduct and improve character. Charles's father also counsels his son against choosing to wed an accomplished woman: "The *exhibiting,* the *displaying* wife may entertain your company, but it is only the informed, the refined, the cultivated woman who can entertain yourself; and I presume whenever you marry you will marry primarily for yourself, and not for your friends: you will want a COMPANION: an ARTIST you may hire" (19). His father's final word on wives, however, resorts to another architectural metaphor to underscore his primary point that while a good Christian wife is not "ornamental," she is an object nonetheless, solid and functional: "Do not be contented with this superstructure, till you have ascertained the solidity of the foundation. The ornaments which decorate, do not support the edifice!" (20). In fact, the Christian wife, who functions generally as a metaphor for the home, is here explicitly "built." The reasons for this metaphorical association are clear: the "happy" family requires the wife and mother as its (pro)creative force and civilizing influence. The home is one mark of civilization and community that, like the Church, organizes "meaningful" existence. The phrase "built like a brick house," a male assessment of the female body, intimates a different admiration for women, but one which similarly assigns the site of home to the female.

With the advice of his parents firmly in mind, Charles enters the world searching for a particularly constructed mate, rather like Rousseau's Emile (whose love affair with Sophie contains parallels to this story). The daughters, who know Latin but very little about domestic management and whose culinary talents are rudimentary at best, exemplify Charles's father's fears about intellectual women: "Though no epicure, I could not forbear observing that many of the dishes were out of season, ill chosen, and ill dressed" (33). In fact, it is the topic of learned women that gives rise to one of Charles's few humorous comments: "I jumped to the conclusion, and was in an instant persuaded that my young hostesses must not only be perfect mistresses of Latin, but the *tout ensemble* was so ill arranged as to induce me to give them full credit for Greek also" (33). In an attempt to find some merit in a dinner party, Charles tries to discuss Virgil with the daughters but finds that he has been mistaken in assuming the extent of their knowledge: the girls do not know how to manage a table *or* read Latin. Their choice of books affirms the fears of those who distrust literature: these girls reportedly read titles such as *Tears of Sensibility* and *Perfidy Punished*. Charles thus learns his first field research "lesson" about women: "It is very possible for a woman to be totally ignorant of the ordinary but indispensable duties of common life without knowing one word of Latin; and that her being a bad companion is no infallible proof of her being a good economist" (34–35).

"Elegant" women as well as bookish women suffer from Charles's disapproval, as he says of one hostess who has a fine meal prepared and is perfectly amiable: "Of course she completely escaped the disgrace of being thought a scholar, but not the suspicion of having a very good taste" (40). Charles then spends time with bad mothers and daughters who are not religious and pretend otherwise, and enjoys, as well, all manner of interesting London diversions: museums, lectures, preachers, and parliamentary orators. He also meets some "agreeable" daughters who might have excited more interest if he had not remembered his father's injunction to delay marrying until he had visited his father's friend, Mr. Stanley. Not surprisingly, then, Charles fails to find a suitable wife in London society. These girls represent the "faulty construction" which both Charles's father and moralists generally feared; their "ornaments" displayed to attract masculine attention are also meant to distract the discerning man away from their lack of internal substance.

At the relatively isolated Stanley-Grove, Charles finally meets his perfect wife. Lucilla Stanley is the kind of young woman Charles had yearned for when confronted with so many worldly females: a domestic, *private* daughter, who, in his own words, "bless[es], dignif[ies], and truly adorn[s] society" (132)—yet she never goes into society. She is "rather perfectly elegant than perfectly beautiful. . . . Her beauty is countenance: it is the stamp of mind intelligibly printed on the face" (185).[44] Within a week of living at Stanley-Grove Charles is rationally "in love," yet he refrains from speaking to Mr. Stanley until he can determine if his partiality is justified (but not whether she returns his love). Charles's passions are subdued by the gravity of his religious feelings: as he reflects early in his search, the choice of a mate "might perhaps affect my happiness in both worlds" (12).

The elaborate courtship plot that predominates in many eighteenth-century novels (among them *Pamela, Evelina,* and *Grandison*), is simplified and minimized in *Coelebs.* Charles's ruminations on the tenor of his courtship is measured and calmly reasonable. In the Evangelical tradition there is little of the excitement, intrigue, suspense, or coincidence that appears in other novels. Evangelicalism determines that in choosing a wife, sexual passion be subordinated to other issues such as domestic management, piety, and humility. (It is in fact a credit to Richardson's skill as a writer that we do not doubt, for example, Harriet Byron's love for the "beauties" of Sir Charles Grandison's body as well as his mind.) Charles understands the conventional romantic image of love to be brilliant yet insubstantial in comparison with the superior form of love tempered by religious feeling:

> I am aware that love is apt to throw a radiance around the being it prefers, till it becomes dazzled, less perhaps with the brightness of the object itself, than with the beams with which imagination has invested it. But religion, though it had not subdued my imagination, had chastised it. It had sobered the splendors of fancy, without obscuring them. It had not extinguished the passions, but it had taught me to regulate them.—I now seemed to have found the being of whom I had been in search. My mind felt her excellencies, my heart acknowledged its conqueror. I struggled, however, not to abandon myself to its impulses. I endeavoured to keep my own feelings in order, till I had time to appreciate a character, which appeared as artless as it was correct. (191–192)

The conclusion of the book contains a series of episodes in the lives of the Stanley family and of Charles, their live-in guest. This narrative structure is similar to that of *The History of the Fairchild Family,* but in *Coelebs* the form is somewhat regulated by the courtship plot that concludes with the conventional marriage. We learn the habits of the family and how charity composes the largest part of their daily lives. Comparisons are made between the happy religious family and those who are wealthier but who lack the regulating force of religion. To this end, as in conduct books and novels, More's novel displays a seemingly endless parade of inappropriate girls, accompanied by seemingly endless commentary on the proper conduct of a wife.

Coelebs promotes an essentially rational view of marriage, one that is centered on religious principles of loving and fearing God, and a traditional separation of duties and spheres of the masculine and feminine. As a marriage manual for girls, however, *Coelebs* follows many tenets of the conduct novel and conduct literature itself: it is a virtue for an unhappy married woman to suffer silently and continue to "promote good works" within her husband, no matter how badly she is used. Just as Eliza Haywood's Betsy Thoughtless's estimation as a conduct-book heroine is raised when she submits to her husband's undeserved ill-usage (*The History of Miss Betsy Thoughtless,* 1751), so Mrs. Carlton demonstrates the wifely virtue of selflessness in *Coelebs.* Unlike Betsy Thoughtless, Mrs. Carlton is a Christian wife, and, as such, suffers with the understanding that she is doing her duty for her eventual heavenly reward. Betsy's conduct was regulated by less religious means; as a matter of good breeding and politeness she is determined to do her duty as a wife. In an Evangelical novel, of course, the good wife is rewarded by her husband's reformation; in the conduct novel, the heroine is rewarded by the inappropriate mate's death, thus allowing her to marry the worthy suitor (Betsy's husband does reform, but on his deathbed). Mrs. Carlton's response to Mrs. Stanley's offer of companionship clearly delineates the difference between the conduct novel and its Evangelical "sister": the conduct-novel heroine needs the "conduct voice" to guide and teach her to make moral choices, but the Evangelical character already possesses these abilities through religion and the Bible— God's word: " 'The grace I most want,' added [Mrs. Carlton], 'is humility. A partial friend, in order to support my spirits, would flatter my conduct: gratified with her soothing, I should, perhaps, not so entirely cast myself for comfort on God. Contented with human praise I might rest in it . . . ' Then turning to the Bible which lay before her, and pointing to the sublime passage of St.

Paul, which she had just been reading 'our light affliction which is but for a moment, worketh for us a far more exceeding and eternal weight of glory' " (252–253).

Lucilla Stanley, as well, at eighteen years old, possesses all of the womanly virtues and characteristics of a good Christian wife so that Charles need not examine or instruct her in the way that the worthy suitor must in the case of such conduct-novel heroines as Evelina and Betsy Thoughtless. For the Evangelical wife selflessness is equivalent to duty. (Mrs. Carlton is described as having a nearly "annihilated" self.) In the conduct novel, although the heroine may be naturally very good (like Evelina) she needs additional instruction in order to rise to the moral (and sometimes material, as we have seen) height of her suitor. The story of her education thus constitutes the narrative. *Coelebs in Search of a Wife,* however, functions as a conduct novel for the girl reader in that the characters serve as consistent models of behavior and right conduct. As a result of Lucilla's superior education and her retired status, Charles does not need to raise her in order to deserve her, and although Charles is on a quest of sorts, he does not resemble Tom Jones because he possesses a firmly formulated character at the novel's start. Lucilla and Charles are therefore "made for each other." In fact, at the novel's close, after Charles has made his intentions known to Lucilla and been accepted by her, the reader discovers, with Charles and Lucilla, that they have indeed been made for each other, that their fathers had educated them in the hopes that they would one day marry. This communion had been foreshadowed by Charles's discovery of Lucilla's love for *Paradise Lost.* Lucilla tells Charles that she has been particularly impressed with the portrait of Eve in her state of innocence as "the most beautiful model of the delicacy, propriety, grace, and elegance of the female character which any poet ever exhibited" (288).[45]

Mr. Stanley gives Charles one month of cooling his heels, to wait and to watch Lucilla before he allows his friend's son to acquaint her of his regard. Lucilla's youngest sister, however, gives him an unexpected opportunity to reveal his love. The description of Charles in the heat of passion, confronted by the woman he desires and finally able to talk of love, is clearly modelled on the romance, albeit the conduct-book romance rather than, for example, B's panting love-talk. Orville, by contrast, is energetic, yet exceedingly polite when he and Evelina come to an understanding: "I revere you! I esteem and admire you above all human beings!—you are the friend to whom my soul is attached as to its better half! you are the most amiable, the most perfect of women! and you are dearer to me than language has the power of telling" (351–352).

For the sake of propriety, More is not able to have her hero profess his feelings in such detail: "I respectfully detained her. How could I neglect such an opportunity? Such an opening as the sweet prattler had given me it was impossible to overlook. The impulse was too powerful to be resisted; I gently replaced her on her seat, and in language, which if it did any justice to my feelings, was the most ardent, tender, and respectful, poured out my whole heart. I believe my words were incoherent; I am sure they were sincere" (295–296).

In spotlighting the responses of the heroines, however, the greatest similarities can be found between them. The conduct-book girl heroine at the declaration of love is always in some manner surprised and reluctant to speak in return, as I have discussed in the previous chapter. The proffering of one's hand also signifies in a very literal way the relinquishment of one's entire body to the husband's "coverture"; in the face of such significance, the heroine is necessarily silent. A prostitute is thought to be passionate; a heroine is confused.

In her letter to Reverend Villars in which she relates Orville's declaration of love, Evelina describes her own behavior. At first she nearly loses all control over her body: "I scarce breathed; I doubted if I existed,—the blood forsook my cheeks, and my feet refused to sustain me: Lord Orville, hastily rising, supported me to a chair, upon which I sunk, almost lifeless" (352). Once she regains some measure of composure, Orville repeats his entreaties, though Evelina's humility does not allow these to be transcribed: "I cannot write the scene that followed, though every word is engraven on my heart: but his protestations, his expressions, were too flattering for repetition: nor would he, in spite of my repeated efforts to leave him, suffer me to escape;—in short, my dear Sir, I was not proof against his solicitations—and he drew from me the most sacred secret of my heart!" (352). Charles describes Lucilla's reaction to his lovemaking as near speechlessness and disorder: "She was evidently distressed. Her emotion prevented her from replying. But it was the emotion of surprise, not of resentment. Her confusion bore no symptom of displeasure. Blushing and hesitating, she at last said—'My father, Sir—my mother.' Here her voice failed her. . . . She ventured to raise her timid eyes to mine, and her modest but expressive look encouraged me almost as much as any words could have done"[46] (296). These blushing and timid looks are tacit approval of Charles's love. Mr. Stanley, of course, consents to the marriage. It is at this point, before Charles is asked to leave for his home, that Mr. Stanley brings out a packet of the correspondence between Stanley and Charles's father in which Charles's and Lucilla's early education are described. These letters, a fictive account of an education, would in their entirety comprise another version of the conduct book on the early education of children (in the manner of Rousseau's *Emile*). In the final letter Stanley explains to Charles (at his urging) how Lucilla, a beautiful and intelligent girl, can be happy in the sober and retiring life they lead at Stanley-Grove. Lucilla represents indeed the picture of all that is proper, certainly of all that is private and homebound. She keeps busy with charity work, gardening, and helping her mother with the children and household accounts, but says little and rather blends with the background. One of Charles's first descriptions of Lucilla recalls a remark More once overheard Dr. Johnson make about Mrs. Garrick: Charles states, "As to her dress, it reminds me of what Dr. Johnson once said to an acquaintance mine of [sic] a lady who was celebrated for dressing well. 'The best evidence that I can give you of her perfection in this respect is, that one can never remember what she had on' " (188–189).[47] That is, Lucilla is barely discernible from her pretty surroundings, from her sisters as they grow, from other one-dimensional heroines whose principles of religion and right conduct gird them so firmly that they, like mannequins, gain momentary glances for their arresting qualities—an angelic countenance, a stylized pose, a heavenly attitude—but who exude very little warmth and gain little sympathy from their readers.

Yet for all of its heavy-handed didacticism promoting Christian girlhood, *Coelebs* was an extremely successful publishing venture: it sold out twelve editions in the first year alone.[48] Although the reviews of the book were in general unfavorable—the *Edinburgh Review* called it a "dramatic sermon" with "marks of negligence and want of skill"—its popularity was unchecked.[49] Robert Colby deems *Coelebs* the "most widely read novel of the first quarter of the nineteenth century, running up at least sixteen editions between its first publication in 1808 and 1826. . . . It sold out 30 editions in America."[50] More's fame spread even to America: "Lion-hunters from America, where her fame was well-established, came in a steady stream to pay their respects to the author of *Coelebs*."[51]

We can theorize many reasons for *Coelebs*' success. As mentioned above, novels, while extremely popular—especially with women and girls—were often held suspect as corrupting, or even slightly immoral. The images and ideals of romance often proposed in novels of the day were thought to influence the thinking and actions of impressionable girls who could come to expect that kind of excitement and suspense in their own lives. Romantic heroines could not be easily translated into the kind of good English wives and mothers most would consider proper or desirable. Conduct-book writers and reformers of female education, then, were very concerned with the pervasive influence of the novel, and *Coelebs* seemed to be a creative antidote: not only was the book religious and sober, but it also contained a romance (such as it was) and a marriage. The religious were also pleased with *Coelebs* as it demonstrated that happiness and love were not antithetical to a spiritual life, and upheld the domestic religious model as the only sure method for peace and contentment in this world. *Coelebs,* then, was a moral book that every one ought to read, and for that reason was most certainly established in households as a classic, rather like Milton, or other edifying and conservative works of literature.

It is difficult to ascertain, however, whether the intended audience of *Coelebs*—girls on the brink of their social and sexual life—other than the most unnaturally pious, enjoyed it or not. The question, remains, then, whether this conscious attempt to meld the conduct book with religious tract and novel was at all successful in communicating its ideology. As a genre, the evangelical conduct novel did not succeed past *Coelebs* and perhaps a few others (Mrs. Sherwood's *History of Susan Gray*, 1801, is another example), but there are considerable aspects to this form that were influential in the development of the novel—most notably, the increasingly emphasized roles of the character of the Christian heroine and of the trope of the conversion, which, again, informed the novel for girls in writers such as Jane Austen in the canon and Mary Brunton largely outside of it. In terms of the novel's development, their books for girls or featuring a girl heroine hold a unique place between the conduct novel/Evangelical novel and the domestic Victorian novel, containing aspects of the former and prefiguring the latter.

As we have seen, *Coelebs* promotes an ideologically static world of female value, shunning materialistic values that reward outward ornaments of show and display in favor of a system of worth based on a combination of Christian and domestic virtues. By shifting attention to a girl's interior—her education and morals—the Christian/domestic ideology allows for a certain class liquidity: a deserving girl could be discovered in any social class. At the same time, this spotlight on internal values also reveals the moral judgments passed on girl characters to be in the service of a kind of aggressively practiced "eugenics" of virtue, rejecting and disposing of flawed characters and creating superlatively "pure" couples who will produce, outside the boundaries of the texts—whether *Tracts,* conduct novel, or domestic fiction like *Mansfield Park*—sterling children.[52] Charles's status allows him to consider the girls of London society, but his moral code rejects these choices as unsuitable. Instead, he chooses his perfect mate from the same squirearchy to which he was born. In feudal economics, of course, this instability would be highly threatening (as the fervor over *Pamela*'s publication attests), but in a gender-based economy where the commerce is *female worth,* the Christian/domestic ideal transcends strict class boundaries. The heroines of Jane Austen's *Mansfield Park* and Mary Brunton's *Discipline* were created within this paradigm of female value and therefore participate in this class liquidity: Fanny is rightfully elevated from working-class Portsmouth to the landed gentry as direct compensation for her moral worth, and Ellen Percy must lose her fortune (gotten in trade) before she converts to "active" Christianity and ascends to the Scottish aristocracy.

III

If you are good, Jane Austen promised, you will be happy.

Fay Weldon, *Letters to Alice on First Reading Jane Austen*

Mary Brunton wrote only three novels before her death of childbed fever in 1818: *Self-Control* (1810), *Discipline* (1815), and *Emmeline* (1819). *Discipline,* a bestselling story of a spoiled and coquettish heiress's loss of fortune, conversion to Christianity, and marriage to a worthy older man, was influential to Austen's creation of *Emma* (1816).[53]

Discipline clearly continues the Evangelical/conduct novel trajectory I have outlined above. In *Ideas and Innovations: Best Sellers of Jane Austen's Age,* Ann Jones notes that one of Evangelicalism's tenets was self-examination; this theme is explored in both Brunton's and Austen's fiction: for example, in Fanny's inner debate over whether or not to take part in the theatrical.[54] In response to the charge that *Discipline* was "too religious," Brunton admits that promoting religious ideas was the novel's main objective: "For the great purpose of the book is to procure admission for the religion of a sound mind and of the Bible, where it cannot find access in any other form."[55] *Discipline* was written in the first person and the narrator and heroine, Ellen Percy, often directly addresses the reader, evoking the intimacy and didacticism of epistolary fiction (Charlotte

Brontë uses this style in *Jane Eyre* to the same purpose). *Discipline* includes aspects of many conduct novels' plot conventions: Ellen Percy, the heroine, has many faults which relate to the flawed education she has received at the hands of her mother; there is a conduct voice in the form of a family friend who offers a good example and religious and feminine training; Ellen's conversion to Christianity is necessary to her gaining a proper husband and material wealth; the novel ends with her marriage to the worthy suitor who has completed her education. Brunton is not, however, following a formula in this novel. There are many idiosyncracies in *Discipline*: the emphasis in the latter part of the book on the Scottish highland, the melodramatic plot that overshadows the religious themes as Ellen moves northward, and the transformation of the hero from father-figure to mythic god. Nevertheless, *Discipline* occupies an important place in the development of the girls' novel, the novel as a genre (in particular for Jane Austen), and as a literary work in itself.

In the spirit of the conduct book, but with the directness of an Evangelical tract, Ellen disclaims the label of egoist in telling her story "to warn others of the danger of their way."[56] Ellen's tale begins, as do so many others, with the narrative of an unfortunate maternal education. Her mother was a pious and generous woman, but so meek and tender that she could never discipline her daughter or even reprove her. Thus Ellen grows up a spirited, willful, stubborn, and manipulative child who cannot be controlled by either parent. In her reflections upon her youth, Ellen identifies her early education as the root of all her faults, thereby emphasizing the causal relationship between education and happiness.

Ellen's strongest characteristic is her intelligence—a twist on the conduct-book heroine who is often vivacious (like Betsy Thoughtless), or exemplary (like Lucilla Stanley). Her intelligence is not counted for much, though, as her father explicitly comments, "It is a confounded pity she is a girl. If she had been of the right sort, she might have got into Parliament, and made a figure with the best of them. But now what use is her sense of?" (4). Not only is Ellen's intelligence disregarded because she is not the "right sort" (male), but she is characterized elsewhere in the novel as both misguided and misused by it. In her youth, Ellen's cleverness was demonstrated by her devastating wit. If she were not the possessor of so much physical beauty, the sharp-tongued, astute Ellen might have resembled More's "Amazon" Miss Sparkes, or Burney's "manly" Mrs. Selwyn—much-maligned for her "masculine" wit and shrewdness.

Mrs. Percy dies of a languishing illness after tending to eight-year-old Ellen, who had caught a fever from her own willfulness. In an Evangelical deathbed scene, Mrs. Percy has her young daughter pray with her before she dies. The next scene, when the unknowing Ellen embraces her mother's corpse, invokes the Evangelical tracts where death—either "beautiful" or horrible—is widely used as a pedagogical tool in creating fear and a self-loathing in its (girl) readers. The child Ellen is not moved to conversion by her mother's death, yet as the novel progresses and she strays further from strict propriety, the image of her mother is enough to startle her into self-reflection.

Ellen continues to make the mistakes that young heroines who are not properly educated or regulated by sober reason often commit. For example, Ellen takes as her bosom companion one Juliet Arnold who has been "educated to be married"—that is, she has learned all of the (useless) "accomplishments which were deemed likely to attract notice and admiration" and that are so denigrated by conduct-book writers and Evangelicals alike (16). The *public* exposure that arts like these necessitate is contrary to the ideology of enclosure imagined to be a crucial aspect of right conduct and a bar to learning the "truly" feminine arts of domesticity, modesty, and maternity. A telling example of Ellen's willfulness and near depravity is her contrivance—against strict orders to the contrary—to attend a masquerade ball without a chaperon. Not only does Ellen disobey but, more important in establishing her character as unwomanly and improper, she displays her body by masking her identity.[57] Ellen and her bad companion, like Betsy Thoughtless and her Miss Forward, read forbidden novels and generally comport themselves in a way most odious to conduct-book writers and Evangelicals, learning little of worth in the "polite seminary" that they both attend. At sixteen, Ellen leaves school to become mistress of her father's household. Her father has made his fortune in business, and for this reason Ellen feels inferior in the face of the "old money" of her school rival, Lady Maria de Burgh. (In "retaliation," Ellen makes a conquest out of Lord Frederick de Burgh, Maria's brother.) Ellen has Juliet Arnold to stay with her and together they live the fashionable, dissipated life of endless parties, amusements, and social calls. The object of this fun is display and flirtation. Ellen vows never to marry and lives only for her own enjoyment and the control of others: "I rather imagine, that in me, as in certain heroines whom I have read of at school, a deficiency had been made on one side [of her heart], on purpose that I might wound with greater dexterity and success" (45). These gay and vivacious behaviors do not pass unnoticed, however, by the conduct voice of the novel, Miss Mortimer, Mrs. Percy's closest friend who has been invited to live with the family as another companion for Ellen. Miss Mortimer is a pious woman, an Evangelical, in fact, who tries, to little avail, to curb Ellen's improper and impious actions.

Ellen and Miss Arnold insult Miss Mortimer and her "fanaticism" and call her a "Methodist" (20). Like Lucilla Stanley, Miss Mortimer is the model for the perfect woman: she is soft-spoken, gentle, devout, intensely private, and selfless. Her only deficiency in terms of conduct-novel heroinism is her lack of physical beauty and her "advanced age." The beautiful Ellen, however, must absorb Miss Mortimer's qualities before she can be said to possess *all* of the attributes of heroinism.[58]

Until she attains these qualities, however, Ellen cannot win the hand of the worthy suitor, in this case, Mr. Maitland, a friend of her father's and much older than she. Maitland's greatest feature is his superabundance of masculinity (he is not generally thought handsome, but athletic and "craggy." All of these qualities create resemblances between Maitland and Brontë's Rochester and Austen's Knightley). A sober Christian man who is attracted to Ellen's beauty, Maitland wishes to form her into a Christian wife. He cannot accept her until this conversion occurs, and to this end he and Miss Mortimer act as correcting influences on Ellen. She respects Maitland above all others, but refuses to change her habits to suit his "Evangelical" program for marriageability: "The wife of a Christian must be more than the toy of his leisure;—she must be his fellow-labourer, his fellow-worshipper" (140).[59]

A necessary first step in Ellen's "purification" is social "mortification." It is important to note that Ellen's spiritual conversion takes place after a *material* fall and that her relinquishing of petty values, consumerist ideals, and selfish indulgence for sacrifice, labor, and duty can occur only within the powerful vacuum created by economic loss: her father's business is ruined and they become penniless. Mr. Percy's response to his loss of fortune is to commit suicide. Now orphaned, Ellen goes to live with Miss Mortimer and there, through Miss Mortimer's example, realizes that she has sinned in forgetting God. It is only through a return to virtue by way of conversion to Christianity and the tenets of Evangelicalism in her thoughts and actions that Ellen can ever hope to be happy again (and, it is implied, regain a home and marry Maitland):[60] "In the sunshine of my day I had refused the guiding cloud; and the pillar of fire was withdrawn from my darkness. I had forgotten Him who filleth heaven and earth,—and the heavens and the earth were become one

The Happiness of Virtue

96

dreary blank to me" (173). Miss Mortimer, who had been languishing for some time with an undisclosed illness, dies an Evangelically "happy" death, but not before she has imparted all of her religious conduct wisdom to Ellen (207, 209). Ellen is now, however, truly homeless, and must rely on the kindness of strangers to find her a place as a governess and music teacher in order to survive.

From the death of Miss Mortimer, the plot of *Discipline* veers from its original ideological framework to take some decidedly melodramatic turns. In her travels to Scotland to find a teaching position she is for some time committed to a insane asylum (which she bears with fairly good grace as she determines that her imprisonment is part of God's will to combat her sin of pride). It is interesting to note that the "hyperbolic" form of enclosure and privacy represented by the insane asylum—complete separation from humanity and imprisonment in a diseased mind—tends to be a gendered trope. In the insane asylum, "rampant" female sexuality is controlled and defused: Maria in Wollstonecraft's *Maria: or, The Wrongs of Woman* is imprisoned in an insane asylum for daring to challenge her husband's rights over her body, and Ellen is restrained because of a woman's (Ellen's employer's) jealous fears that Ellen will seduce her husband. Ellen also discovers her old friend Juliet Arnold—who had abandoned her once the Percy fortune was lost—now penniless and the victim of a sham marriage and mother of a sickly child; meets a Scotch "princess" who prevails upon her to visit her home, the Castle Eredine; and finally, marries this princess's brother, none other than Mr. Maitland, who becomes, ultimately, a mythic figure rather than a worthy suitor. She becomes a true Highlander, learning Gaelic and the ways of the humble Scottish cottagers. In the final third of the novel, Brunton shifts emphasis from an Evangelical program of reform to a typical melodramatic romance—with the embellishments found in "landscape" novels such as Edgeworth's and Scott's—and where a man, not God, is all in all to the heroine. Ellen's last speech encapsulates conduct and religious messages of *Discipline*—laced with a certain ethnocentrism: "Having in my early days seized the enjoyments which selfish pleasure can bestow, I might now compare them with those of enlarged affections, of useful employment, of relaxations truly social, of lofty contemplation, of devout thankfulness, of glorious hope. I might compare them!—but the Lowland tongue wants energy for the contrast" (375).

Jane Austen's *Mansfield Park,* written in 1811–13 and published in 1814, was contemporaneous with both *Coelebs in Search of a Wife* and *Discipline.*

Although not generally considered a children's or girls' author, Austen wrote novels (in particular, *Mansfield Park*) easily situated within the historical and literary context of the conduct novel and Evangelical novel described above. There are critics who maintain that Austen would never create so formulaic a character as a conduct-book heroine without the "saving grace" of irony.[61] Margaret Kirkham flatly states, "If Jane Austen created a conduct-book heroine, it cannot have been without an ironic intention of some kind."[62] In fact, it does not seem at all ironic that Fanny Price's moral strength and retiring nature are rewarded by an appropriate marriage that reflects conduct-manual ideology and discourse. If we remove Fanny from her context and examine her ironically as an undeserving moral prig, however, the novel loses all coherence (which is what critics who refuse to acknowledge this context generally contend). To understand the character of Fanny as part of a didactic tradition gives meaning and form to the novel; removing this tradition necessitates undue importance on an ironic intention not fully realized in the novel. Marilyn Butler reads Austen's letters as evidence for the importance of religion in her life, if not her absolute Evangelicalism: "Jane Austen's own letters in her last decade exhibit a new willingness to speak directly of religion and some remorse for the sprightliness and even malice she had freely allowed herself in the 1790s. She also composed prayers that illustrate the Evangelical habit of self-scrutiny."[63]

Austen's fiction is concerned with the intersecting considerations of moral conduct, education, and sexuality of her girl heroines.[64] Like More's Lucilla, Fanny is a Christian girl heroine awaiting a Christian man. Rather than representing an outdated and musty heroine of a bygone literary tradition, Fanny reflects, as Marian E. Fowler rightly suggests, the "current taste in heroines."[65] Like the biblical "virtuous woman" evoked in the epigraph to chapter 3, Fanny is valuable indeed.

The different philosophies of female education and their results are clearly displayed and compared within the first few pages of *Mansfield Park*. Fanny Price, the poor relation of the wealthy and privileged Bertram family, lacks education in the sense that she has had very little formal instruction, and has no "accomplishments"—she cannot play a musical instrument, or sing, or draw. The Bertram daughters, by contrast, have been educated in the latest fashion. They read and speak French, can recite history, paint, sing, and play the piano, among other fashionable abilities. Given the expense of such training it would seem a weighty burden to undertake the care of one more girl in the family, yet, as Mrs. Norris explains, this economics of female education attempts to "guarantee" financial security for the girl by creating value: "Give a girl an education, and introduce her properly into the world, and ten to one but she has the means of settling well, without farther expense to any body."[66] A fashionable education is expected to pay for itself by securing a husband (and financial stability) for the girl. Fanny's educational deficiencies are revealed (and reviled) by her more worldly cousins at the earliest moment. Julia and Maria make no attempt to hide their surprise and shock at ten-year-old Fanny's ignorance: "Fanny could read, work and write, but she had been taught nothing more; and as her cousins found her ignorant of many things with which they had been long familiar, they thought her prodigiously stupid and for the first two or three weeks were continually bringing some fresh report of it into the drawing-room. 'Dear Mamma, only think, my cousin cannot put the map of Europe together or my cousin cannot tell the principal rivers in Russia—or she never heard of Asia Minor—or she does not know the difference between water-colours and crayons!'" (54).

This disparity in educational background alienates Fanny from her girl cousins and sets up the brilliant contrast between her "natural" education and their artificial accomplishments as is made manifest in their temperaments and ultimate fates.[67] Edmund alone recognizes the value of Fanny's "primitivism" and the qualities that she possesses: "He talked to [Fanny] more, and from all that she said, was convinced of her having an affectionate heart, and a strong desire of doing right; and he could perceive her to be further entitled to attention, by great sensibility of her situation, and great timidity" (53). Indeed, Fanny does not want to become "more" than she is, and resists learning accomplishments of display (55). This fear of public enterprise is a conduct-book ideal, and, as such, marks Fanny as a conduct-book heroine. Fanny's value is negotiable only within private space. At first, Fanny's moral makeup is denigrated everywhere outside of her schoolroom. Her influence will ultimately expand, however, to include the interior of Mansfield itself.

In the shallow world of fashion and pleasure that describes Mansfield Park under the direction of Mrs. Norris and with the tacit approval of the languid Lady Bertram, Fanny's quiet nature and yielding temperament render her different from the others in more than just outward accomplishments. The talents of the Misses Bertram, however, delivered without any accompanying lessons in conduct, are seen as indicative of a lesser nature: "it is not very wonderful that with all their promising talents and early information, they should be entirely deficient in the less common acquirements of self-knowledge, generosity, and humility. In every thing but disposition, they were admirably taught" (55).

Although regarded by nearly everyone at Mansfield Park as inconsequential and ignorant, Fanny, as a member of the household, is taught a basic curriculum with her cousins. It is Edmund, however, who undertakes the role of her teacher. A model of sober propriety, he chooses Fanny's reading material (as Orville does for Evelina)—as befits a good conduct hero and eventual worthy suitor: "[Edmund] knew [Fanny] to be clever, to have a quick apprehension as well as good sense, and a fondness for reading, which, properly directed, must be an education in itself. Miss Lee taught her French, and heard her read the daily portion of History; but he recommended the books which charmed her leisure hours, he encouraged her taste, and corrected her judgment; he made reading useful by talking to her of what she read, and heightened its attraction by judicious praise" (57). Through it all, Fanny changes very little. It is to her credit as Christian girl heroine that she remains "unspoiled" by wealth and privilege, but those in authority feel that her static nature and personality indicate immaturity. Sir Thomas insensitively remarks to Fanny: "If William [Fanny's brother] does come to Mansfield, I hope you may be able to convince him that the many years which have passed since you have parted, have not been spent on your side entirely without improvement— though, I fear, he must find his sister at sixteen in some respects too much like his sister at ten" (67).

As the Mansfield children grow, Fanny's differences from her cousins are less easily discernable than her earlier ignorance of facts and figures. As the girls reach marriageable age, conduct and behavior attain greater significance. Fanny stays at home with Lady Bertram while Maria and Julia attend balls and other social functions with their aunt Norris. Her private world within Mansfield Park which had thus existed until her eighteenth year, and her role within it as a kind of property of the estate to be used or not according to the whims and wishes of its more public inhabitants, is interrupted by the arrival of the Crawford siblings. These wealthy young people enliven the society of Mansfield Park, and even Fanny is brought somewhat forward under their scrutiny. Inquiring after one of the crucial questions of the novel as it pinpoints the tension between public and private space, Mary Crawford cannot ascertain exactly how to label Fanny: is she "out" or "not out"?

Manners as well as appearance are, generally speaking, so totally different. Till now, I could not have supposed it possible to be mistaken as to a girl's being out or not. A girl not out, has always the same sort of dress; a close bonnet for instance, looks very demure, and never says a word. You may smile—but it is so I assure you—and except that it is sometimes carried a little too far, it is all very proper. Girls should be quiet and modest. The most objectionable part is, that the alteration of manners on being introduced into company is frequently too sudden. They sometimes pass in such very little time from reserve to quite the opposite—to confidence![68] (81)

The distinction is actually an important one in terms of the social and sexual politics of early nineteenth-century aristocratic life (and increasingly, as the lower classes began to emulate the aristocracy in terms of fashion, custom, and education, the social status of girlhood became a middle-class concern as well). Without a clear demarcation between those girls who are part of the market economy of sexual politics—those whose fortunes and bodies are "for sale" for possible "purchase" through marriage—and those who have not yet entered the market because of age (or who never will enter the market because of lack of fiscal potential)—the regulating factor of sexual coupling, family heritage, and fortune and legacy, and even the continuation of the class system are threatened. While I argue that the novel is at pains to suppress "coming out" in favor of "staying in"—a morally superior status—Austen relies upon the rigid adherence to the system Mary Crawford outlines as one more arbiter of moral worth, as well as a metaphor for female behavior. Any "public" girl who acts differently than a "private one," that is, has gone out too far.

If Fanny is "out," she cannot belong only to the world of Mansfield Park, but can be claimed by the rigors of public life: parties, flirtation, suitors, London society. If Fanny is "not out," she remains autonomous within her role as "underdaughter" to Lady Bertram. Fanny plays both parts: the demands upon the Bertram daughters as they become absorbed in the marriage market extend themselves rather faintly to Fanny. Henry Crawford becomes the object of desire for both Maria and Julia, although Maria is engaged to Mr. Rushworth. The appearance of the Crawfords and Edmund's decided interest in Mary Crawford also complicate Fanny's life. The interplay of these competing and conflicting desires culminates in the private theatrical which the Crawfords and Bertrams contrive to present and which proves a moral "watershed" for Edmund and Fanny.

While under the influence of Mary's beauty and vivacity, and struggling to fit her behavior within the constructs of his defined system of conduct, Edmund loses some of his moral strength. He earnestly quizzes Fanny on her impressions of Mary and asks for her judgment of Mary's conduct (94–95). Fanny therefore ascends to the stature of teacher and conduct instructress as her own conduct never wavers or falters. In *Mansfield Park* (as well as in *Emma* and *Northanger Abbey*), Austen promotes an ideal sexual love based on supposedly disinterested instruction (for the heroine's moral good). Edmund's desire to help Fanny grow up results in her sexual desire for her teacher; the same can be said of Orville in *Evelina,* Henry in Wollstonecraft's *Mary, a Fiction,* and Maitland in *Discipline* (although these heroes admittedly have a stake in the outcome of the girls' education). The sexual desire that is created through mentoring (and in *Mansfield Park,* this intimacy is so private that it approaches an incestuous relationship, as many scholars have noted) also allows for sexual desire.[69] Only after Fanny is acknowledged as a vital moral force in the family does Henry Crawford become romantically attracted to her.

As in most matters of the household, Fanny is an outsider to the preparations for the home theatrical, but the difference is not that she has been uninvited, overlooked, or ignored, but that she firmly refuses to participate: "Fanny looked on and listened, not unamused to observe the selfishness which, more or less disguised, seemed to govern them all, and wondering how it would end. For her own gratification she could have wished that something might be acted, for she had never seen even half a play, but everything of higher consequence was against it" (156).[70]

The play is suggested as a cure for boredom, but its significance lies within the promotion of acting and sexual innuendo as appropriate family employment. As such, the play offends Fanny's sense of right and wrong. Her response is very similar to More's in *Strictures Upon the Modern System of Female Education*: "This world is not a stage for the display of superficial or even shining talents, but for the strict and sober exercises of fortitude, temperance, meekness, faith, diligence, and self-denial."[71] To Fanny's dismay, however, Edmund makes very little argument or "remonstrance" against the play. He is uneasy over the idea of staging a theatrical, but feels unable to stop the production once he imagines how entrancing Mary Crawford will appear in costume, and watches how well she acts her part. At this juncture, Fanny's stature as moral instructress expands and she becomes Edmund's teacher and confidant during the agonizing days of witnessing the distressingly improper conduct of the woman with whom he is infatuated. Edmund tries to rationalize Mary's behavior and understand her in light of what he knows to be right conduct. The damaging effects of a poor education thus show themselves clearly as they are embodied in Mary Crawford (and ultimately, in the Bertram sisters as well): " 'I know her disposition to be as sweet and faultless as your own, but the influence of her former companions makes her seem, gives to her conversation, to her professed opinions, sometimes a tinge of wrong. She does not *think* evil, but she speaks it—speaks it in playfulness—and though I know it to be playfulness, it grieves me to the soul.' 'The effect of education,' said Fanny gently" (275).

Evidence of the negative effects of fashionable education include the eagerness to act in a drama wholly improper and culminate, in the case of Julia, in a hasty elopement with the frivolous Mr. Yates, and in the case of Maria, in an adulterous affair with Henry Crawford. Sir Thomas is forced to realize how badly he had managed his daughters's education through "the anguish arising from the conviction of his own errors in the education of his daughters was never to be entirely done away" (447). The conduct-book lessons and the Evangelical principles of sobriety and religious conviction that inform *Mansfield Park* are brought together in a meditation on female education. Sir Thomas is made suddenly aware that Mrs. Norris's constant flattery and the indolence of his wife have not been beneficial to his daughters' upbringing, and yet he realizes that there are things more important still to the creation of a girl's good character and sound principles:

Here had been grievous mismanagement; but, bad as it was, he gradually grew to feel that it had not been the most direful mistake in his plan of education. Something must have been wanting *within,* or time would have worn away much of its ill effect. He feared that principle, active principle, had been wanting, that they had never been properly taught to govern their inclinations and tempers, by that sense of duty which can alone suffice. They had been instructed theoretically in their religion, but never required to bring it into daily practice. To be distinguished for elegance and accomplishments—the authorised object of their youth— could have had no useful influence that way, no moral effect on the mind. He had meant them to be good, but his cares had been directed to the understanding and manners, not the disposition; and of the necessity of self-denial and humility, he feared they had never heard from any lips that could profit them. (448)

In the manner of any good conduct-book heroine, Fanny is religious, sober, and modest, and enjoys, finally, the private possession of the successful female education Hannah More had earlier described in *Coelebs*: "A woman whose whole education has been a rehearsal, will always be dull, except she lives on the stage, constantly displaying what she has been sedulously acquiring. Books, on the contrary, do not lead to exhibition. The knowledge a woman acquires in private, desires no witnesses; the possession is the pleasure."[72] Part of Fanny's valuable private knowledge is an understanding of a good home. While she has suffered under antiteachers in her "mothers" (her birth mother, Mrs. Norris, and Lady Bertram), and elder "sisters" (the Bertram girls and Mary Crawford), Fanny has learned by the time she reaches marriageable age what belongs within and without a true home. Insincerity (acting), rivalry, and independence are to be cast out of the home, while family feeling, duty, and delicacy are to be gathered in. Fanny's developed sense of "taste" in matters of sentiment and action, as well as physical place, also reveal her housewifely fitness. For example, *Mansfield Park*'s final turn toward a newly constituted-family unit—constructed by the expulsion of undeserving former members—reifies Fanny's earlier insight into "home reform": she has been offended by the moral and physical dirtiness of her Portsmouth family. Ruth Bernard Yeazell considers Fanny's domestic discernment to be additional evidence of her modesty and purity. In fact, the creation of "spatial boundaries, of arbitrary lines between the dirty and the clean" constitutes the moral work of the novel.[73]

Fanny's success is both personal and, at the same time, relentlessly and *privately* textual: her "story" becomes emblematic of the ideological imperative of home values that propels the machinery of conduct literature for middle-class and lower-class girls. Certainly the successes of Betty Brown and Fanny Price (and even Pamela Andrews) are not so utterly distinct as their class positions might lead us to believe. Their tales relate an identical method of achieving material and spiritual rewards: maintaining a conscious and consistent "moral" (and lawful) fortitude in the midst of a fallen (and commercial) world. By its rigid structure, eudemonism—the theory that virtue and happiness are inseparable—upholds literature for girls and women as we have seen it staged in Austen, Brunton, Fielding, More, and Sherwood.

In his discussion of Jane Austen and her world, John Wiltshire, evoking Lionel Trilling, asserts that early-nineteenth-century society was "oriental . . . because of the premium placed on outward decorum, the stylisation of manners, and the consignment of distress to a private area, and indeed because the body is the only area of true privacy allowed."[74] I would argue that "true privacy of the body" is a luxury of the upper classes, yet this idea of bodily privacy serves as a point of departure for chapter 5, which changes focus from an assessment of the Christian girl heroine and the literary Evangelical inheritance to a reading of the social function of humor and theatricality in nineteenth-century series books for girls. In eighteenth- and nineteenth-century girls' fiction generally, the female body exists to be read and interpreted. The "sanctity" of the body that Wiltshire describes as operative in Jane Austen's social world is not found in mid- to late nineteenth-century books for female children and adolescents. My discussion will pinpoint the use of humor and representations of dramatic play in girls' texts, arguing that for female characters and their readers, growing up, while comical, is serious business indeed.

5

The Daughters of the New Republic

Girls' Play in Nineteenth-Century American

Juvenile Fiction

~~~

Learn well your grammar,   *Starve your canaries.*

And never stammer,   *Believe in fairies.*

Write well and neatly,   *If you are able,*

And sing most sweetly,   *Don't have a stable*

Be enterprising,   *With any mangers.*

Love early rising,   *Be rude to strangers.*

. . . . . .   *Moral*: Behave.

Lewis Carroll, "Rules and Regulations" (1845)

I plod away, though I don't enjoy this sort of thing. Never liked

girls, or knew many, except my sisters; but our queer plays

and experiences may prove interesting, though I doubt it.

Louisa May Alcott

In the previous chapter I discussed Fanny Price's moral character in its relation to private "closing in"; this chapter will explore the "acting-out" found in nineteenth-century American fiction. I will focus on examples of theatrical play in books for boys and girls, arguing that "staging play"—the authors' use of the rhetoric of acting, laughing, and playing—though comic, attempts to model female characters (and their readers) into aestheticized set pieces. And yet, literary theatricality, as Joseph Litvak asserts, does not function in fiction as "prop" only. In *Caught in the Act: Theatricality in the Nineteenth-Century English Novel*, Litvak persuades us that "if theatrical structures and techniques underlie or enable various coercive cultural mechanisms [such as patriarchy], the same structures and techniques can threaten those mechanisms' smooth functioning" by undermining cultural norms, as well as "narrative flow."[1]

That most curious and, at times, dramatic girl heroine, Lewis Carroll's Alice, serves as a helpful touchstone for play, comedy, and theatricality in girls' and boys' books. In order to negotiate Wonderland, Alice must reorganize her "game attitude" to learn that games, competition, and contests—mainstays of child culture—have very different outcomes belowground than Alice might have anticipated.[2] Adults and aboveground children expect games and competition to originate in a state of equality and end in a state of distinct difference: at the outset of any contest everyone has *equal opportunity* to win, but only one person is allowed finally to do so. In the Caucus-race, however, players can begin running from any position and at any time. The race's conclusion is arbitrary and no individual wins.[3] Alice is discomfited—quite literally—to learn that she must provide equivalent prizes for each contestant: "Alice had no idea what to do, and in despair she put her hand in her pocket, and pulled out a box of comfits (luckily the salt water had not got into it), and handed them round as prizes. There was exactly one a-piece, all round."[4] The Dodo requires that Alice must also conjure her own prize from pocket-leavings; but she finds that relinquishing her thimble—a reminder of aboveground duty and labor—will result only in its return to her. (The awarding of the "absurd" thimble prize that the prepubescent Alice would easily forego in favor of a more traditional, *desirable* reward, has none of the sexual tension of the older and proper Wendy Darling's similarly "cheapened" thimble gift in *Peter Pan.*)

Certainly Alice hails from a culture where social values are radically different from those of Wonderland. Incidents resulting from the distinction between life above and below the ground abound in the text, of course. There are the obvious (and hilarious) parodies of didactic children's verse popular in the nineteenth century found to be unspeakable in Wonderland ("How doth the little busy bee" and "You are old, Father William," for example), but the fundamental disparity between the two worlds which frustrates Alice and serves to emphasize her status as foreigner can be found in the inversion of an essential aboveground law: to play fair. Within the games of the Caucus-race, the Mad Hatter's tea party, the Queen's croquet game, and especially the trial, the rule of "play fair" is turned on its head. I have inverted the perhaps conventional phrase "fair play" into "play fair" in order to emphasize the childlike urgency attached to the adherence of its values and to dramatize the importance of complex and complicating "play."

I will turn here to consider the ideal of "play fair" in its many incarnations in fiction for girls from 1866 to 1876, focusing on Louisa May Alcott's *Little Women* (1868–69), Thomas Bailey Aldrich's *Story of a Bad Boy* (1870), Susan Coolidge's *What Katy Did* (1872), Mark Twain's *The Adventures of Tom Sawyer* (1876), and Elizabeth Stuart Phelps' *Gypsy Breynton* (1866). "Play fair" in the books for girls can include the Alicean understanding of playing by the rules, but its perhaps greater significance lies in the content of those rules as they embody gendered ideas of "play" (as both antic pastime and theater), and of "fair"—what is just and at the same time aesthetic. These representative juvenile authors held a similar belief in the *opposite* of "play fair"—which is not, as we might imagine, "play unfair" (as it yet remains for the preadolescent Alice), but "play ugly." That is, these texts explore the means by which girls' play (as opposed to boys' play) can increase or decrease feminine "beauty" and thus feminine (social) value.[5]

Certainly "play fair" in the sense of play by The Rules is a demand redolent of American ideals as well as childish ones. The conflicts that created the new republic were based, in part, on the myths that surround the requirement of play fair (on either team) in the relationships between nation and colony, federal government and state government, white master and black slave. The tension between an American and British version of justice in play has been dramatized in another fictional croquet game, one between British and American adolescents. In Alcott's *Little Women*, Jo plays croquet with some British friends of Laurie's and in so doing demonstrates the superiority of American manners and morals. In the closely contested game Fred Vaughn nudges his ball through a wicket and sends Jo's ball into the bushes. Jo has observed Fred's treachery and calls his attention to it, but is able to control her temper, tersely responding "We don't cheat in America; but *you* can, if you choose" (125), hammering a wicket "with all her might." Jo is triumphant at last, however, as she self-righteously remonstrates, using Fred's insulting language against him, " 'Yankees have a trick of being generous to their enemies,' said Jo, with a look that made the lad redden, 'especially when they beat them,' she added, as, leaving Kate's ball untouched, she won the game by a clever stroke" (125).

Horatio Alger's books for boys are literary models that obviously support the American economic ideology of "play fair," that is, social and material advancement through capitalist enterprise and "desert." *Ragged Dick: or, Street Life in New York* (1868), for example, relates the rise of a young street urchin bootblack who achieves, in one year's time, a bank account, literacy, a fine suit of clothes, a home, and a job in a countinghouse making ten dollars a week. Although his good fortune has been aided by a chance occurrence—he is employed in the countinghouse as a reward for saving the owner's son from drowning—Dick never stops calculating the means for his continued advancement "up the ladder": "Dick left the counting-room, hardly knowing whether he stood on his head or his heels, so overjoyed was he at the sudden change in his fortunes. Ten dollars a week was to him a fortune, and three times as much as he had expected to obtain at first. . . . He reflected that with the stock of clothes which he had now on hand, he could save up at least half of it, and even then live better than he had been accustomed to do; so that his little fund in the savings bank, instead of being diminished, would be steadily increasing. Then he was to be advanced, if he deserved it."[6]

In Catharine Maria Sedgwick's *Live and Let Live; or, Domestic Service Illustrated* (1840), also set in New York City, however, a comparable plot that traces the trajectory of material success through industry is mitigated by the gender politics operative in descriptions of domestic rather than "commercial" work. Lucy Lee, Sedgwick's heroine, is the eldest daughter of an intemperate father and a saintly mother. The family has been reduced from independence to extreme poverty, so Lucy is sent out to work. The novel does not tell the story

of the family's climb to success, but narrates instead the useful domestic training Lucy learns while a servant. Her trials and suffering as a hired domestic
are in the service of an ideology that not only privileges work over leisure, but
also understands any domestic work—even that which is produced for an
employer—as inherently feminine and therefore valuable: "Lucy, while serving
others, was educating herself. Besides the daily exercise of difficult virtues, she
was increasing her value by learning to perform domestic offices."[7] Like Dick,
Lucy also performs a rescue of a wealthy family's son (the child's French governess had been poisoning him with laudanum), and is offered great sums of
money to oversee the child. Lucy knows, however, that her best opportunity
for advancement lies in service to a good family where she learns domestic
economy rather than in surrogate motherhood—an instinctive rather than instructed role. Her sufferings repaid, and her few faults corrected, Lucy, now
perfectly happy, moves west and establishes her own household with her
tradesman husband in the land of economic opportunity.

American play fair can also be found in nineteenth-century conduct and
domestic manuals that preach a "gospel" of equal opportunity for their middle-
class readers: merit, not entitlement, creates the American class system.
Though we are reminded here of the Pamelian trope, it is Pamela's swift and
hyperbolic rise that dates and locates her ascent in an earlier time and within
the (rejected) aristocracy. The representation of American girls' and boys' play
in juvenile fiction, informed by Alice's "play fair" and the American "theater
of equality," can be found in nineteenth-century conduct manuals and pulp
fiction, as well as in domestic ideology.

The (consciously) humorous Carroll poem that serves as an epigraph to this
chapter, "Rules and Regulations" (1845), playfully treats the breathless delivery
of some of girlhood's many injunctions and cautions. It is interesting—yet
perhaps not surprising—that the long second (and final) stanza from which
my selection is taken anticipates the concerns of domestic and didactic fiction
for girls found in *Little Women*. Certainly the self-important Amy March is
exhorted to "learn well your grammar," and the girls are generally taught the
benefits of "be enterprising, / Love early rising," and "Don't waste your money,"
among other bits of advice offered in the piece. However, like Alice's fall from
"coherence" to a kind of incoherence belowground, the poem begins to descend into nonsense; that is, it gleefully suggests conduct *unbecoming* such as
"Don't push with your shoulder / Until you are older" and "Starve your canaries" in its rush to conclude with the ironically stern distillation of child-

hood's many rules: "*Moral*: Behave."[8] This inversion of conventional didactic games playing lightens Carroll's verse into a gentle satire on overregulated girlhood and those who dourly speak such commands rehearsed in the poem.

The nineteenth-century American writers of girls' fiction who employed humor as a didactic tool chose to reject or to augment traditional forms of literary instruction such as the sentimental story or the religious narrative. Nancy Walker compares wit with sentimentality and argues that wit functions as an empowering element of women's fiction: "If sentimentality in literature is a result of powerlessness, wit may be seen as its opposite: an expression of confidence and power. . . . Humor [for the "witty" writers] functioned as an antidote to the pious religiosity of the sentimental novel and poem."[9] Certainly, the girls' book in general included sentimental as well as religious messages (usually of service and charity), yet the conscious use of humor in literature could soften the blow of didactic necessity. One of the complexities of the comic in nineteenth-century girls' books is that although wit and humor can move the female character to mirth and play in the novel, she generally laughs at herself or must overcome her faults and wrest self-control out of her joy, as the eighteenth-century moralist John Gregory asserts (see below), without losing her sense of humor or her sense of place. This tension between self and society and, ultimately, self and eternity, is poignantly expressed by Alcott's theatrical metaphors when she discusses her early aspirations for acting: "I have come to the conclusion that its not worth trying for at the expense of health & peace of mind, & I shall try to be contented with the small part already given me & acting that well try to mix the tragedy & comedy of life so wisely that when the curtain falls I can jump up as briskly as the stage dead always do, & cheered by the applause of my little audience here, go away to learn & act a new and better part in the Lords theatre where all *good* actors are *stars*."[10] I will set the scene for my discussion of the literary enactment of play fair by exploring the tenets and particulars of nineteenth-century American conduct discourse, arguing that the "rules and regulations" of the new republic allow for both the careful creation and ultimate destruction of the funny girl, the tomboy.

I

Wit is the most dangerous talent you can possess. It must be guarded with great discretion and good-nature, otherwise it will create you many

enemies. . . . Wit is so flattering to vanity, that they who possess it become intoxicated, and lose all self-command.

John Gregory, *A Father's Legacy to His Daughters* (1774)

Women are too good to be humorists.

"Feminine Humour," *Saturday Review* (1871)

We leave Fanny Price and girls' fiction safely enclosed within a clearly articulated domestic and religious ideology that had been refined from the dramatic
gestures and lessons of *Pamela,* travelling through the foibles of the conduct
novel, and through evangelical precept and practice, only to cross the waters
and enter the turbulent world after the Revolution. Here, the establishment of
an indigenous children's literature slowly evolved in response to the ideals of
the newly formed nation. Samuel Goodrich, who wrote the immensely popular
Peter Parley children's books, noted in his journal that the proportion of Brit-
ish- to American-authored children's books shifted from 70 percent British,
30 percent American in 1820, to the reverse by 1850.[11] Not surprisingly, the
didactic writers of American books for children, like their British counterparts,
concentrated their literary efforts in imparting a moral education for the future
citizens of the new republic.[12] Anne Scott MacLeod, in her book *A Moral Tale:
Children's Fiction and American Culture,* explains:

> Nationalist fervor asked for American authorship, concern for the train-
> ing of young Americans in the obligations of citizenship called for edu-
> cation. And the general agreement among Americans that the most
> important qualities of a good citizen were moral rather than intellectual
> tended to put the creation of books for children into the hands of those
> designated as the keepers of the moral conscience of American society.
> Since women and churchmen had been assigned the major responsibility
> for the moral training of the young, the writing of children's books, bent
> as they were to moral didacticism exclusively, was taken up largely by
> women and clergymen.[13]

One essential difference between the mid-nineteenth-century British books
for children and the American books is not in the fundamentally didactic
nature of all realistic works for children, but rather in the greater emphasis on
the *future* found in nineteenth-century books written for American children;
this characteristic is reflected by the emphasis placed upon fulfilling the moral

responsibilities thought to be inherent in the maintenance of a recently established democracy.[14] It was believed that the youngest members of the new political system must be taught that upholding this system was morally sanctioned. The growing American nation, however, was fraught with economic, social, and demographic movement: fortunes were made and lost seemingly overnight, the issue of slavery was threatening national unity, and the rapid growth of urban areas and cultivation of the wilderness all combined to create if not an actually unstable atmosphere, at least the emotional equivalent. Children's literature of this period was formulated in response to the fears of change and the unknown, and reflected the desire for stability and stasis: "The exuberance of the young United States, its social fluidity, its fiercely competitive spirit, and its mounting tensions rarely appeared directly in juvenile fiction, yet they were all there in the reverse images of order, cooperation, and sober attention to duty and conscience that were repeated in every book."[15] This fear of "social breakdown," moral decay, and political destruction and the means by which they could be controlled were clearly delineated in advice books, the popular American counterpart to the English conduct manuals for girls. As Frances Cogan notes in *All-American Girl: The Ideal of Real Womanhood in Mid-Nineteenth-Century America*: "Between 1820 and 1852, the *Bibliotheca Americana* listed more titles for advice books than for any other genre, and such books directed their advice to middle-class audiences who made up as much as three-fourths of the population and 'set the cultural tone and level of society.' "[16]

Cogan argues convincingly that, in opposition to the well-acknowledged "cult of True Womanhood" and its ideals of passive, delicate, and intellectually ignorant girls and women, advice books promulgated a variant ideal that she has called the "ideal of Real Womanhood."[17] The "real" woman also reflects the American belief in democratic play fair; she is solid, down-to-earth, and productive, as opposed to the sentimental, romantic, and aristocratic true woman. There were many requirements necessary to meet the exacting standards of real womanhood: domestic capability, physical and intellectual exercise, as well as conventional feminine "accomplishments" including modesty, piety, and chastity. Cogan describes the ideal of real womanhood as "a popular, middle-of-the-road image that recognized the disparities and the dangers protested by early feminists but tried to deal with those ugly realities in what it saw as a 'female' way. It placed itself, therefore, firmly in the 'separate sphere' controversy by claiming a unique sphere of action and duty for women, but one vastly extended and magically swollen past the dimensions of anything meant by that term to devotees of competing True Womanhood."[18] The real womanhood expressed in advice books written especially for adolescent girls and reflected in the books written by women for a female audience (again, usually featuring a girl heroine) is inherently domestic. Unlike the exclusive and insular world of Mansfield Park that absorbs and ultimately rejects its inhabitants by turn according to their behavior and beliefs, the American "cult of domesticity" operates as an all-inclusive system of moral, religious, and social values that also constitutes a persuasive work ethic. As Nina Baym explains: "The domestic ideal meant not that woman was to be sequestered from the world in her palace at home but that everybody was to be placed in the home, and hence home and the world would become one. Then, to the extent that woman dominated the home, the ideology implied an unprecedented historical expansion of her influence, and a tremendous advance over her lot in a world dominated by money and market considerations, where she was defined as chattel or sexual toy."[19] The nineteenth-century American domestic ideology for girls reflected the areas of concern such as health, education, and household management as well as those rules determining piety, charity, dress, and manners we have seen illuminated by seventeenth- and eighteenth-century British conduct books. One of the most striking differences between the earlier conduct books of English heroines and the advice books of the new republic is a preoccupation with physical fitness and health found in the latter.[20] Domestic ideology held that American girls embodied the potential for a certain majestic motherhood ultimately attained by Alcott's tomboy, Jo March, who is clever, strong, and skillful in her role as ur-mother to the Plumfield boys.

For the girls who were to become pillars of their homes, maintaining a healthy body and mind was considered a moral duty.[21] William Alcott, a popular author of advice books in America, wrote in *Letters to a Sister* (1850): "But if you are morally bound to attend to bodily health, whatever may be your present condition, and however great your present possessions, in this particular, are you not morally culpable for neglect? Are you not, at least, blameworthy, if you do not act up to the dignity of your present convictions of what is physically *right*?" (my emphasis).[22] For the advice writers, health was not, however, simply freedom from disease. Varying degrees of vigorous exercise were advocated to train girls in physical strength. Dio Lewis stood at one end of the spectrum, arguing for such mechanical means to fitness as the pangymnastikon (a two-ring exercise device popular in Germany, its country of origin) and his own invention, the iron "gymnastic crown," worn for fifteen minutes morning and night to improve posture.[23] A homeopathic physician, Dr. Lewis wrote anecdotal and humorous books for young women, such as *Our Girls* (1871), in which he gave paternal advice on girl's health and fitness, through discussions of dress, nutrition, and body size, and how these matters related to employment and matrimonial prospects. In his discussion of the necessity for thick-soled shoes, for example, Dr. Lewis good-humoredly chides those who would idealize girls as overly delicate or ethereal: "Some people seem, somehow, to suppose that girls do not really step on the ground, but that, in some sort of spiritual way, they pass along just above the damp, unclean earth. But, as a matter of fact, girls do step on the ground just like boys. I have frequently walked behind them to test this point, and have noticed that when the ground is soft, they make tracks, and thus demonstrate the existence of an actual, material body."[24]

It is this focus on the material body which also separates the "real" girl from the "true" girl.[25] The physically fit and healthy girl not only enlarged her capacity for work and service, but also enhanced her beauty and chances on the marriage market. An almost universal complaint against American girls was that although they were thought to be the prettiest national type (in comparison with English and Continental girls), they often neglected their beauty through sheer idleness and indolence. The anonymous *Young Girl's Book of Healthful Amusements and Exercises* (1840) includes illustrations of a girl doing calisthenics and, as an enticement to regularly performing these exercises, suggested that exercise would fulfill every girl's desire for (male) attention: "And if the young girls into whose hands this little book may fall, wish to be admired for their personal beauty and graceful carriage, as well as to have the rosy hue of health tinge their cheeks, they will not neglect the opportunities they may have for daily exercise, and as much as possible in the open air."[26]

The work ethic of the cult of domesticity elevated housekeeping to the level of a profession (see chapter 6). Yankee values such as economy, frugality, and organization infused the popular housekeeping manuals (which often also included general advice for girls). Lydia Maria Child's *Frugal Housewife* (the first of at least 33 editions was published in 1829; later editions were entitled *The American Frugal Housewife*) preached the new "American evangelicalism" of prudence: "The true economy of housekeeping is simply the art of gathering up all the fragments, so that nothing is lost. I mean fragments, of *time,* as well as *materials*. Nothing should be thrown away so long as it is possible to make any use of it, however trifling that use may be; and whatever be the size of a family, every member should be employed either in earning, or saving money."[27] Thus, the female members of a household—probably not earning money in the commercial sphere—could (and must, according to this philosophy) participate in the market by avoiding expense. This saving creates value. Child's reverence for hard work and ingenuity is revealed in the following example where a few homely ingredients combined with female labor could improve old fabric and even increase its original value: "Skim-milk and water with a bit of glue in it, heated scalding hot, is excellent to restore old, rusty black Italian crape. If clapped and pulled dry, like nice muslin, it will look as well, or better, than when new."[28]

As the title indicates, Catharine Beecher and Harriet Beecher Stowe's *American Woman's Home: or, Principles of Domestic Science; Being a Guide to the Formation and Maintenance of Economical, Healthful, Beautiful and Christian Homes* (1869) raises the care and management of the home to the level of science.[29] In their discussion of the absolute necessity of fresh air in the house regardless of the weather outside, the sisters (although this is primarily Catharine Beecher's work, one imagines her sister Harriet was probably included as author to help the book sell) discuss in detail, with the help of illustrations, the respiratory system and its exact function.[30] Analogous to maintaining the health of the body, establishing a healthy home was also considered morally imperative. In a chapter entitled "A Healthful Home," Harriet Beecher Stowe's "House and Home Papers" is quoted, demonstrating in fiction the serious ill-effects of improper ventilation: "Little Jim, who, fresh from his afternoon's ramble in the fields, last evening said his prayers dutifully, and lay down to sleep in a most Christian frame, this morning sits up in bed with his hair bristling with crossness, strikes at his nurse, and declares he won't say his prayers—that he don't want to be good. The simple difference is, that the child, having slept in a close box of a room, his brain all night fed by poison, is in a mild state of moral insanity" (49–50). Here unhealthy domestic space—through irrational enclosure—is linked to madness, whereas clean air promises redemption. Reminiscent of Hannah Woolley's *Gentlewomans Companion*, the *American Woman's Home*'s compendium of domestic management and moral philosophy leaves nothing to chance, but documents and discusses every aspect of the middle-class New England home, from "Habits of System and Order" to the

care of infants, children, servants, and gardens, and expands feminine influence to include "The Christian Neighborhood."[31]

Another significant aspect of the advice books for girls was the promotion
of democratic ideals within its program for moral reform, feminine behavior,
and domestic management. For example, *American Woman's Home* considers
early rising to be a habit especially suited for the new republic: "This practice
[of early rising] which may justly be called a domestic virtue, is one which has
peculiar claim to be styled American and democratic. . . . But in aristocratic
countries, especially in England, labor is regarded as the mark of the lower
classes, and indolence is considered as one mark of a gentleman. This impression has gradually and imperceptibly, to a great extent, regulated their
customs, so that, even in their hours of meals and repose, the higher orders
aim at being different and distinct from those who, by laborious pursuits, are
placed below them" (191).

Many of the advice books are lavish in their praise of the domestic American
woman and the opportunities that exist for her in America: Reverend George
Washington Burnap, in *Lectures on the Sphere and Duties of Women, and Other
Subjects* (1841), felt that although women ought not to seek suffrage, "better
provisions ought to be made to secure to them their property, I have no
doubt."[32] The sentimental Burnap also considered women the "very poetry of
the world" and America, with its "free" society, as the "Paradise of Women."[33]
Catharine Maria Sedgwick, who, like Lydia Maria Child and many other ad-
vice-book authors, also wrote for children, related an incident in *Morals of
Manners; or, Hints for our Young People* (1846) that demonstrates her national
pride in American manners and American labor: "Last winter, an elderly lady
met with [a street filled with water too wide to step over]. A labouring man
was passing. There was no plank at hand. He set his foot in the water for a
stepping-place, and extending his hand to her, begged her to put her foot on
it! You may have heard of Sir Walter Raleigh's gallantry to Queen Elizabeth,
how he threw the cloak from his shoulders into the mud for her to step upon.
We think our American labourer's courtesy exceeded even Sir Walter Raleigh's."[34] Sedgwick later reminds her child readers of their accountability as
inheritors of a democratic political system and its rewards for hard-working
citizens: "You have a great responsibility as American children. It is not here
as in the old world, where one man is born with a silver spoon, and another
with a pewter one, in his mouth. You may all handle silver spoons, if you will.
That is, you may all rise to places of respectability."[35] An American girl's knowl-

edge gained in the "home school" could be critical to the success of her family members; her influence upon her brothers and sons might determine the degree of their honor in whatever society the fluid American "class" system made available to them: "A Farmer's boy accustomed, at home, to a neat table and well-conducted meal, will not in any way discredit himself, nor be abashed or flurried if he chance, in after life, (as he well may,) to be the guest of the President of the United States."[36]

As I have argued above concerning the formation of nineteenth-century American children's literature, the instability and liquidity of the American economy, where fortunes were made and lost with alarming frequency, also affected the advice books for girls, which almost unanimously advocated for its readers training in some marketable skill or trade in the unhappy event that some evil befall the girl and her family. Lydia Howard Sigourney in *Letters to Young Ladies* (1833) considered the "sphere of Woman [to be] eminently practical" and that "young ladies should make themselves the mistresses of some attainment, either in art or science, by which they might secure a subsistence, should they be reduced to poverty."[37]

It is not only in response to the threat of reduced fortune that girls were encouraged to increase their knowledge and skills beyond domestic management, but also to render their happiness somewhat independent from these duties. As Mary Wollstonecraft had rather grimly noted in *Thoughts on the Education of Daughters*, a girl's marriage might not be satisfactory or companionable, but rather a trial to be borne and thus a girl's (or woman's) abilities to transcend her suffering through reading and study would be a comfort and a virtue.[38] In *Means and Ends, or Self-Training* (1839), an advice book written for girls aged ten to sixteen, Sedgwick writes: "Be sure to be so educated that you can have an independent pursuit, something to occupy your time and interest your affections; then marriage will not be essential to your usefulness, respectability, or happiness."[39] She suggests the study of arithmetic as useful and beneficial, opening employment possibilities traditionally closed to women and serving to "inspire a love of order and accuracy, and thus aid[ing] women where they are most defective."[40]

The ideal Real Womanhood depicted in the advice books was biased in favor of the middle-class: wealth and its "benefits" were seen as tending to make its possessors idle and morally weak. Sedgwick sternly admonishes her wealthy readers: "Depend upon it, that if you are totally ignorant of domestic affairs, you are nearly as unfit to be an American wife and mother, as if you were lame in both feet and hands."[41] Grace H. Dodge's *A Bundle of Letters to Busy Girls on Practical Matters* (1887), written expressly for the working girls of New York City, gives domestic advice mediated by the strictures harsh economic times imposed upon these readers. The hints and strategies offered are meant to make up for the lack of time a factory or office girl had to spend on learning domestic and personal management, yet also to convince these girls that home values are best. The book thus cautions readers about the temptations and dangers particular to urban girls with an income—spending money on trifles, drink, fashionable clothing, and running with a "fast" crowd.[42] The distressed circumstances of many of the girls of Dodge's "Practical Talks" (published in the same volume) is evident from the advice given: "Buy a morning paper, read it, and then keep it for a cold spell of weather, and thus make your news useful. Girls can tuck it inside of a thin coat, and for a few hours it will keep them warm and comfortable."[43] One discourse replaces another: Dodge's indispensable pearls of wisdom transform the words of disposable newspapers into useful articles.

As Cogan points out, much of the literature written by women in nineteenth-century America was addressed to a middle-class audience (the evangelical and temperance tracts were an exception) and featured middle-class characters. This is an accurate description of novels written for girls in the same period. The active, intelligent, playful, and loving tomboy, a popular conception of nineteenth-century girlhood, embodies, in part, the ideals of Real Womanhood and conduct ideology, even as she strains against their boundaries. She will become, with time and training, a capable American woman. Eliza Stuart Phelps's preface to a new edition of the *Gypsy* books (1895) calls Gypsy "quite a Tom-boy, if I remember correctly." Although Phelps cannot answer the hypothetical questions her "modern readers" pose about Gypsy's adult life and choices ("Did [Gypsy] edit a Quarterly Review, or sing a baby to sleep?"), she emphatically describes Gypsy as the same Real Woman that advice books portray: "Gypsy never grew up to be 'timid,' or silly, or mean, or lazy; but a sensible woman, true and strong; asking little help of other people, but giving much; an honor to her brave and loving sex, and a safe comrade to the girls who kept step with her into middle life."[44]

The formulaic aspects of the novels that feature tomboys include a girl heroine of about twelve years old who prefers boyish games and pursuits to the duties of the domestic girl. She is always lively, intelligent, and charming; the most famous example is certainly Alcott's Jo March. The tomboy is also the possessor of good sense of humor, enjoying practical jokes and the ironies of life. A "tomboy" is not the same thing as a boy, however. The earliest (now obsolete) uses cited in the *Oxford English Dictionary* define "tomboy" as "a rude, boisterous, or forward boy" (sixteenth-century definitions are given). Subsequently, we see a shift in the definition from boisterous boy to "immodest woman." But there were also positive connotations and uses of the term in nineteenth-century texts—for instance, in Charlotte Yonge's *Womankind* (1876): "What I mean by 'tomboyism' is a *wholesome* delight in rushing about at full speed, playing at active games, climbing trees, rowing boats, making dirt-pies and the like" (my emphasis), yet the tomboy is always measured against a male standard; her charm is that she is a proto-boy. The possessor of some of his qualities but few of his prerogatives, a tomboy merely plays at being a boy. The tomboy is naturally humorous as she gender-bends girlhood into androgyny. If she were truly masculine without the saving grace of comedy, of course, the tomboy would be an unreclaimed outsider.[45]

It was thought that girls generally could not be trusted with the freedom of boy-life. Sarah Elbert compares Alcott's works with Twain's and argues that "neither boyhood nor girlhood in Alcott's novel represent the sacred liberty found in Twain's Mississippi odyssey. Plumfield has a small, tame stream with a playhouse refuge in the willow tree overhanging its banks; grownups and children climb up and share confidence with one another. In Twain's scheme of things neither girls nor white adults can really be trusted. Only boys and "niggers," both social outcasts, are existentially free."[46] And yet the figure of the adventuresome and independent boy is an important symbol of the new republic. It is his very nature as a "sanctioned rebel" that insures his place as the cornerstone of American society.[47] The girl, however, is not trusted to enjoy freedom or believed to possess the ability to maintain it. She needs and, so the ideology goes, deserves to be regulated and domesticated. Alfred Habegger, in his book *Gender, Fantasy and Realism in American Literature,* calls the comic nineteenth-century tomboy "*really* peculiar" in that she "become[s] a boy."[48] She is therefore both "funny peculiar and funny ha ha." He suggests that the "masculinization" of these characters is the key to their humor, but assumes a male standard of comic behavior against which he judges the tomboy.[49] Yet, the comedy of the tomboy is certainly more complex than Habegger would have us believe. More fruitful to an understanding of the humor of Jo, for example, is Judy Little's concept of "liminality" (borrowed from anthropology):

"The liminal phase of a rite characteristically emphasizes the annulled identity of the persons undergoing the rite and expresses sometimes their freedom from the usual norms of behavior."[50] The liminal aspect of the tomboy is exactly this freedom from conventional gender roles. This transitional phase in the tomboy's life—for most nineteenth-century tomboys do grow into some form or other of the conventional women—may be the only space in which the women novelists writing for children were allowed what Little calls the "renegade comedy" of Virginia Woolf and Muriel Spark (among others): "comedy in which the liminal elements are never resolved, comedy which implies, or perhaps even advocates, a permanently inverted world, a radical reordering of social structures, a real rather than temporary and merely playful redefinition of sex identity, a relentless mocking of truths otherwise taken to be self-evident or even sacred."[51] Theatrical play is a fitting venue for the tomboy as it is similarly comic in a liminal, renegade way.[52] The demands for precise female behavior in nineteenth-century aestheticized girls' culture are clearly articulated in didactically staged scenes of drama, acting, and tableau.[53] The stage and its counterpart, the schoolroom platform, function as sites of chastening laughter for girls, while for boys, acting (out) and theatricality are celebrated as male "rights" of passage.

Ernest Earnest overlooks girls' fiction when he writes in *The American Eve in Fact and Fiction, 1775–1914* that "unlike the real girls of the time, a nineteenth-century fictional heroine almost never makes a wisecrack."[54] The tomboy does joke; her play, however, has an elegiac quality: as she grows up, albeit resistingly, within the time frame of the novels she enlivens, her comic aspects undergo a transformation from "free play" to a kind of "cost management."

II

Carelesly to nod, gape, or go away whilst one is speaking, is both an act of incivility and stupidity; to laugh, or express any Tom-boy trick is as bad or worse.

Hannah Woolley, *The Gentlewomans Companion* (1675)

Boys is boys.

Thomas Bailey Aldrich, *The Story of a Bad Boy* (1870)

The Daughters of the New Republic

Nineteenth-century books for girls such as *Little Women, Gypsy Breynton,* and *What Katy Did* were written within the ideological paradigm set forth in the advice books of mid-nineteenth century America. Nineteenth-century novels for girls, like the conduct novels of the eighteenth century discussed in chapter 3, organize and categorize female experience by combining the tenets of "real womanhood" with narrative. Both advice books and juvenile novels were created, in part, as responses to the fear of female "disorder" and its dangers to the family, society, and the nation. The inclusion of play and comedy in girls' books, which potentially functions as moments of disruption, and subversion of patriarchy, also raises considerable anxiety over the selfsame instability of the community or political system. Robert Martin's treatment of the British Victorian's fear of laughter for its unruly and threatening nature can also be applied, I believe, to nineteenth-century American texts for girls: "When one realizes that chaotic emotion and decorum will always be in conflict, then superimposes upon that knowledge the awareness that even conflict is part of a unified world, it finally becomes safe to laugh at comedy, either in the world around us or in literature. That realization, that safety, was precisely what the Victorian middle class lacked. It was dangerous to laugh because laughter revealed the fundamental dislocation of both the individual and society."[55] The following pages consider the pervasive inclusion of fascinating and dangerous comic theatricality in the construction of texts for girls. I compare examples of play and humor in these books with that of the quintessential boys' book of the nineteenth century, *Tom Sawyer,* and with the now lesser-known *Story of a Bad Boy* by Thomas Bailey Aldrich.[56]

That adolescent or preadolescent boys and girls historically were not encouraged to share reading material emphasized the "segregation" they would experience in later life through the separate-sphere economies of the domestic and the commercial. The subject matter for "boys' books" was generally adventure, school days, and success stories, whereas girls' books were concerned with the home, family, and romance.[57] In addition to the distinctions in subject matter between boys' and girls' books, humor was employed differently in gendered texts. Alfred Habegger identifies and discusses the gender-relational quality of much of American humor, and uses as examples the boys' books of the 1870s and 1880s, where "the distinguishing mark of the boy is the tireless enterprise he devotes to practical jokes."[58] Girls, on the other hand, have little to do with humor, save "manly" Jo, who, in Habegger's view, "is the exception that proves the rule—that humor was a masculine trait."[59]

Yes, virtually everything seems funny in the boyish world of *Tom Sawyer,* from the narrator's wry tone, and stock characters (the "model boy," the "old maid"), to Tom's superstitions and various capers that propel the plot. As James Cox writes in *Mark Twain: The Fate of Humor,* the humor of *Tom Sawyer* lies "precisely in the discovery of a character who could create the world as play."[60] Tom's conventional but effective tricks open the book: "My! Look behind you, aunt!"[61] when he wants to escape punishment; and his innocent fantasies close it: in his gleefully solemn discussion of "turning robber," Tom defines "initiation" for Huck—"It's to swear to stand by one another, and never tell the gang's secrets, even if you're chopped all to flinders, and kill anybody and all his family that hurts one of the gang." Huck responds, "That's gay—that's mighty gay" (218). And in between these scenes occurs the famous whitewashing incident—which has become part of the American idiom for ingenuity and cleverness—turning the Protestant work ethic upside down. We laugh at the jealous boys' naivete and Tom's ability to discover their weakness, for we all share the desire for what another is enjoying. We also laugh with the trickster to see that he has again succeeded in getting what *he* wants: the boys' treasures, an idle day, and the opportunity to shock Aunt Polly with his industry. This swindle constitutes an even exchange—each boy barters what he has for something of greater value—but only Tom actually comes out ahead because he knows, as does the reader, that in a youthful fantasy, work is worthless. The episodic series of summer days all create a boy's world full of warmth and good fun, even when coupled with the danger and treachery represented by Injun Joe. Evil is ultimately conquered, justice served, and, to fulfill the idyll completely, Tom and Huck find a treasure that enriches them beyond their dreams.[62]

Within the innocent world of *Tom Sawyer,* social instability is overcome by the enactment of Old Testament justice and morality where the good are saved—Tom and Becky find a way out of the cave—and the bad are damned in tragic irony: Injun Joe starves to death, trapped behind an iron door Judge Thatcher has had built as a safety measure. The external evil that surrounds Tom can be safely eradicated, without disturbing him psychologically. In the lives of the Alcott little women, Katy Carr of *What Katy Did,* and Gypsy Breynton, however, corruption is housed within so that women become the *embodiment* of error.[63] This fundamental difference between the boy's adventure and the girls' learning experience is reflected in the function of humor in these texts. Humor serves, in *Tom Sawyer,* to help us laugh at the "boy" in each of us, at caricatures of people we all recognize, and at Mark Twain's wry tales of childhood. In an adolescent girl's world, by contrast, humor teaches us the necessity of exorcising the evil in ourselves and becoming selfless little women.[64] In this way, literature functions similarly to the proliferate advice books for girls, which also respond to the seemingly timeless need for control over female behavior. The modifications of female behavior called for by the novels, however, are also expected to come primarily from within, through self-regulation and examination, that is, by "conquering the self beautifully."

I am not asserting that girls' books are humorless; little women *do* have fun and are funny. And the American advice books do not, in general, caution against laughter or pleasure, but advocate, rather, the suppression of high spirits. Sedgwick, in *Means and Ends,* warns girls against talking excessive "non-sense" and describes a broadly conceived rule against "rowdyism."[65] Seeming to fear the disruptive and "peculiar" female body, William Alcott coyly advises against running once a girl reaches physical maturity: "She must not, after she is old enough to need a brassiere, indulge in 'any form of motion more rapid than walking,' for fear of betraying somewhere below the neck some 'portion of the general system which gives to woman her peculiar prerogative, as well as her distinctive character.' "[66]

In addition to the body, the stage is another locus for negotiating humor and self-regulation. Any actual or metaphorical platform for the performance of comic or tragic theatrical gesture is a common "playground" in books for male and female juveniles. This space, Johan Huizinga has eloquently argued in *Homo Ludens,* is sacred and therefore set apart from the unremarkable or mundane: "Just as there is no formal difference between play and ritual, so the 'consecrated spot' cannot be formally distinguished from the play-ground. The arena, the card-table, the magic circle, the temple, the stage, the screen, the tennis court, the court of justice, etc., are all in form and function play-grounds, i.e. forbidden spots, isolated, hedged round, hallowed, within which special rules obtain. All are temporary worlds within the ordinary world, ded-icated to the performance of an act apart."[67] Theatricality is a natural trope in literature for young people because childhood is a time of trying different identities on for size. Authors and readers alike scrutinize the adolescent girl, evaluating the beauties or frailties of her nature. Huizinga conjectures that the aesthetic of "beautiful" play may result from its inherent organization: "It may be that this aesthetic factor is identical with the impulse to create orderly form, which animates play in all its aspects."[68] The "orderly form" of play, of course, is found within its determining rules—which can be simple or unbearably complex or arcane (for example, rope skipping and a Congressional hearing are both organized games). As in my earlier definition of "play fair," this aestheticism informs the instances of staged play in *Little Women, Gypsy Breynton,* and *What Katy Did.* It is in the theatrical, as well, that the potentially subversive nature of female comedy can also operate. Here the rules of the game of patriarchy may be challenged and at least partially overcome.[69]

After the March girls decide to spend their money on Christmas gifts for their mother rather than on themselves, they gather together to rehearse Jo's annual Christmas play. This original melodrama, "The Witch's Curse: An Operatic Tragedy," calls for each sister to play two roles: Jo is both hero and villain, Meg is a witch and the "cruel sire," Amy is the heroine and a spirit, Beth is a servant and a "black imp." The girls' amateur theatricals fill their apparent need for drama (like Alcott's own need) in lives narrowed by economic constraint, and, I would argue, social injunctions against seeking public applause.[70] The plays enable the sisters not only to exercise their imaginations, but also to construct mechanical and artistic sets and props to enhance their productions (16). Most important, Jo is able to indulge her fantasies of masculine privilege, anger, and action by playing male roles, wearing "his" shoes and sword: "No gentlemen were admitted; so Jo played male parts to her heart's content, and took immense satisfaction in a pair of russet-leather boots given her by a friend, who knew a lady who knew an actor. These boots, an old foil, and a slashed doublet once used by an artist for some picture, were Jo's chief treasures, and appeared on all occasions" (16–17). Heroism and villainy are all the same to Jo: delightful for their distinction from her own domestic drama. Elizabeth Lennox Keyser understands Jo's dual role in the production to represent not only her wish for "male freedom," but also her divided nature.[71] Playing both the good and the bad male characters, I believe, however, does not reveal Jo's internal conflict—as she is the creator of the two characters who are ultimately sides of the same (male) coin—but rather indicates her masculine identification and her understanding of comic masculine excess where passion and rage are both exhilarating emotions. First writing and then cross-dressing and wielding the phallic sword "frees" Jo to act the male and playfully expose his folly at the same time. As Elaine Showalter notes about "Behind a Mask," one of Alcott's pseudonymously published "blood-and-thunder" tales, " 'Behind a Mask' can be seen as a narrative meditation on the possibilities for feminist subversion of patriarchal culture, on the ways for women to express themselves, or at least their power. Through role-playing, if women are trapped within feminine scripts of childishness and victimization, Alcott suggests, they can unmask these roles only by deliberately overacting them."[72]

Although the theatrical might seem to be empty of didactic intention, within or without the novel, playacting can be reclaimed as practical: "It was excellent drill for their memories, a harmless amusement, and employed many hours which otherwise would have been lonely, or spent in less profitable society" (17). The explanation is a subtle comment on many things: that amusement may be harmful, that memories need drilling, that one might not "profit" from associations with persons other than family members. The March girls are carefully watched, and even their play must be based on training the self for "little womanhood."[73]

The attending difficulties in adapting the play to Marmee's parlor with four girls playing every role make for an amusing scene. We laugh again when, on its opening and closing night, the narrator treats us to a description of the melodrama and its disasters: "Timidly she crept from her lattice, put her hand on Roderigo's shoulder, and was about to leap gracefully down, when, 'Alas! alas for Zara!' she forgot her train,—it caught in the window; the tower tottered, leaned forward, fell with a crash, and buried the unhappy lovers in the ruins!" (19). The play's comic function clearly goes beyond Jo's liberation through disguise. Although the comic tone and atmosphere of *Little Women* is certainly not sarcastic or biting, the female reader herself is established in a superior position to the penitent or ridiculous character (Amy as the awkward Zara tumbling to the floor in a heap is one example): *she* would not be so foolish; she would know better. In this way, the comedy of the text requires that the author and the reader be placed next to each other, in opposition (but not antagonism) to the character. Martin discusses nineteenth-century theories of the relationship between the author and reader in humorous writing: "There is always an implied self-superiority in the individual who laughs at others. . . . Not only is the quality of mind of the reader or audience important in understanding the reaction to wit, but there must be a kind of likeness between the minds of the author and the reader."[74] Without this meeting of the minds, humor falls flat. The March girls thus participate in a gendered household economy of time; time used wisely—even playtime—creates value. Eliza W. R. Farrar's *Young Lady's Friend* (1836) relates how a girl who takes one extra hour a night to sleep, "in a life of three score year and ten, shortens her conscious existence *nearly four years*."[75] The implication here is that the girl's time is too precious to waste in idleness, and that only industry—labor—accrues meaning.

Most of the humorous scenes of the novel take this notion of training one step further: the laugh is almost always *on* one of the girls. That is, an adventure (or *mis*adventure), while comical, is often funny in a rueful sense.[76] The girl is made to realize, ultimately, how serious her "shortcomings" are. Lest she forget, Marmee delivers a gentle but unambiguous lecture in order to impress further the lesson on the penitent daughter and on the reader. The value gained through useful play has currency beyond the family and community, as well. The game of Pilgrim's Progress that girls engage in is, as Greta Gaard notes, also a "play" crucial to the girls' spiritual development.[77]

In the household, however, multiple lessons are left to be learned by the struggling Pilgrims. Underlying the comical vignette of Meg and Jo's preparations for a fancy New Year's Eve party is a lesson suggesting that not only is vanity and social climbing wrong, but its net result—marred beauty— represents physical and social loss rather than material gain. Meg desires a "cloud of little ringlets" about her face, but when Jo attempts to create the effect with hot tongs, Meg's hair is burnt off instead: " 'Serves me right for trying to be fine. I wish I'd let my hair alone,' cried Meg petulantly" (25).[78] "Natural value" is reinforced by the end of the chapter. Meg and Jo's poverty forces them into numerous preparations and tricks to disguise it—wearing one clean glove a piece and holding the stained one in their hands, standing against the wall so no one will notice Jo's burned gown, wearing last year's outgrown high-heeled slippers. Even so, however, the Marches recognize that they are more fortunate than their wealthier friends. By appearing either as they are, or in "decorous disguise," the girls realize that not only do they enjoy themselves as much as "fine young ladies," as Jo says, but they also enjoy "profitable poverty"—the oxymoronic state proposed by the novel whereby men of value appreciate and reward honest poor girls with their approbation and offers of marriage. The message here and, ultimately, of the entire novel, is that she who can laugh at her material poverty and mask it, using domestic sleight of hand, and who can realize that a poverty of "womanly" character cannot be hidden, will laugh longest, all the way to her wedding day.[79] To act as a modest, polite young lady is not to act at all, but to illuminate the beauties of the national female character described in advice books for girls.

As in *Tom Sawyer,* but for a different purpose, humorous school pranks are described in each of the girls' books under discussion. The school platform and schoolyard function as sacred playgrounds and the sites of staged play in books for both boys and girls. In *Little Women,* Amy, the only March girl to attend school, falls into trouble for bringing twenty-four delicious pickled limes to class. These limes are the fashionable currency of the day, and to own many is to be rich in friends and social power; they have been forbidden, however, by the schoolmaster. We laugh with Amy's older sisters over what a self-important and prissy schoolgirl finds meaningful: "Why, you see, the girls are always buying them, and unless you want to be thought mean, you must do it, too. It's nothing but limes now, for every one is sucking them in their desks in school-time, and trading them off for pencils, bead-rings, paper dolls, or something else, at recess. If one girl likes another, she gives her a lime; if she's mad with her, she eats one before her face, and don't offer even a suck. They treat by turns; and I've had ever so many, but haven't returned them, and I ought, for they are debts of honor, you know" (66). But Amy's fall, which quickly loses its humor, is long and hard. The limes had been declared a "contraband article" (67) by the schoolmaster; and, after a jealous rival tells him of their existence in Amy's desk, she is both physically punished and publicly humiliated by having to stand on the platform until recess. This scene dramatizes social embarrassment with a twist: unlike *Jane Eyre*'s saintly Helen Burns who wears the too-harsh label "Slattern," and unlike Jane herself who is unjustly branded a liar by Mr. Brocklehurst and placed on a stool as an example to the students, Amy (like Gypsy and Katy) "deserves" her punishment of scorn and humiliation. While Amy is removed from school, the school prank is used for didactic purposes by Marmee, the novel's moral arbiter. Later, in response to her mother's lecture, Amy responds, "I see. It's nice to have accomplishments and be elegant, but not to show off or get perked up" (71). At stake for the dramatic and artistic Amy is her social value; we are reminded here of the many warnings against the displaying woman in *Coelebs:* "You will want a COMPANION: an ARTIST you may hire" (19). Ironically, the reformation of the showy schoolgirl is effected by placing her *on display.* The female reader is meant to consider her own failures as well as the benefits of changing from a girl concerned with display to a modest young woman. Alcott's chapter ends neatly at this point, after the lesson has been carefully delineated in the theater of humiliation and presumably digested by character and reader alike.

Although we smile with indulgence at Tom Sawyer's showing off— an essential element of boyhood that often serves to insulate the boyish man (like

Mark Twain) from growing old[80]—the female character must avoid or repress her desire for applause or attention. Thus playacting or dressing up is also explored and regulated in girls' fiction. Certainly assuming different identities is an important aspect of playfulness. The desire for, yet fear of, the anarchy of disguise is also at the center of the carnivalesque, or adult play: "[In disguise] the 'extra-ordinary nature of play reaches perfection. The disguised or masked individual 'plays' another part, another being. He *is* another being."[81] Gypsy's school prank in *Gypsy Breynton* constitutes such an identity switch: one morning she falls in the pond after her raft sunk, and, penitent after this mishap, which makes her late for school, Gypsy resolves "not to do a single funny thing all day."[82] However, tempted by her classmates' outerwear hanging in the hall, she dresses as an old woman and affects a country Yankee accent to test her powers of mimicry and disguise: " 'I come to see the young uns,' piped the old woman. 'I ben deown teown fur some eggs, an' I heerd the little creaturs a sayin' of their lessons as I come by, an' thinks says I to myself, says I, bless their dear hearts. I'll go in an' see 'em, says I, an' I'll thank ye kindly for a seat, for I'm pretty nigh beat out.' "[83] She points a finger at her best friend and demands that she recite Alice's nemesis, "How doth the little busy bee."

Gypsy is delighted by the apparent success of her playacting. Her satisfaction has surely come, in part, from swapping identities. Terry Castle defines the pleasure of masquerade as emanating from "the experience of doubleness, the alienation of inner from outer, a fantasy of two bodies simultaneously and thrillingly present, self and other together, the two-in-one."[84] Like Jo, Gypsy has chosen a subversive double—in her case the strong-minded "widdy." Yet once discovered, Gypsy's punishment for masking her true self—a powerless schoolgirl—is severe: she is treated as if she has doesn't exist, and must watch in silence as absent marks go "down on her report, when she was right in the room and had learned her lessons" (70).[85] Gypsy's performance on the school stage has no utility other than as an example of "play ugly": by acting as another, Gypsy has repudiated her self.[86] She is remonstrated for inappropriate behavior and unkindness to her teacher. Gypsy asks for a scolding, but receives something of greater weight: the self-knowledge that she is morally corrupt.

Disguises, mistaken and assumed identities, and dramatic playgrounds (Jackson Island, the river, the circus) populate Twain's *Adventures of Huckleberry Finn* (1884). Huck dresses as a girl to ease his anxiety over St. Petersburg events, but cannot mask his boyishly accurate throwing arm or his inability to thread a needle correctly. Undaunted by his detection, Huck readily assumes another disguise—that of a runaway apprentice—and rushes to alert Jim of their danger on Jackson Island. (We are reminded here of Jo's half-hearted joke that Mr. Lawrence should look for two runaway boys if he and Laurie do not patch up their quarrel. The joke lacks enthusiasm, however, as Jo had just reminded Laurie that she could not run off to Washington with him as "prunes and prisms' are my doom, and I may as well make up my mind to it" [213].)[87] The King and the Duke are effective, if inept, actors on the social stage (their *Hamlet* is a notable theatrical failure), swindling and weaving lies as they go. Even Jim, who carries his "identity"—his black skin—at all times, plays a sick Arab for a time. Exposure of these various frauds would have much greater consequences for the characters of *Huckleberry Finn* than for the little women of girls' novels. The difference in detection is between death and imprisonment for Jim and Huck, and embarrassment or shame for the girl characters. And yet, in spite of the dangers, the comic vision is unrelenting in Twain, whereas comedy is mitigated and finally undercut by social convention in the girls' books.[88]

Twelve-year-old Katy Carr in *What Katy Did* also learns the benefits of taking responsibility for her actions and of asking for forgiveness. As a result of "profaning" the schoolroom by leading her schoolfellows in a particularly uproarious activity called the "game of rivers," Katy suffers from the realization that she has greatly disappointed her teacher. She gains relief from her self-hatred only after uncontrollable weeping and pitiful confession. Tom Sawyer, by contrast, is rewarded for *his* theatrical school prank acted in front of the Sunday school classes and visiting dignitaries by *attaining* his desires and *retaining* center stage. After winning the envy of his peers and the attention of the girl he loves by audaciously pretending to have memorized two thousand verses of Scripture, "his success tarnished slightly but still intact, Tom remains the central attraction."[89] His punishment, unlike the girls', is never described or witnessed, and the reader is led to believe that the only lesson Tom learns (and this over and over) is that happiness and humor lie in acts of bravado and self-interest.

Aldrich's Tom Bailey also relishes the stage. Tom and his friends are seized with a passion for acting and transform his grandfather's barn into a theater where the boys perform such heroic pieces as "William Tell." After mistakenly shooting his fellow actor in the mouth with an arrow, Tom's first thought, unlike the sentiments of self-loathing penitent players of girls' fiction express, is to imagine a subsequent dramatic platform for his heroic display: "I looked upon [the victim] as a corpse, and, glancing not far into the dreary future, pictured myself led forth to execution in the presence of the very same spectators then assembled."[90] In fact, although Tom's grandfather shuts the theater down, Tom is able to make a final impassioned speech defending drama and his innocence before the curtain literally closes the show: "[t]he place was closed; not, however, without a farewell speech from me, in which I said that this would have been the proudest moment of my life if I hadn't hit Pepper Whitcomb in the mouth. Whereupon the audience (assisted, I am glad to state, by Pepper) cried 'Hear! Hear!' "[91] Harm is never caused by accident in *Little Women*, by contrast. Amy's near-death by drowning is laid directly at Jo's door for her anger and inability to forgive. Jo ultimately fears not the loss of her artistic powers—as Tom Bailey does—but that she will "do something dreadful some day, and spoil my life, and make everybody hate me" (79). The adult lesson Jo learns is to be unforgiving of her own faults while forgiving the faults of others.[92]

The lessons that the March girls, Katy Carr, Gypsy Breynton, and other (especially serial) heroines learn successfully reform their characters. Each girl grows up in the course of her novel, whereas Tom Sawyer and Huck Finn remain eternal boys.[93] As the girls develop, the didactic use of humor in scenes of childish escapades and pranks, awkward situations, and misunderstandings falls away and is often replaced by another, more serious, teacher: in the words of the invalid Helen (from *What Katy Did*)—"The School of Pain." After disobeying her aunt's orders to stay off the dangerous woodshed swing, Katy's back is severely injured in a serious fall. She is partially paralyzed for two years, but mysteriously recovers after assimilating the lessons of Real Womanhood.[94] As Elizabeth Janeway writes, "But Katy must 'grow up,' and to grow up properly she must be chastened until she is ready, even eager, to fit herself into the pattern of womanhood then admired. It is not a pattern that upholds frivolity, silliness, or incapacity."[95] Katy's lessons in selflessness, even as the reality of her disability diminishes her ability to play, takes place on the "stage" created by her bed or wheelchair. As Auerbach notes, "a compulsively theatrical age made a pageant even of the sickroom,"[96] and certainly the drama of Katy's illness and her improvement overshadows the book so that "child's play" evolves into the domestic theater by the novel's end. Jo, too, at the heart of the comedy of *Little Women*, suffers and languishes after the death of her beloved sister until she begins to find some consolation in trying to emulate Beth's selfless attention to duty and domestic chores:[97] "Brooms and dishcloths never could be as distasteful as they once had been, for Beth presided over both; and something of her housewifely spirit seemed to linger round the little mop and the old brush, that was never thrown away. As she used them, Jo found herself humming the songs Beth used to hum, imitating Beth's orderly ways, and giving the little touches here and there that kept everything fresh and cozy, which was the first step toward making home happy" (434). Like Alice, little women such as Katy, Gypsy, and the March sisters each fall through self-reflection into socialization, safety, and a narrowly determined female role, as opposed to the "sons of Liberty" who climb up to freedom: "It is the nature of the girl to fall through her looking glass into selfhood; Lewis Carroll's Alice does so as readily as Jane Eyre, becoming a queen through this fall, as does Jane in her own stern way. It is the nature of the boy to diffuse himself into the horror of space; Stevenson's Jim Hawkins becomes a self on the sea, Kipling's Kim in a boundless India that is full of treacherous secrets."[98] Although the heroines grow in authority through their falls, it is only Alice—the youngest and most autonomous of the characters (and the only created by a male author)—whose post-lapsarian identity is not directly related to home and domesticity.

There is very little in the way of play or humor in the second part of *Little Women* (entitled *Good Wives*), other than these selfsame absurdities of home and domesticity—most notably found in Meg's mistakes with the kitchen, household accounts, and children. Her husband, John Brooke, like David Copperfield, marries a "child-bride" (a *little* woman!) and her blunders, while amusing, ultimately fail to be very funny: the dangerous undertone in the relations between husband and wife surface when Marmee suggests that Meg should learn to fear John's anger.[99]

John W. Crowley defines the boy's book as creating "a child's world that is antagonistic to the world of adults"[100]; Cox writes that much of the humor in *Tom Sawyer* comes from the perspective of burlesque against "adult rituals."[101] But in the girl's book, the separation between the woman and female child is not so very distinct. All of the heroines of the texts I have been discussing may be rightfully called "little women." They begin training for their heavily determined roles quite early in life—no matter how they may rebel along the way. (This is taken to an absurd level when Meg's daughter, Daisy, begins sewing at age three.) The ultimate lesson we find even in good-humored children's or young adult novels of the late nineteenth century is that girlhood really is not funny. Typically, the function of humor in fiction for girls is different from that of boys' texts: it does not provide the release of laughter, but points to some deficiency in the character which must be, in the words of Father March, "conquered beautifully" (19) before the girl can fulfill her destiny as a virtuous and selfless woman.[102]

By emptying themselves of the humorous transgressions of their gender-ambiguous tomboy status, Jo, Katy, and Gypsy play fair; the rules are determined from outside and absorbed within. Alice never assimilates: she claims her prerogative at the trial, another playground, and makes a scene, stealing the show from the rule-laden King and from the monstrous maternal figure of the Queen (who never refers to the lively royal children Alice admires in the procession, and who aggressively dispatches many of her childlike subjects to their deaths). Comic fantasy allows Alice to declare her superior authority to the Wonderland residents—they are "only a pack of cards" and she is the player. The comic realism of *Little Women, Gypsy Breynton,* and *What Katy Did* also directs the girl character toward authority, privileging the limited authority of womanhood rather than the autonomous child at play making and breaking rules at will. Roger Henkle's argument about the intermittent nature of play in the *Alice* books more accurately describes Alcott's fiction or Carroll's life, for example, than Carroll's books: "Play can only temporarily remove us from outside reality, as Carroll himself repeatedly discovered, because authority (characterized in those adult women—Queens and Duchesses) will interfere and impose its angry will."[103] Alice is angry at the conclusion of both her tales and this self-righteous anger awakens her from the playing field of dreams she found both amusing and frustrating. Little women assume authority at the close of their stories as well, but finally, it is an acceptance of both the authority of the repressing mother (not the laughing medusa) and the symbolism of the familial patriot (not the ingenue on stage) that plays them fair.[104]

In his discussion of *Alice* and schizophrenic language, Gilles Deleuze places Alice "on edge":

At the beginning of *Alice in Wonderland,* the search for the secret of things and events goes on in the depths of the earth: in deeply dug wells and rabbit holes, as well as in the mixtures of bodies which penetrate each other and coexist. As one advances in the narrative, however, the sinking and borrowing movements give way to lateral, sliding movements: from left to right and right to left. . . . One might say that the former depth has spread itself out, has become breadth. . . . Consequently, there are no adventures of Alice; there is but *one* adventure: her rising to the surface, her disavowal of the false depths, and her discovery that everything happens at the borderline.[105]

The girl, too, is notable for her borderline, or liminal, status. The mildly transgressive boy represented by Tom Sawyer and Tom Bailey is welcomed in American culture and its humorous texts; the erring girl is also invited to stay— but only if she agrees to remain within strictly set boundaries of feminine behavior. Humorous girls, especially tomboys, straddle the border between nature or wilderness and culture. Unlike Tom and Huck, who can choose to escape, girl characters must, in the words of Jo March "stop at home." They cannot leave home because their duties lie within. One significant aspect of these duties, discussed in the next chapter, is maintaining cleanliness in the home. "Little women must cleanse and order the larger world in order to gain even half a day to themselves."[106] The prevalent trope of the equivalence of the clean house and pure mind in American literature and culture is another levelling aspect of nineteenth-century society. Any woman can—and every woman should—keep clean.

6

"The True Meaning of Dirt"

Putting Good and Bad Girls in Their Place(s)

*"That's the reward for your services," said Mother Holle, and
closed the door. So then the lazy girl went home, but she was
all covered with pitch and when the rooster on the rim of the
well saw her he crowed: "Cock-a-doodle-doo, / Our dirty girl is
home anew." And the pitch refused to come off, and it stuck to
her as long as she lived.*

"Mother Holle" (German folk tale)

*It is sublime work to save a woman, for in her bosom
generations are embodied, and in her hands, if perverted, the
fate of innumerable men is held. The whole community,
gentlemen, personally interested as they are in our success
because the children of the virtuous must breathe the*

atmosphere exhaled by the vicious, will feel a lively sympathy

for you, in your generous endeavors to redeem the erring

mothers of the next generation.

Bradford Peirce to the Massachusetts Legislature (1857)

After being banished in Portsmouth for her refusal to accept Henry Crawford, Fanny Price is horrified and disgusted by the disorder and dirtiness of her mother's home. She is summoned back to Mansfield Park to comfort the Mansfield inhabitants after they receive the news that the recently married Maria has run away with Henry. Times of moral crisis such as this one, Ruth Bernard Yeazell argues in *Fictions of Modesty,* necessitate separating the good (the clean) and bad (the dirty) from each other, thus emphasizing their distinction: "It is not surprising that in this interval of heightened anxiety and suspense Fanny Price should see dirt."[1] In the case of either guilt or innocence, then, the clean and dirty must be appropriately acknowledged and placed. In *Some Practical Suggestions on the Conduct of a Rescue Home* (1903), turn-of-the-century social reformer and co-leader of the National Florence Crittenton Mission (from 1896) Dr. Kate Waller Barrett defines "the true meaning of dirt" as "matter out of place."[2] This chapter argues that this definition of dirt illuminates central ideologies surrounding various aspects of the Woman Question—in particular those of female sexuality and domesticity—in terms of three "institutions" for girls: the rescue home for bad (read "sexual") girls, reformatories for juveniles and women, and the domestic science movement. The cult of cleanliness that informs this "dirt"-seeking organization has a very clear idea of where "dirt" ought to be placed.[3] For instance, a room open to the effluvia of the outdoors is dirty, just as a girl with "lazy" morals or idle habits is dirty (even her breath and her body, as the epigraphs to this chapter indicate). Both the room and the girl are impure. Barrett's system allows for the reclamation of dirty girls, however, by putting them "where they belong"—in a rescue home—and re-naming them "daughters." That some girls are dirty implies an earlier mismanagement or misplacement of them, an assessment that eventually gives rise to the conflation of female sexuality with domesticity so prevalent in nine-teenth-century theories of gender: the place where all girls (women) belong is in a home.[4] That home, as I will discuss below, whether a female penitentiary, rescue home, or Yankee bungalow, had certain uniform structures. And the females who were to live in these places also had qualities in common.

However, the unselfconscious placement of women in the home became problematic by the mid-nineteenth century during the fervor over women's roles created, in part, by the Woman Question debate as it was furthered by Wollstonecraft, the Grimké sisters, Susan B. Anthony, Elizabeth Cady Stanton, and others. The eloquent and vibrant voices of these and other reformers on the subjects of woman's rights, suffrage, abolition, and female education made the argument for separate spheres based solely on duty—as it had been conventionally rehearsed—seem faint and pallid.[5] The domestic science movement, led by Catharine Beecher, was able to animate the separate-sphere ideology by transforming housekeeping into a important, demanding, and intellectual career that only the female could fulfill.[6] Kathryn Kish Sklar writes in her biography of Beecher: "Women in America had always experienced such inequity [between the sexes], but they had never before needed to reconcile it with a growing ideology of popular democracy and equal rights."[7] As reformers wrote and agitated for greater participation in the political processes of democracy, the domestic science movement co-opted what seemed most appealing about life outside the home—social responsibility, important decision making, service to others, paid labor—and then "shrunk" these desires to fit inside its walls by professionalizing and systematizing the running of the home.[8] To further these ends, domestic training manuals proliferated in antebellum America: "Many women expressed the feeling that the traditional rhythms of housekeeping were being supplanted by a new time—and task—discipline, one they associate with the world of paid business."[9]

In her influential first treatment of the subject of domesticity, *A Treatise on Domestic Economy for the Use of Young Ladies at Home, and at School* (1841), Beecher outlined in detail her system of domestic management: "Here for the first time was a text that standardized American domestic practices—prescribing one system that integrated psychological, physiological, economic, religious, social, and political factors, and in addition demonstrating how the specifics of the system should work."[10] This standardization and systemization of domesticity elevated its moral and political significance to a "science," and in turn raised the "significance" of the women—young and old—who practiced it. Beecher writes that "every woman should imbibe, from early youth, the impression, that she is training for the discharge of the most important, the most difficult, and the most sacred and interesting duties that can possibly employ the highest intellect."[11]

As the title of her treatise indicates, Beecher felt that the movement could best be started and sustained by including domestic science as part of the curriculum of the new female seminaries springing up in the Northeast and West.[12] In this way, the concerns of domestic science were included in the general ideologies of enlightened female education that would properly train young women in the values and ideals of the new republic (see chapter 5): self-reliance, hard work, (relative) egalitarianism, and independence (within the framework of separate spheres).

A proper education for the daughters of the new republic was *useful* above all—the "ornamental" education of accomplishments ultimately found to be so limited for the Bertram sisters in *Mansfield Park,* was sneered at by nine-teenth-century educational reformers as wasteful and even harmful. By contrast, the education offered in *A Treatise on Domestic Economy* enabled a diligent girl to leave school (at approximately sixteen years of age) eminently qualified to fill her God-given role as housekeeper, whether it be for some member(s) of her immediate or extended family or for her new husband.[13] The knowledge that the student of domestic economy gains, Beecher argues, has great value because of its practical nature. She finds some of the gains made in the general curriculum of female seminaries shocking in light of what she understands to be a deplorable ignorance of crucial domestic skills:

> And let the young women of this Nation find, that Domestic Economy is placed, in schools, on an equal or superior ground to Chemistry, Philosophy, and Mathematics, and they will blush to be found ignorant of its first principles, as much as they will to hesitate respecting the laws of gravity, or the composition of the atmosphere. But as matters are now conducted, many young ladies, who can tell how to make oxygen and hydrogen, and discuss questions of Philosophy or Political Economy, do not know how properly to make a bed and sweep a room; while they can "construct a diagram" in Geometry with far more skill than they could construct the simplest article of female dress.[14]

Like the ambitious advice books by Child, Lewis, Sedgwick, Sigourney, and others, and harkening back to Woolley's compendium, Beecher's *Treatise on Domestic Economy* includes a wide-ranging array of subjects necessary for a thorough understanding of domestic management: "the preparation of healthful food," "cleanliness," "domestic exercise," "the management of young children," "the propagation of plants," "muscles; their Constitution, Use and Connection with Bones [with] Engravings and Description," and "the care of domestic animals, barns, etc."

Beecher's various books and speeches on domestic science established a discourse of domesticity in which nationalism and a kind of proto-feminism became inseparably entwined.[15] In her first two chapters, "The Peculiar Responsibilities of American Women" and "Difficulties Peculiar to American Women," Beecher discusses both the primacy of American democracy and the American woman's place in its hierarchy:

> The success of democratic institutions, as is conceded by all, depends upon the intellectual and moral character of the mass of the people. If they are intelligent and virtuous, democracy is a blessing; but if they are ignorant and wicked, it is only a curse, and as much more dreadful than any other form of civil government, as a thousand tyrants are more to be dreaded than one. It is equally conceded, that the formation of the moral and intellectual character of the young is committed mainly to the female hand. The mother writes the character of the future man; the sister bends the fibres that hereafter are the forest tree; the wife sways the heart, whose energies may turn for good or for evil the destinies of a nation. Let the women of a country be made virtuous and intelligent, and the men will certainly be the same. (13)

Informed by the writings of Alexis de Tocqueville, Beecher refers to the relation of women to men as "equal" but at the same time necessarily subordinate, a viewpoint shared by many female reformers of the mid-nineteenth century: "It appears, then, that it is in America, alone, that women are raised to an equality with the other sex; and that, both in theory and practice, their interests are regarded as of equal value. They are made subordinate in station, only where a regard to their best interests demands it, while, as if in compensation for this, by custom and courtesy, they are always treated as superiors" (9). According to Beecher, the means by which woman achieves "equality" with man is through her important work in the "home," whether it be a family dwelling, a school, a room of one's own, or someone else's house: "The woman who is rearing a family of children; the woman who labors in the schoolroom; the woman who, in her retired chamber, earns, with her needle, the mite to contribute for the intellectual and moral elevation of her country; even the humble domestic, whose example and influence may be moulding and forming young minds, while her faithful services sustain a prosperous domestic state; —each and all may be cheered by the consciousness, that they are agents in accomplishing the greatest work that ever was committed to human responsibility" (14). The domestic science movement elevated woman's work to the status of nation building through the "construction" of the country's citizens and through the management and caretaking of democracy's essentially undemocratic family relationships.

Beecher conflates all women into one group—whatever their class, national origin, or race—and raises them all through separate-sphere ideology that attempts to elevate the status of homemaking and women's roles generally. In so doing, however, she elides the very real and significant social and economic distinctions between women based upon the very differences she is at pains to ignore. As Sklar notes, "by defining gender identity as more important than class, regional, or religious identity, and by ignoring altogether the imponderables of American racial divisions, she promoted the belief that the society's only basic division was that between men and women."[16]

Beecher is able to dispatch breezily any questions about the noticeable differences between the life and work experiences of servants and "ladies" (separate entrances into the household, for example), by relegating inequalities to the service of the all-important "order," and by attempting to convince the servant class that they are actually happier this way: "[Servants and the lower class] should be taught, that domestics use a different entrance to the house, and sit at a distinct table, not because they are inferior beings, but because this is the best method of securing neatness and order and convenience. They can be shown, if it is attempted in a proper spirit and manner, that these very regulations really tend to their own ease and comfort, as well as to that of the family" (201).

Domestic scientists held that it was important for woman's labor first to be rendered systematic—increasing its value—and then made invisible—dispersing labor's value by denying its existence as *work*.[17] For example, in her description of an imaginary female seminary's laundry room, Beecher sentimentalizes the scene of labor by painting it in neorepublican pastels that elevate washing to all that is enjoyable and artful: "Let [aristocratic daughters and mothers] see some thirty or forty merry girls, superintended by a motherly lady, chatting and singing, washing and starching, while every convenience is at hand, and everything around is clean and comfortable. Two hours, thus employed, enables each young lady to wash the articles she used during the previous week, which is all that is demanded, while thus they are all practically initiated into the arts and mysteries of the wash-tub" (32–33). Here "washing and starching" become equivalent activities—and sanctified ones—to "chatting and singing."

The powerful ideology of labor, which disguises itself as female duty, physical exercise, or career opportunity, is delineated carefully in fiction of the mid-nineteenth century. For example, Harriet Beecher Stowe's *Minister's Wooing* (1859), although set in late eighteenth-century New England, concisely communicates the general rule (which has all the force of a moral law) that housework should be completed in the morning to allow for afternoon study, repose, and social obligations: "Everything [in the kitchen] seemed to be always done and never doing. Washing and baking, those formidable disturbers of the composure of families, were all over within those two or three morning-hours when we are composing ourselves for a last nap—and only the fluttering of linen over the green yard, on Monday mornings, proclaimed that the dreaded solemnity of a wash had transpired. A breakfast arose there as by magic; and in an incredibly short space after, every knife, fork, spoon, and trencher, clean and shining, was looking as innocent and unconscious in its place as if it never had been used and never expected to be."[18]

Stowe's definition of the Yankee term "faculty" contains the mystical elements of a romanticized domestic practice. This labor is magical in that it transforms the worker by virtue of its very imperceptibility—work does not change the body, clothes do not cost money, labor does not take time ("everything seems to be always done and never doing"). The domestic woman, like the charitable one, is not diminished, but accrues excess value through this invisible work that can then be "spent":

To her who has faculty nothing shall be impossible. She shall scrub floors, wash, wring, bake, brew, and yet her hands shall be small and white; she shall have no perceptible income, yet always be handsomely dressed; she shall have not a servant in her house,—with a dairy to manage, hired men to feed, a boarder or two to care for, unheard of pickling and preserving to do,—and yet you commonly see her every afternoon sitting at her shady parlor-window behind the lilacs, cool and easy, hemming muslin cap-strings, or reading the last new book. She who hath faculty is never in a hurry, never behindhand. She can always step over to distressed Mrs. Smith, whose jelly won't come,—and stop to show Mrs. Jones how she makes her pickles so green,—and be ready to watch with poor old Mrs. Simpkins, who is down with the rheumatism.[19]

Domestic science and reform ideologies thus participate in one of the prevailing idealistic notions of postrevolutionary America found in the advice books as well: that as a "new" system the new republic's social makeup was perfectible. As Sklar writes: "As a postrevolutionary generation bent on extracting practical benefits from their theoretical innovations, many Americans believed that elementary matters like diet and health should be as susceptible to improvement as anything else in the new age, and that wherever possible they should be made perfect."[20] Beecher and the institutional reformers contend that there is one correct system of household management and one "system" of female character. Both ideologies of female behavior—within the family and within the institution—of course, endorse domesticity as the "perfect" female lifestyle. In this way we see that the institutions of domesticity are expanded to include not only the domicile of the family, but also the female seminary and, finally, houses of correction for female criminals, prostitutes, and unwed mothers.[21] Those "good girls" who live in houses like that of Stowe's Katy Scudder, and who thus have extra time on their hands, are expected (as Beecher carefully points out in her chapter entitled "Charity") to expend that time usefully and charitably in exchanging domestic knowledge, services, and goods in the pursuit of satisfaction and happiness.

The ideology of the "social gospel" made current by both men and women in conduct books, sermons, periodicals, Evangelical tracts and novels from the eighteenth century onward emphasized the "feminine" nature of charitable works (see chapter 1). Home management skills were considered well-suited to put the house of the poor in order.[22] The British reformer Elizabeth Fry, an ardent advocate of women's managerial work in charity and social causes, wrote, "May the attention of *women* be more and more directed to these labours of love; and may the time quickly arrive, when there shall not exist, in this realm, a single public institution [where women] . . . shall not enjoy the *efficacious superintendence* of the pious and benevolent of THEIR OWN SEX!"[23]

As charitable institutions, the Magdalen Hospital and the National Florence Crittenton Mission (NFCM) of late nineteenth-century America both sought to convert girls whose sins were sexual—either prostitutes or seduced and abandoned girls—to Christian values, and to train them in such domestic arts laundry and sewing.[24] Begun by Charles Nelson Crittenton, a successful wholesale druggist turned social activist and philanthropist, the Florence Crittenton Homes (established in 1883 and named for a beloved daughter who died of scarlet fever at the age of four) attempted to reform prostitutes and unmarried pregnant girls to religious and domestic values. In *Fifty Years' Work With Girls* Otto Wilson provides a complete (and complimentary) history of the Florence Crittenton Homes. Earlier American rescue homes included the Penitent Females' Refuge (1822), the Boston Temporary Home for Fallen Women (1838), and the House of Mercy (1865). The Catholic Protective Society, the Empire Friendly Shelter (for African-American women), the Salvation Army Rescue Homes, and the Society of the Epiphany also participated in the work of saving the fallen from the streets. Although both the Magdalen Hospital and the Mission sought, in Linda Mahood's words, to "colonize the poor" by isolating one segment of the female (generally) working class from the others, a comparison between the two institutions yields significant ideological differences in their organization.[25] The time span and geography that separates them clearly accounts for some of these differences; however, the notable ways in which Barrett's Rescue Home distinguishes itself from institutions like the Magdalen Hospital, the London Female Penitentiary (1807), and the British Female Penitent Refuge (1829) are in its "republicanisms," or as Barrett calls it, "the democratic spirit of our Home" (26).[26] The girls seeking admittance to a Florence Crittenton home remained essentially nameless, and discussion of their past lives was expressly forbidden by the Crittenton staff. The Magdalen Hospital also maintained this requirement, and the reasons are easily imagined: dwelling upon a past, sinful life would impede progress in Christian humility and could give rise to unnecessary melancholy or, worse yet, revive desires for the company, drink, clothing, and freedom that the old life produced or promised to produce. The American rescue home, however it might have feared the negative effects of storytelling, nevertheless stoutly believed in the legal right to privacy: "Everybody has a right to discuss, or not, their private affairs, and the world is entitled to know that only which it can find out by watching the actions of persons. The Constitution of the United States asserts that everybody has an equal right to the pursuit of life, liberty and happiness" (53).[27] The success of the National Florence Crittenton Mission was in part due to its leaders' vigilance in detecting vice and publicizing the pervasiveness of its unhealthy presence, thereby rallying support for their institutions that attempted to transform the public's image of the fallen girl from unreclaimed, willful sinner to pathetic victim.[28] One example of this kind of useful propaganda is Barrett's cancellation of a trip to the International Council of Women held in Berlin in 1904 in order to hurry to the World's Fair in St. Louis, where it had been rumored that innocent young girls were being rounded up as prostitutes to service the crowds attracted to the Fair. As Otto Wilson writes in his brief life of Barrett, "It was [the Florence Crittenton apologists'] great achievement that they presented the fallen woman not simply as a vessel of sin, a person of mature judgment who had deliberately sold her soul to the devil, but as a human being, sometimes perversely erring but in the great majority of cases merely a child victim of the seducer or of circumstance."[29] This redefinition also had been the greatest hope and challenge of the British charities of earlier times, yet we are reminded here of the obstacles to reform that Sarah Green had remarked to her niece: the failure of such charities as the Magdalen Hospital to reform its clients was largely due to the penitents "not meeting with sufficient charity and encouragement from the rigidly virtuous of their own sex!"[30]

To counteract such antisororal sentiments, the reformer and woman's rights activist Caroline Kirkland, in her stirring fundraising tract, *The Helping Hand: Comprising an Account of the Home for Discharged Female Convicts and an Appeal on Behalf of that Institution* (1853), called upon every privileged female to accept her responsibility toward all other women, or be implicated in their misery: "Among the most precious of Women's Rights is the right to do good to her own sex. . . . Sad it is that [the] fallen woman hopes less from her sisters than from her brothers . . . women should consider themselves as a community, having special common needs and common obligations, which it is a shame to turn aside from under the plea of inability or distaste. *Every woman in misfortune is the proper object of care to the happier and safer part of her sex.* Not to stretch forth to her the helping hand—not to defend her against wrong and shield her from temptation—is to consent to her degradation and to become, in some sense, party to her ruin."[31]

The Florence Crittenton Mission attempted to demonstrate in its institutions the "strengths" of American society: home and family. While the Magdalen Hospital replicated the class structure of outside society inside the institution (penitents of a higher class were separated from the other girls and given special treatment), the American rescue home, by contrast, self-consciously mixed the girls, the matron and her assistants, and the domestic workers of the home, mimicking family structure.[32] Everyone ate at the same time, except for those girls whose turn it was to wait on the others. Barrett writes, "The most important reason [for everyone to eat together], of course, is that we want to be in a true sense a family, with the matron as the mother, presiding at the head of the table" (21). Like such fictional schools as Fielding's "Little Female Academy" and Alcott's Plumfield, the maternity home's artificial familial structure was especially maternal in cast: the matron played "mother," while at the same time the middle-class female reformer also "mothered" the young unwed mothers who were the objects of the institution's reformative program.[33]

Conduct of a Rescue Home outlines Barrett's understanding of the proper organization of a rescue home to house fallen teenaged mothers. A pervasive ideological feature of her pamphlet, which includes specific organizational advice on such issues as the duties of the treasurer, the setup of the kitchen, and "one day in detail," is the means by which the institution is described as systematically deinstitutionalized so that the Home becomes a "home." Although Barrett explicitly discusses some institutional features that the Home can and should avoid (for example, the girls are to make many smaller batches of bread using conventional recipes rather than adhering to the "bakery plan" [107]), in general this deinstitutionalization occurs subtly, so that "home" and "Home" are used interchangeably both semantically and connotatively within any given sentence. The institution ("Home"), therefore, is invested with the same emotional and social value as is the dwelling place of related persons. The story of a girl who had left the rescue home but who ultimately reflected her training there by gaining a position of trust in a "respectable" family "had given me [Barrett] much peace, as it proves to me what an effect a true Home has upon a girl" (94–95). In this way, Barrett extends the commonplace judgment that a girl's home "makes" her a social success or failure to the fallen girl who admirably reflects her [h]ome: "Although Kate Barrett held foremost 'that Trinity which God intended, father, mother, and child,' she advanced a second option—'that beautiful Trinity which is so potent—Mother, Child, and Home.' "[34]

Anita Levy's comment about Victorian sociologists' reaction to transgressive female behavior—"to complement the good woman in the home, sociology imagined the bad woman in the street"—marks a useful transition from my discussion of "home values" to a consideration of penal institutions.[35] One response to "street girls," as we have seen with Barrett and the evangelical reformers, was to put them back in the Home; another response was to incarcerate them. In either case, the "bad" woman was a figure to control. In *Literature and Crime in Augustan England,* Ian Bell argues that the work of the eighteenth-century social reformers, though progressive in its attempts to change the means of punishment, can also be understood as confirmation of the state's *right* to control and to punish: "While it is still possible to see the reformers as instigating a decisive and transforming break with precedent, it is just as interesting to see them as maintaining and developing the state's right to punish, albeit presented as the right to impose punishments which have more utilitarian justification."[36] The American women's prison reform movement of the late nineteenth century, led by Josephine Shaw Lowell, participates in a similar kind of moral conflation of physical incarceration and moral regeneration, in each case highlighting domestic skills central to its success.[37] As Stanley Cohen notes in *Visions of Social Control: Crime, Punishment and Classification,* by the mid-nineteenth century, in contrast to eighteenth-century practice, institutions became places of "*first* resort, the preferred solution to problems of deviancy and dependency."[38] Adolescent chastity offenders—or girls who it was feared would fall—not only made up the greatest number of prisoners incarcerated in the reformed women's penitentiaries, they also received longer sentences than those who had committed theft or a violent crime.[39] As Freedman writes in *Their Sister's Keepers*: "The chastity offenders included young women sentenced for 'stubbornness' when their relatives could not control their behavior. Sixteen-year-old Eliza L., for example, committed for two years as a 'stubborn child,' had been 'weak and licentious rather than deliberately bad.' Another sixteen-year-old who had run away from home was sentenced at her grandmother's request. The length of these sentences reflected officials' belief that the young, promising cases deserved fuller treatment."[40] This theory of "preventative incarceration" was also a main tenet of the Crittenton Mission's ideology, which sought to contain girls who had made "one mistake" in becoming pregnant, in order to rescue them from prostitution: "The eyes of the Florence Crittenton workers were more and more turned toward the erring girl rather than the confirmed professional. It was logical, too, that in reaching out a rescuing hand the Mission could accomplish most by coming into the girl's life at that precise point where the old life was most threatened with disintegration through terror and despair— the months when she realized that her misstep must soon become evident to the world."[41] Fearful lest the "misstep" become a fall, the Crittenton worker was ready to catch the girl and set her aright on redemption's path. Through domestic labor, maternal feeling, and prayer, the girl could be saved.

The new penology of late nineteenth-century and Progressive Era female prisons emphasized rehabilitation over punishment. This ideology accompanied the rise of the New Woman in reform activism; women's jobs were increasingly paid professional positions rather than volunteer work. Examples of such professional women include Katharine Bement Davis, superintendent of the Bedford Hills, New York, reformatory, and Jessie Donaldson Hodder, superintendent of the Framingham, Massachusetts, reformatory. These two women were in the forefront of the struggle for anti-institutional female prisons.[42] In her discussion of Davis's Bedford Hills facility (established on the cottage system in 1901), Freedman describes the doctrine of practical lessons and shared education: "To make classes more palatable, the Bedford Hills staff adopted Progressive educational methods. All tasks, both in the classroom and outside it, were to be shared by inmates and teachers. The staff was expected to do as much menial work as their charges, and instructors tried to make subject matter relevant to the lives of the women. Daily institutional experiences became the subjects of the lessons."[43] This ideology was shared by the Crittenton rescue homes in their uniting of the "family system" with practical domestic training.

Upon admittance to a Florence Crittenton Home—and every (white) girl seeking asylum was admitted on a trial basis[44]—the girls were told that the rescue home belonged to them alone "and that all is required of any is that each one shall do her part in making it a real Home" (16). This statement privileges Beecher's ideology of "homemaking": participation in the primacy of domestic duties, the cult of cleanliness, the drive for self-improvement through the study of the Bible and "good books," and the romanticization of motherhood. If a girl did not have this knowledge, however, the rescue home would train her in it. In discussing the training that the girls received in the Home, Barrett packs her meaning once again, in a manner consistent with her ability "to get twenty-five hours out of the twenty-four." By calling the girls "ladies" and then enumerating the skills necessary to become a lady, she is able at once to raise the reputations of the fallen girls *and* firmly place the idea of the lady within domestic, middle-class ideals: "We believe that every lady should know how to cook, wash, and iron, if she does not know anything else, and as we expect our girls to be ladies in the highest and truest sense, they must all learn to do these things, and do them well" (26).[45] The nineteenth-century British system, by contrast, while mimicking as much as possible middle-class ideals about female behavior within the institution for penitent prostitutes, did not expect the girls to be transformed into ladies but rather into improved domestics.[46] Beecher also confronts the issue of "ladylike" behavior and domestic work by countering the argument that labor is degrading to women. Domestic labor, she writes, is for everyone (female): "The last method suggested for lessening the evils peculiar to American women, is, a decided effort to oppose the aristocratic feeling, that labor is degrading; and to bring about the impression that it is refined and lady-like to engage in domestic pursuits. . . . But as soon as ladies of refinement, as a general custom, patronise domestic pursuits, then these pursuits will be deemed lady-like" (39–40). Barrett's system for the rescue home also trains the girls to be gender- rather than class-identified. She describes enforced menial labor as a means to this identification, and as a condition of moral reform and repentance: "If a girl comes to us well dressed and with manicured nails and tells us that she has never been accustomed to do any sort of work in her life, we are sure to put this girl at the wash-tub, because we will never be able to do anything with her until she has learned to believe in the aristocracy of hard hands and the dignity of labor" (37).[47]

In order to establish a Home that will both appear and operate, for all intents and purposes, as a "home" for "ladies," Barrett prefers an extant structure rather than a new building, otherwise, "a great many institutional features are apt to creep in" (7). As Barrett's casual and cheerful claim "no home is complete without a baby" (9) would ostensibly have it seem, each Rescue Home's large and commodious nursery is present primarily to create the best structure of a home, rather than to accommodate the illegitimate children who unwittingly make their mother's presence in a rescue home necessary.[48]

In her introduction to *Some Practical Suggestions on the Conduct of a Rescue Home*, Barrett reinforces her idea that "bad girls" are no different from unfallen ones and deserve the same love, attention, and strict parental guidance that girls within families should receive: "The training and discipline which is good for our own girls is the best kind to use in a Rescue Home." Barrett made the transmission of this idea her life's work through writing newspaper articles and speeches and making appeals to town administrators all over the country. (This zeal bled into a second generation, as two of Barrett's children—a son and a daughter—were involved in the Crittenton Mission after their mother's death.) In a "homely" manner, as opposed to the dramatic gestures of the early nineteenth-century sermonist, Barrett persuades her audience (the mothers and fathers of the unfallen) of her charity's mission by emphasizing the daughterly role that (any) girl plays in society. One small example of this ideal of the universal daughter is demonstrated by the theory of Home decoration: "When we remember with what fastidious care we try to have our own daughter's room the most attractive in the house, and how we love to think of the purity of the furnishings as emblematic of the purity of her who occupies it, we will understand how necessary it is, when we are dealing with God's daughters, to use the same watchful care in the little detail of their lives" (13–14).

Another telling example of the conflation of daughters affected by the "institution that is not an institution" is that the matron is instructed to refrain from asking the girl seeking admittance to the Home her name, but rather to ask, "What name did you love best for your mother to call you when you were a little girl at home?" (19). The efficacy of using the baby name, or maternal nickname, is that the girl is reminded of her mother and her pure "home self." The recalling of these memories seeks to prompt the girl to better actions in the future and to aid in her redemption. At the same time, Barrett recognizes the limitations of girls—fallen or "upright"—when she comments, "We cannot hope to do more with a girl after she has fallen than it would have been possible to have done with that same girl before her trouble, but we ought to be able to do as much with her" (84). Assuming a "practical" stance in this sentiment, Barrett admits to the probability of deviations from the ideal feminine conduct in both the pure and the penitent.

Nineteenth-century reform ideology for juvenile delinquents, too, stressed the need to return the erring child to childhood, just as the fallen girl must be restored to the place of the daughter, in order to enable positive behavioral change. The object of juvenile reform expressed by the British reformer Mary Carpenter in *Juvenile Delinquents, Their Condition and Treatment* (1853), not surprisingly, closely resembles theories held by the Florence Crittenton Homes. In both cases, the inmate must "be gradually restored to the true position of childhood. He must be brought to a sense of dependence by reawakening in him new and healthy desires which he cannot himself satisfy, and by finding that there is a power far greater than his own to which he is indebted for the gratification of these desires."[49] Healthy children and domestic girls are raised in homes, therefore sexual girls must be placed in Homes to re-establish both their rights as "citizens" as well as their duties as subordinates.

Of course, no institution can totally succeed in its attempts to disguise itself, whatever its good intentions. Although Barrett's leadership in the Crittenton Mission's establishment of the extensive network of rescue homes (together with that of the Mission's founder, Charles Nelson Crittenton) takes its place alongside the efforts of other inspirational and effective female institutional reformers of late nineteenth- and early twentieth-century America—including Dorothea Dix, Katharine Bement Davis, Jessie Donaldson Hodder, Jane Addams, and Josephine Shaw Lowell—the fact that each rescue home operated as a self-sufficient house of correction should not be overlooked. Certainly, a rescue home is like a juvenile reformatory, is like a women's prison, is like a penitent prostitute's penitentiary, is like a lock hospital (for venereal-diseased prostitutes—also generally organized as a house of moral correction and as an industrial plant), is like a female seminary where domestic science is taught. Freedman's description of the requirements of the rescue homes thus sounds familiar: "The Florence Crittenton Homes, originally for rescuing prostitutes, searched inmates on entry, forbade profane or slang language and coarse jesting, required 'family worship' morning and evening, censored letters and watched visitors, and taught 'plain sewing and simple working,' table setting and orderly kitchen work. Bible readings required attendance, as did the 'general work of the Home.' "[50] The separate "franchises" in the Mission's "corporation" were responsible for earning money toward their upkeep; however, donations for the charity were eagerly sought from members of the community and from those successfully trained girls who left the Home and gained employment elsewhere. The suggested methods of self-sufficiency were laundry work or sewing, as was the case in the model furnished by the Magdalen Hospital and other "female" institutions. Such labor was understood to be valuable for females in general, and for those in need of moral training in particular: "Apart from its remunerative features, the laundry may also be used as a 'means of grace.' There is nothing that settles a restless, high-strung spirit, like weariness of the flesh" (Barrett, 28). The inmate of the rescue home was compelled to learn a new economy to replace the one she had "willingly" acquired at an early age: from the sale of the (sexual) body in exchange for money, pleasure, and love, to the sale of the (laboring) body in exchange for money, shelter, and (the reform ideology insists) self-respect and eternal reward.

After two years of training, the now-reclaimed Christian girl was expected to leave the Home with her child and take a position as a servant, thereby becoming independent of the Home (except insofar as she would like to visit or donate money toward its upkeep). The Homes, however, according to Barrett, were to be *relatively* forgiving of those girls who either failed while out on their own, or who never felt able to leave. Of a girl who desired the protection of the Home, Barrett wrote, "she is our child for life when once she has come under our care" (51).[51] In general, the Florence Crittenton Homes, as Barrett conceives of them in her pamphlet, were "humanized" institutions. The girls did not wear uniforms or a distinctive dress that set them apart from ("respectable") society at large; the only clothing requirement was that everyday wear must be washable cotton in order to facilitate the practical matters of hygiene and laundry work. Barrett is not free from ideological assumptions about female dress and class, however, when she equates the diseases of promiscuity with unwashable fabrics, and health with inexpensive materials: "There is nothing more depressing than a number of women, many of whose faces bear the marks of disease, dressed in woolen clothes that cannot be readily cleansed. . . . On the other hand, to see a girl dressed in a seven-cent gingham, neatly made, rustling in its spick and spanness, is exhilirating, like a breath of fresh air" (41).[52] In fact, it is the matron, assistant matron, and workers who wear uniforms in the Home: the matron dresses entirely in white, and the assistant matron and workers wear a blue gingham dress, white apron, and "dainty little cap" that is understood to be a "badge of authority" (43).[53]

Regularly scheduled entertainment for the girls was an important feature of Barrett's "humanistic" organization of the rescue home. One night a week was set aside as "play night," special snacks were served (apples, peanuts, or candy), and a social event was planned. When Barrett lists the different committees (some examples are the educational, nursery, and devotional committees) that made up the organization of each Home, she describes the entertainment committee as the most important (80).

And yet it is exactly "entertainment by committee" that reveals each Home's insistent institutional nature. The ideological makeup of the "institution that looks like a home" (as well as that of women's prisons and "domestically enhanced" female seminaries) recalls a kind of idealistic belief in the restorative powers of the loving nuclear family.[54] However, the institution must also operate as social apologist for the weaknesses of that preferred system. While the family rejected its bad girls, the institution took its place and created a "homelike" atmosphere in the place of the home. As Barrett writes, the "true meaning of dirt" is "matter out of place." The Florence Crittenton Mission swept turn-of-the-century "dirty" girls into its own place (its "Home") and renamed them as its own daughters: inheritors of a reformed feminine ideology that both accepted them as ladies and continued to keep them in place.

Afterword
"Still Harping on My Daughter"

Pamela's Sisters

It is with some anxiety that Polonius remarks Hamlet's seeming obsessive concern with Ophelia—"still harping on my daughter"—hoping to discover in his bitter comments the lovesickness that is causing the prince's madness. Hamlet has been reading a book before he begins his conversation with Polonius, and from that moment until the Players enter, his discourse centers on "daughters" and their degenerations. It is perhaps from this book that he is reminded of the ballad that tells the story of Jephthah—of a father who for a battle won has promised God to make an offering of the first animate thing he sees upon returning from war. This promise results, as these promises often do, in the sacrifice of the female:

> When *Jepha* did perceive and see
> his Daughter first and formostly,
> He rent his cloths and tore his haire,
> and shrieked out most piteously.
> For thou art she (quoth he)
> Hath brought me low, alas for woe,
> And troubled me so,
> that I cannot tell what to do to doe.[1]

153

The father's benefit—victory—has already been granted by God and Jephthah's nameless daughter then must function as the place holder in her father's relationship with God. She freely accepts her role as bartered object—as do the heroines of such folktales as "The Girl Without Hands" and "Beauty and the Beast." In *Hamlet,* however, Ophelia does not have any choice—any voice—in the matter of her sacrifice to Hamlet's bitterness and misogyny. Hamlet unfairly conflates the dutiful daughter with the rejected one—innocents both—and, in an act of reinscribing and assigning, renames Ophelia (by association with Polonius) Jephthah's daughter—the sacrifice to God's law, and the father's will, that will result in the daughter's (self)annihilation.

My turn to Shakespeare here should in no way imply a valorization of the male canon; I want instead to emphasize the way in which culture has historically suffered from a similarly Hamletian lovesickness for the (place of the) girl. Hamlet's fascination with and ultimate denial of the daughter (the female) culminates in the "nunnery" speech in which Ophelia is understood as entirely determined by a hypothesized sexual disposition—as either a nun or bawd: "If thou dost marry, I'll give thee this plague for thy dowry: be thou as chaste as ice, as pure as snow, thou shalt not escape calumny. Get thee to a nunnery, farewell."[2] Here Hamlet effectively eradicates Ophelia's virtue, which is otherwise unquestionable, and her only "reward" becomes a grand, tragic and finally self-destructive loss of self.

During the writing of this book I have returned to *Pamela* again and again, finding in her story of "virtue rewarded" the elements of girls' culture I wanted to explore: among them, charity as an aestheticized gesture, narrative coherence, courtship and commerce, religious sensibility, theatrical play, and domestic duty. One hundred and seventy years after *Pamela,* Jean Webster's novel for girls, *Daddy-Long-Legs* (1912), relates in epistolary form another story of one teenager's "rise in the world." These novels can serve as bookends to my own fascination with girlhood. *Daddy-Long-Legs* contains in truncated form many of the elements of *Pamela* and of the narrative and historical treatments of girlhood discussed above. Jerusha Abbott (known as Judy) is a foundling who has lived at the John Grier Home for all her eighteen years of life. An intelligent and spunky girl, she has been allowed to stay on at the home and attend the village school in return for her labor as domestic help in the institution. The book opens on a "Blue Wednesday": "a day to be awaited with dread, endured with courage and forgotten with haste. Every floor must be spotless, every chair dustless, and every bed without a wrinkle. Ninety-seven squirming little orphans must be scrubbed and combed and buttoned into freshly starched ginghams; and all ninety-seven reminded of their manners, and told to say, 'Yes, sir,' 'No, sir,' whenever a Trustee spoke."[3] Jerusha is largely responsible for these preparations, and the Blue Wednesdays seem to stretch on in front of her with no end. Her fortunes change dramatically, however, as an eccentric trustee decides to send her to college to be educated for a future career as a writer (he had enjoyed a composition she had written entitled "Blue Wednesday"). His only stipulations are that he remain anonymous, and that she write him letters every month.

Jerusha Abbott is one example of a girl heroine who "knows the score" of female sociability—as Fanny Price does, acknowledging its appropriateness, as Jo March also does—and chafes at the restrictions it brings. Once she is informed of her good luck by the stiff matron who is as well-versed in conduct discourse as any moralist, she is able to step back and clearly articulate her position with panache: " 'I trust that you are properly grateful for this very rare good fortune that has befallen you? Not many girls in your position ever have such an opportunity to rise in the world. You must always remember—' 'I— yes, ma'am, thank you. I think, if that's all, I must go and sew a patch on Freddie Perkins's trousers' " (8). Her "peroration in midair," the matron can only stare at the place where Jerusha had been. Jerusha later informs her benefactor in her first letter that reveals her scorn of such advice: "Mrs. Lippett told me how to behave all the rest of my life, and especially how to behave toward the kind gentleman who is doing so much for me. I must take care to be Very Respectful" (10). The book then chronicles their seemingly one-sided relationship as Jerusha writes lively illustrated letters about college life to the mysterious and unknown philanthropist she calls "Daddy-Long-Legs."

The parallels with *Pamela*'s formal structure are greater than perhaps has been made obvious here: Jerusha's benefactor is an extremely wealthy older man (though not the elderly bald-headed creature she imagines him to be) who holds her future completely in his hands. He is able, through his secretary (a benign Mrs. Jewkes), to send presents, deny requests, and even "imprison" Jerusha in his country "estate" (a farm he owns where he sends Judy for the summers, regardless of her wishes). The "daddy" of her destiny, "Master Jervie," as he is called—like Pamela's master, B—falls in love with the girl he has "raised," and she with him. Pygmalion stories such as these, created from the "frisson" of class and gender conflict, continue to interest us with their fairy tale marriages and happy endings.

Daddy-Long-Legs also reminds us of the institutions for "dirty girls," and the "home imperative" discussed in this book generally and in chapters 1 and 6 in particular.[4] While an inmate of the John Grier Home, Judy often imagines a place called "home," but ultimately cannot conjure a respectable image, never having lived in either its physical or emotional space: "She pictured herself in a fur coat and a velvet hat trimmed with feathers leaning back in the seat and nonchalantly murmuring 'Home' to the driver. But on the doorsill of her home the picture grew blurred" (2). *Daddy-Long-Legs* is really about losing the institution and earning a family, a *meaningful* name (her "own" name has been chosen by the matron of the home from the phone book and a tombstone), and a place in the world. Pamela must maintain her good name; Evelina must reclaim hers; the Evangelicals must proclaim theirs; and the Magdalens must create names anew. It is this production of names—sometimes imposed from without, sometimes prompted from "within"—that can be said to crystallize the cultural work involved in the construction of girls' lives and girlhood.

When the girl is "successfully" integrated into the socially sanctioned place already prepared for her—"no place like home"—the story ends happily. Renaming, however, can also act as a prohibition, leading to madness or death thus disallowing the "happy ending" in its more explicit and relentlessly tragic rejection of the girl. If Pamela stands as the model of the "comic" girl heroine, then Ophelia has come to model the tragic.

Although I, too, may be guilty of the charge of "harping" on daughters and their "sins" and sighs, it is solely with delight that I have studied female adolescence in literature and its historical context. Informed by and in conversation with the innovative scholarship on gender and history, women's writing, female subjectivity, and sexuality, this book will, I hope, convince readers of the literary and historical significance of a different "margin"—that of the "underaged"—and along with studies by Gorham, Pickering, MacLeod, Nelson, and Reynolds, among others, help to bring the cultural and literary contexts of youth to light. Beverly Lyon Clark makes the point that feminist theory and scholarship has overlooked children and children's literature in her article "Fairy Godmothers or Wicked Stepmothers? The Uneasy Relationship of Feminist Theory and Children's Criticism": "Yet—as if children are still so thoroughly beyond the pale—feminists who theorize marginality have paid virtually no attention to the position of children. Such feminist and cultural critics often address race, gender, and class. But not age, not children."[5] We have seen a much-needed proliferation of books and articles treating postcolonialism and gay and lesbian studies. I would hope that we will soon be reading and talking about youth studies within the model set up by cultural studies wherein we examine literary, cultural, and ideological practices of childhood and adolescence.

Many of us were girls, others have daughters or sisters. In this era of discovering that in adolescence girls are in danger of "losing their voices" and "hitting the wall," it is important to reflect upon the girl of the past, on Pamela and her sisters, on the virtue of their disciplines and the discipline of their virtues.[6] I have introduced or reintroduced some notable girls or girl characters from the past: Pamela, Alice, and Jo, of course, but also Jenny Peace, Lucilla Stanley, Betty Brown, Gypsy Breynton, Jerusha Abbott, and the "erring girl," to name a few. I have described some of the institutional, literary, instructive, legal, and domestic forces that have helped to create girls' culture in England and America, from the late seventeenth to early twentieth centuries. Although my work here has not been primarily concerned with the "lived culture" of everyday life for eighteenth- and nineteenth-century girls, the book takes as its subject the social construction of girlhood that produces the effect of the "lived experience." The institutions and practices—textual and actual—that I discuss are best understood not only as products of cultures but also as its producers. Lovesick ourselves, we can read the discourses of girlhood—those stories about earlier "becoming" girls and their struggles and silence, their beauties and virtues, their foibles and failures, even their victimization and valor—everywhere inscribed in culture. We cling to the "girlish" and emulate it, celebrate it, even as we promote "maturity" and desire "mastery." There is a world of girls—past, present, and future—to inhabit, enjoy, interpret, and yet explore.

Notes

Introduction

1. Barrie, *Peter Pan,* 13.

2. Carroll, *Complete Works,* 879.

3. Auerbach, *Romantic Imprisonment,* 155.

4. Carroll, *Annotated Alice,* 155.

5. In the early 1980s, two useful books by social historians on Victorian and Edwardian English girlhood were published: Deborah Gorham, *The Victorian Girl and the Feminine Ideal* (1982), and Carol Dyhouse, *Girls Growing Up in Late Victorian and Edwardian England* (1981). Their detailed work on images of girlhood, educational opportunities, biographies of girls, family life, etc., has informed my understanding of girls' culture. Although I treat the same general subject, this study offers in-depth readings of literary and cultural moments of girlhood in the eighteenth and nineteenth centuries in addition to offering brief historical contexts. For an illuminating discussion of boys' literature and the figure of the boy, see Claudia Nelson, *Boys Will Be Girls.*

6. Beverly Lyon Clark addresses directly the invisibility of children's literature in scholarship and offers "thirteen ways of thumbing your nose at children's literature," including "pretend the works you are addressing are not children's literature—or, better yet, redeem them from their pitiable status as children's literature" and "construct anthologies that pretend full general coverage yet omit children's literature" (Clark, "Thirteen Ways," 240, 242). I find Clark's brief essay to be both fascinating and funny, yet ultimately uncomfortable for scholars (working in children's literature and generally) precisely for the accuracy of her observations.

7. Anna Williams, in "Verses to Mr Richardson on his History of Sir Charles Grandison" in the January 1754 issue of the *Gentleman's Magazine,* after scorning the "loose wits of a degen'rate age," praises *Pamela* thus: "Thou, zealous friend of long insulted truth, / Didst first appear the guardian of our youth; / 'Twas thine, a juster lesson to impart, / To move the

passions, and to mend the heart" (Williams, "Verses to Mr. Richardson," 40). Such examples concerning the regulation of girls' reading are myriad in eighteenth- and nineteenth-century conduct literature and educational treatises. Another example of typical rhetoric against "delusionary" light reading occurs in Maria Edgeworth's *Practical Education* (1798): "Sentimental stories, and books of mere entertainment . . . should be sparingly used, especially in the education of girls. This species of reading cultivates what is called the heart prematurely, lowers the tone of mind, and induces indifferences for those common pleasures and occupations which, however trivial in themselves, constitute by far the greatest portion of our daily happiness" (quoted in Hill, *Eighteenth-Century Women*, 60–61).

Judith Rowbotham, in *Good Girls Make Good Wives: Guidance for Girls in Victorian Fiction*, discusses the ways in which didactic fiction for girls filled the need for "productive recreation" that moralists and educators had described (Rowbotham, *Good Girls*, 17–18). The conduct novel, as a hybrid genre, certainly functioned in this way. Kate Flint's *Woman Reader, 1837–1914* is a wonderfully detailed and comprehensive analysis of gender and reading. See also Kimberley Reynolds for a discussion of boys' and girls' reading in the late Victorian and Edwardian periods (Reynolds, *Girls Only?*, 92–110).

8. *Story of a Great Philanthropy*, n.p.

9. Hunter, "Readers and the Beginnings of the English Novel," 266.

10. Alcott, *Little Women*, 8. All further references to this edition are made in the body of the text.

Chapter 1
The Pleasure of the Act

1. Head, *The Miss Display'd*, 4–5. The verse under the frontispiece illustration reads "Love not Lewd Women, for yo'ule find em worse / Than all that's Bad, attended with a Curse."

2. Head, *The Miss Display'd*, 90.

3. Cornelia's alluring features are carefully described as both natural and metaphoric: "That through the natural whiteness and smoothness of her Front, Neck, and plump Breasts, a man might with wonderful delight perceive the azure of her Veins, circling about in their several Meanders; the splendor of her eyes made her Beholders dim-sighted, their radiant influence being so strong and penetrating" (Head, *The Miss Display'd*, 90).

4. This is not to assert that there are no biographies or autobiographies of the male penitent (the earliest example would perhaps be the epistles of Paul). My theory of the narrative of pleasure is concerned with the act of writing about the female body/text that is a way to describe, know, and control it. The pleasure holds sway in terms of both the transgressive body and the "normal"—adolescent girl—body.

5. In a similar pairing of seemingly disparate female figures, Nina Auerbach links the old maid with the fallen woman in *Woman and the Demon*, 150–184. See Auerbach for a densely packed discussion of the fallen woman described in nineteenth-century literature, art, and (authors') lives. See also Sally Mitchell, *The Fallen Angel: Chastity, Class and Women's Reading, 1835–1880*.

6. The anonymous writer of *Ape-Gentle-Woman, or the Character of an Exchange Wench* objectifies the prostitute as "a Hussing piece of puff past" and "one commodity at Several Rates" (*Ape-Gentle-Woman*, 1, 2).

7. Anderson, *Tainted Souls,* 9.

8. I am generally indebted to Michel Foucault's *Discipline and Punish: The Birth of the Prison* for raising some of the issues I am concerned with in this chapter: the "art" of punishment and its representation (104), the "rhythms" of the penal institution (149), the general effects of surveillance. An important distinction between our concerns, however, is my focus on gender and the institution. Foucault, for example, in his fascinating discussion of examination (184–194) fails to discuss the significantly unbalanced power relationship created when female inmates are examined internally, typically by male doctors.

In *The Evolution of Women's Asylums Since 1500,* Sherrill Cohen also notes that Foucault "and his fellow scholars writing on institutions, appear unaware of the existence of an extensive, finely graded network of institutions to correct, help, and supervise females in sixteenth-century Europe" (5–6).

9. Eliza White's "Gertrude; or, Thoughtlessness and Inattention Corrected" (1823) is one example of a nineteenth-century text for young girls that instructs both the character and the reader in the duty and joy of charity. The generally good but flawed heroine, nine-year-old Gertrude Woodford, is very willing to assist her mother and sisters in providing money and clothes for their neighborhood's poor families (she gives away her allowance), but she is thoughtless and careless in sewing little Mary Page's school frock. Ultimately Gertrude fails to complete the dress in time for Mary to go to school. Mrs. Woodford sternly admonishes Gertrude for her selfishness: "Instead of steadily devoting the requisite time to the service of this poor little girl, which you offered to do, and which you perfectly had it in your power to do, you have neglected her for your own diversion" (White, "Gertrude," 142–143). Gertrude is heartily ashamed at her (in)action, accepts her responsibility to the needy, and becomes a perfectly charitable girl.

10. The *Oxford English Dictionary* cites the first usage of this meaning of "charity" in 1154.

11. Quoted in Prochaska, *Women and Philanthropy,* 8. *The Wives of England; their relative duties, domestic influence, and social obligations* (1843) enlists female duty and feminine "nature" in charity's cause: "Men, engaged in the active affairs of life, have neither time nor opportunity for those innumerable little acts of consideration which come within the sphere of female duty, nor are they by nature so fitted as woman for entering into the peculiarities of personal feeling, so as to enable them to sympathize with the suffering of the distressed" (quoted in Prochaska, *Women and Philanthropy,* 7).

12. An obvious psycho/sexual correlation can be made here between this external/internal understanding of gendered charity and physical characteristics: the "significantly" signifying visible male genitalia that delivers both pleasure and product, and the hidden female sex organ that simply delivers.

13. Horne, *Sermon,* 32. All further references to this edition are made in the text.

14. Historian Judith Walkowitz's *Prostitution and Victorian Society* carefully dismantles some of the popular myths about nineteenth-century prostitution—that the prostitute is

either a naive country girl or a seduced gentlewoman—popular because these images of female sexuality are less dangerous than those of an uncontrolled and "unreasonable" female sexuality. In her study she found that the majority of prostitutes were born of lower-class families, and that the average age of initiation into prostitution was approximately sixteen years: "Most [prostitutes in the second half of the nineteenth century] were single, and more often than not their previous occupation had been as casual maids of all work. They were local girls, indigenous to the region. They overwhelmingly lived outside the family—indeed, they would most likely have been half or full orphan. Before going onto the streets, they had already had sexual relations of a noncommercial sort with a man of their social class" (Walkowitz, *Prostitution and Victorian Society,* 19). Henry Mayhew reports that most fallen women came from "the ranks of domestic service" (Mayhew, *London Labour and the London Poor* 4: xxvi).

15. As Walkowitz suggests, "investigators of prostitution were unable to construct a cultural model that would make a poor woman's move into prostitution comprehensible within the terms of her social and cultural world. For these middle-class writers, working-class culture represented a total negation of culture" (Walkowitz, *Prostitution and Victorian Society,* 38). I will discuss in greater detail in chapter 6 the means by which American middle-class reformers of the Progressive Era responded to this need to *create* a culture for prostitutes by availing themselves of the model of domesticity and labor in establishing rescue homes. The rescue home functions as an artificial environment that explicitly emphasizes the servile nature of female duty to the home by bringing the girls "home" and making them work in the service of the home.

16. Van Sant, *Eighteenth-Century Sensibility,* 27. Carroll's poem "Only a Woman's Hair" (1862) considers this biblical scene in his unusual (for Carroll) paean to a lock of hair: "I see the feast—the purple and the gold; / The gathering crowd of Pharisees, / Whose scornful eyes are centred to behold Yon woman on her knees. / The stifled sob rings strangely on mine ears, / Wrung from the depth of sin's despair: / And still she bathes the sacred feet with tears, / And wipes them with her hair / He scorned not then the simple loving deed / Of her, the lowest and the last; / Then scorn not thou, but use with earnest heed / This relic of the past. / The eyes that loved it once no longer wake: / So lay it by with reverent care— / Touching it tenderly for sorrow's sake— / It is a woman's hair" (Carroll, *Complete Works,* 968–969).

17. William Dodd, in a defense of the Magdalen Hospital, attempts to soften the opposition to the institution by defending the inmates and shifting the blame for their sins elsewhere: "The objection [to the hospital] rose from a supposition that those who became prostitutes were betrayed to such a course by love of pleasure, and retained in it by a love of idleness, but this charity has furnished incontrovertible proof, that the supposition itself is erroneous: The greater part of those who have fled to the shelter it affords [have] been seduced by the most artful and insidious contrivances of wretches who preside over marts of prostitution" (Dodd, "Some Account of the Magdalen Hospital," 279–280). The 1816 report of the Guardian Society also emphasizes the number of "stolen girls" housed in their temporary asylum: "Eighteen of the twenty four females now in the Asylum, appear *not to have gone, by their own will,* to the haunts of prolificacy; but to have been actually represen-

tatives, made by persons of their own sex; into houses of ill fame; and laid under personal restraint, till the base purposes for which they were decoyed were effected" (*Report,* 16).

18. Or when reminded that the appeal is made on behalf of white, Christian women who from the "outside" resemble their mothers, sisters, daughters. As partial justification for his catalogue of prostitution in *London Labour and the London Poor,* Mayhew reveals the racist and xenophobic attitudes that can inform reform movements: "Who are those whose souls, in countless numbers, are now glutting the chambers of hell? Not swarthy Indians nor sable Africans, whose deeds of violence and superstition have spread horror and astonishment among civilized nations, but delicately-nurtured Saxon women, who in infancy were lovingly fondled in the arms of Christian mothers, and received 'into the ark of Christ's Church' in baptism" (Mayhew, *London Labour and the London Poor* 4:xxxviii).

19. Hogarth's *Harlot's Progress* (1732) depicts the prostitute's career from naive country girl tricked by a crafty madam, to diseased woman, to corpse. Charles Booth's *Life and Labour of the People in London* (1889) described how girls generally fell into sin: "A girl's first slip may have been due to passion (sometimes), or to sexual softness (more often), or to wantonness (more often still); with man ordinarily though not always as seducer, and with other members of the community—parents, employers, and companions—sharing the responsibility in a hundred ways" (Booth, *Life and Labour,* 129).

20. *Remedies,* 9.

21. Marjorie Malvern dates the first narrative of Mary Magdalen's repentance to the thirteenth century in *Legenda Aurea* by Jacobus a Voragine (translated in 1850) (Malvern, *Venus in Sackcloth,* 89). Malvern also discusses the controversy over Mary Magdalen's biblical identity, as she has been named Luke's anonymous prostitute, Lazarus and Martha's sister, as well as the Bride in the "Song of Songs." Jane Schaberg's article "How Mary Magdalene Became a Whore" takes up the issue of Mary Magdalen's identity as well. Using biblical exegesis she "disproves" that Mary Magdalen was a prostitute at all. Schaberg separates the identities of three different gospel women and asserts that Roman Catholic, Protestant, and Eastern Orthodox doctrine concur that "the Magdalene can no longer be identified as a sinner" (Schaberg, "Mary Magdalene," 51). I am grateful to E. Cleve Want for this reference.

22. The former of these success stories is an example of the reciprocity between Charity/charity and money; that is, the ideology of (c)harity includes the ideal of gain through financial loss. This gain is not only the psychic value of an increased sense of self-worth and self-satisfaction—Edward Pelling, in *A Practical Discourse Upon Charity* (1693) calls Charity a "Virtue that stirs the Bowels" (Pelling, *Practical Discourse,* 7)—but also a "profitable loss" in that it is at the hands of the needy that the charitable person's "Treasure in Heaven" is laid by (Pelling, *Practical Discourse,* 159–60). Thomas Tenison offers a somewhat refined understanding of the benefits of giving in *A Sermon Concerning Discretion in Giving Alms* (1681): "The prudence of Charity consisteth in that Discretion which provideth, preserveth, increaseth wealth, that we may have ability to do good, and to continue in doing of it, and in bearing such useful fruit until we die" (Tenison, *Discretion in Giving Alms,* 14–15). In "The Surest and Safest Way of Thriving, or, the Conviction of that Grand Mistake in many, *that what is given to the Poor, is a loss, to their Estate;* which is directly contrary, as to the experiences

of the Charitable, so to the testimony of *Gods Spirit* in divers places of Scripture," another seventeenth-century commentator on charity, however, asserts that charity provides *both* psychic satisfaction *and* material gains: "But this I say, *that as penuriousness towards the Poor* is the readiest way to poverty; so Christian Charity, rightly performed, is the surest way to plenty and abundance; it being usually rewarded with *Temporal* blessings here, as well as with Eternal hereafter" (Gouge, "Surest and Safest," 10).

Donna T. Andrew describes the practical use of the ideology of "profitable loss" by the London charities: "Charities that did best financially used what might be described as the multimotive or shotgun approach toward convincing citizens to subscribe. Donation to their charity, each proclaimed, would not only be pleasant to the donor, but would also be profitable to him in his capacity as an economic agent, a citizen and a soul, both here and hereafter" (Andrew, *Philanthropy and Police*, 8). See Andrew's first chapter, " 'All Mankind's Concern': Religion, Commerce, and Charity, 1680–1740," for an excellent discussion of early eighteenth-century motivations for charitable donations.

23. Michie, *The Flesh Made Word*, 59.

24. Fictional and biographical stories of penitent prostitutes, as I have mentioned above, were popular in the eighteenth century. Some examples include *The Histories of some of the Penitents in the Magdalen House* (1760), *The Life and Adventures of a Reformed Magdalen* (1763), and Hugh Kelly's *Memoires of a Magdalen: or The History of Louisa Mildmay* (1767) (quoted in Blondel, "Minor Eighteenth-Century Novel," 36).

25. In his multivolume work on the "changing pattern of English social aspirations," *Philanthropy in England, 1480–1660* and *Charities of London, 1480–1660*, W. K. Jordan somewhat petulantly remarks the difficulties of tracing the philanthropic and charitable actions of women: "Women have complicated as they have graced the course of history" (Jordan, *Philanthropy*, 32). These "complications" arise not only as a result of women's gifts represented as the husband's, but also because women's gifts were unquantifiable—often goods and services rather than money. Jordan does manage, however, to amass statistical information on the monetary amount of charitable contributions made by women (separated by county and class), as well as the kinds of charities they supported. For example—in Jordan's inimitable "generosity"—"The women of our era, some of whom rank among the really great and farsighted donors, gave in a pattern which suggests not only independence of judgment, but a maturity of understanding which we find very impressive indeed. Thus they devoted upwards of 44 per cent of all their charitable funds [which ranged between nine and thirteen per cent of all contributions] to the various forms of poor relief, concentrating this considerable sum principally on endowments to secure household aid in their own parishes" (Jordan, *Philanthropy*, 354–355). See also Jordan, *Charities of London*, 28–31.

26. "Charity," 196. The author goes on to assert, in fact, that it is *uncharitable* to deny to women the satisfaction delivered by participating in the charitable enterprise: "To deny this prerogative to any human creature is to bring discord into the moral government of the universe. To assent, is indirectly to admit the injustice of those obstacles which render ineligible to women the varied paths of mental progress and employment, indispensable to the realisation of her human rights to life, liberty, and happiness—rights which the spirit of charity itself cannot but advocate and commend" (196).

27. See the introduction to Peter Mandler, ed., *The Uses of Charity: The Poor on Relief in the Nineteenth-Century Metropolis* for a discussion of charitable giving as part of the domestic role of women.

28. Jordan, *Philanthropy*, 232.

29. For a thorough look at female refuges in nineteenth-century Scotland see Linda Mahood, *The Magdalenes: Prostitution in the Nineteenth Century*. Ann Jessie Van Sant's discussion of the Magdalen House and the philanthropic enterprise dovetails with my own (see chapter 2 of *Eighteenth-Century Sensibility and the Novel*, 16–44). See also Cohen, *Evolution of Women's Asylums*, which traces the history of women's institutions from their earliest examples, in early modern Europe in particular.

30. The London Female Penitentiary Society altered its name to the London Female Guardian Society in 1891 in recognition of the change in the popular meaning of "penitentiary" from house of refuge to house of correction.

31. Van Sant, *Eighteenth-Century Sensibility*, 21. The Poor Law (1601) held that the state was responsible for providing relief to the poor, sick, and aged when their families were unable to do so; the able-bodied poor were required to work.

32. The charity was also very successful, at first, in attracting donations. As Andrew comments, "Perhaps the charity's enormous success in collecting more than £5,000 in subscriptions and donations during its first eight months can be explained by the hypothesis that the care of the fallen and lascivious women engaged the public imagination" (Andrew, *Philanthropy and Police*, 131). We know that Samuel Richardson's imagination was sparked by this concern. He was a generous supporter of the Magdalen Hospital and even had his "good man," Sir Charles Grandison, propose a similar scheme (Richardson, *Grandison* 4:356, 1n). However, within the generally falling number of donations, as the years passed, donations by women slipped from seventeen percent in 1759 to only eleven percent by 1768 (Andrew, *Philanthropy and Police*, 88). Andrew theorizes that the charity survived this narrowing of its revenues by limiting the number of inmates it accepted and increasing the number of girls it sent back into society: "It may be supposed that the administrators of the charity, feeling the financial pinch and perhaps suspecting that some of the women were freeloading, decided to relax their rules and standards, investigate potential jobs less closely, and let girls back into the world more easily" (Andrew, *Philanthropy and Police*, 160).

Cohen notes that the Magdalen House was in operation into the second half of the twentieth century (Cohen, *Evolution of Women's Asylums*, 133). A recent Magdalen institution is the Mary Magdalen Project, established in Los Angeles, California, in 1980 (Cohen, *Evolution of Women's Asylums*, 135).

33. The institution's methods and theories of domestic training as an exercise in moral training have an interesting history. Andrew notes that "[Jonas] Hanway was especially desirous of teaching [the inmates] to make Turkey carpets, and thus, in the best mercantile fashion, both finding employment for the needy and keeping bullion at home" (Andrew, *Philanthropy and Police*, 126). John Fielding's 1758 plan for "preserving those deserted Girls in this Town, who become Prostitutes from Necessity" proposes a public laundry as the best means for the girls to "obtain an honest Livelihood by severe Industry" (Fielding, "Plan for preserving," 49). By the early nineteenth century, the Magdalen charity had abandoned

vocational training, and turned to Fielding's plan: "The governors employed the women as laundry maids, and consequently saw the profits of the institution rise at the turn of the century" (Andrew, *Philanthropy and Police,* 191).

34. The form of the petition used by the Magdalen House to begin the process of admission to the charity was as follows: "To the Committee of the Magdalen Hospital / The Humble Petition of _____ aged _____ years, of the Parish of _____ in the County of _____. / Sheweth / that your Petitioner hath been guilty of such misconduct, as renders her a proper object of the protection of this Charity. / Your Petitioner is truly sensible of her offence, and humbly prays that she may be admitted into this House, solemnly promising to behave herself decently and orderly, and to conform to all the rules of the Institution. / And your Petitioner, as in duty bound, shall ever pray." Stanley Nash gives a good summary of the daily life of the Magdalen inmates in "Prostitution and Charity: The Magdalen Hospital."

35. See Mahood for a brief discussion of the "politics" of the speculum (Mahood, *The Magdalenes,* 126–130). She also quotes from Dr. A. G. Miller's article in the *Edinburgh Medical Journal* (1882) where Miller employs a horrifying metaphor to describe the work of the doctor "with speculum in hand": "The medical man must be conjoined with the policeman in this dirty and degrading work . . . he must go from brothel to brothel, and from door to door, examining patient by patient systematically . . . like a railway porter, with a hammer in hand, examining axle by axle in a newly arrived train, to see whether any may be heated or no" (Mahood, *The Magdalenes,* 67).

36. "By-Laws," 40.

37. If a girl or young woman "misbehaved" after her admission, she was punished— often severely: "Between 1833 and 1835 discipline in the Edinburgh asylum was so bad that the directors resorted to shaving inmates' heads in order to suppress the desire to get out. Head shaving was also practiced in the London Magdalene Hospital and the Dublin Lock Hospital, but was less common in Glasgow" (Mahood, *The Magdalenes,* 80). Head shaving was an effective means of discipline as the inmates were ashamed to go outside of the institution thus marked and "uglified." Milder punishments included "confinement in a room for six hours for the first offense" or "twelve hours in a room for the third" (Nash, "Prostitution and Charity," 622).

38. William Acton's account of the organization of the Government Lock Hospital (October 1868) describes a similar isolation of the inmates of the institution in order to "protect" those both inside and outside the structure: "So admirable are the arrangements at this institution, that one thing only came under my notice that could possibly operate as a drawback to the health and comfort of the inmates. The view from the windows, which are kept constantly closed, is interrupted by means of blinds and whitened glass, and a certain amount of light and air thereby excluded. This is to be regretted, but seems *absolutely necessary,* as, in consequence of the close proximity of the hospital to a much frequented road, great difficulty was experienced previously to the adoption of this course, in keeping the inmates from presenting themselves at the windows, and holding conversations with soldiers and others outside the building . . ." (Acton, *Prostitution,* 95). The emphasis is mine, but the suggestive ellipses are Acton's.

39. An obvious sympathy exists between this surveillance and Bentham's panopticon, with this interesting difference: rather than an inviolate enclosure (as is the case with the panopticon model prison where it is critical that the inmates be seen at all times while they are unable to see their watchers), the Magdalen Chapel partially *reveals* the penitents—not only by (partial) view, but by the sound of their voices, their *stories*. The penitents can see outside their enclosure, but only to look upon those worthy of emulation: those (charitable) persons to whom they owe their "salvation."

40. Dodd, *Advice,* 323.

41. Van Sant, *Eighteenth-Century Sensibility,* 36.

42. Van Sant, *Eighteenth-Century Sensibility,* 33.

43. Except insofar as the stories are removed from the bodies and used for "commercial" purposes. John Fielding's "Plan for preserving those deserted girls in this Town, who become Prostitutes from Necessity" (1758) reprints the texts of the penitents' letters to parents asking them for forgiveness, to the institution thanking it for assistance, to old companions pleading with them for their repentance, as a marketing strategy promoting his plan for a self-sufficient public laundry staffed by former prostitutes.

A. E. Chesterton's *In Darkest London* (1926) comments upon the partial realization of Fielding's dream of the public laundry (within lock hospitals for venereally diseased patients), with all the liberal self-satisfaction for which Fielding could have hoped: "Laundry work helped to underwrite the cost of the women's confinement, but it also served a more symbolic function. Through laundry work, women could do penance for their past sins and purge themselves of their moral contagion: 'clear starching, it would seem, cleanses all sin, and an expert ironer can cheerfully put her record behind her' " (quoted in Walkowitz, *Prostitution and Victorian Society,* 221).

44. William Blair's 1809 response to a Mr. Hale who published a pamphlet against the London Female Penitentiary refutes Hale's claim that once the prostitutes are "sheltered," they will be encouraged to disregard social and moral laws: "The fear of punishment and public exposure being taken away [with the institution of the Penitentiary], he tells us the passions of youth will be unbridled, and they will soon reap the fruits of their unrestrained depravity" (Blair, *Prostitutes Reclaimed,* 38). In this public rebuke of Hale's conservative opinion, Blair tellingly describes the life of the reclaimed prostitute within the institution: "Does he [Mr. Hale] indeed think that the 'tempting prize' held out to all applicants at the Penitentiary, of daily labour, severe discipline, plain dress, homely diet, religious exercises, and total exclusion from gay company, in an enclosed house, resembles the prizes contained in the lottery sanctioned by government; and may probably ruin thousands by seducing them from comfortable abodes in private families?" (Blair, *Prostitutes Reclaimed,* 35).

The debate over the utility of the Magdalen penitentiaries was waged well into the nineteenth century. The *Quarterly Review* positively assessed the ideals of the charitable work described in *A Short Account of the London Magdalene Hospital* (1848), but found the organization and some of its practices wanting. The reviewer also bitterly denounced the legal status of prostitution which barred the law's enforceable right to "rehabilitate" the offender: "[The way of return] is closed for ever to the erring girl. She cannot claim the merciful correction of the law; there are none to catch her and drag her by legal force from her haunts;

there is no penitential prison for her; her sin not being subject to legal punishment, she is denied the means of reformation which, for other offenders, are now mixed with punishment" (*Quarterly Review* 83 [1848], 360).

45. Mayhew, *London Labour and the London Poor*, 4:36.

46. Fielding, "A Plan for preserving," 10. Van Sant describes the means of separation as a "lattice" that would reveal the penitents rather than hide them (Van Sant, *Eighteenth-Century Sensibility*, 32). In order to make her argument that "sympathetic visibility" is at work in the relationship between the penitents and the chapel patrons, the magdalens must be seen. Yet she understands this "visibility" to also occur in the "mind's eye" (Van Sant, *Eighteenth-Century Sensibility*, 33).

47. Dodd, *Advice*, 241–242.

48. *Quarterly Review* 83 (1848), 371.

49. Bender, *Imagining the Penitentiary*, 202.

50. Van Sant, *Eighteenth-Century Sensibility*, 37.

51. Attending religious services at the chapel was a charitable action. Although the use of tickets to admit persons to the service had been discontinued, it was expected that all persons attending the chapel would have contributed to the charity prior to admission ("By-Laws," 32). The by-laws also dictated the psalms and hymns to be sung at the services. The following is an excerpt of one sanctioned hymn (number 18): "O God of mercy! Hear my pray'r, / Thy weak, thy sinful creature save; / Thy voice can raise me from despair, / Raise me triumphant from the grave! / In Vanity's bewild'ring maze, / How long my erring feet have stray'd! / Far from Religion's peaceful ways, / And far from Virtue's guardian aid!" (quoted in Dodd, *Advice to Magdalens*, 305). Nash notes that the "Magdalen made a big show of [religious services] in its early years, and attending Sunday Chapel at the Magdalen hospital became a fashionable and popular thing to do (Nash, *Prostitution and Charity*, 621-622).

52. The "unfortunate man" who founded the Magdalen hospital, the court chaplain Dr. William Dodd, was eventually hanged for forgery (Evans, *Harlots and Whores,* 92). [Green], *Mental Improvement*, 59–61.

53. Chapone, *Improvement of the Mind*, 87.

54. Mayhew recites a familiar and powerful myth when he warns of the potential danger of undomesticated, sexual women: "Woman, waylaid, tempted, deceived, becomes in turn the terrible avenger of her sex. Armed with a power which is all but irresistible, and stript of that which can alone restrain and purify her influence, she steps upon the arena of life qualified to act her part in the reorganization of society" (Mayhew, *London Labour and the London Poor*, 4:xxxix).

55. In the latter part of the nineteenth century this division between male and female roles in the institutions of charity began to break down as greater numbers of women became involved in the administration of charity and social work, and as the imperative to one's "family" began to be redefined on larger terms. This movement coincided with widening opportunities for women in the public sphere, especially in "feminine" roles such as caring for the unfortunate, which allowed, in part, for the increased participation of women in the institution.

Social work for women became increasingly professionalized in the nineteenth century, yet women were often chosen for charity work for their understanding of domestic concerns like uncleanliness. Frank Mort notes a series of lectures given by the Reverend Frederick Maurice in 1855 "for middle-class women as part of his scheme to found a college for training charity workers. . . . The lectures, given by prominent sanitary reformers, harped on as usual about the dual principles of medico-moral improvement. But they sounded a new note by arguing that middle-class women were especially suited for sowing the seeds of sanitary knowledge" (Mort, *Dangerous Sexualities*, 55). See F. K. Prochaska's finely researched account of women's roles in philanthropy in *Women and Philanthropy in Nineteenth-Century England*. See also Jane Lewis, *Women and Social Action in Victorian and Edwardian England*, and Regina Kunzel, *Fallen Women, Problem Girls*.

In *Family, Love, and Work in the Lives of Victorian Gentlewomen*, M. Jeanne Peterson attempts to account for the widespread participation in charity work among middle-class women of all ages: "The search for excitement or the mere impulse to conform to upper-middle-class norms could not, in themselves, sustain women in the demanding and sometimes harrowing work of charity. Christian commitment, an abiding compassion for their fellow creatures, and the need to lead useful lives were the sustaining motives in women's charity work. Adolescent girls and spinsters of sixty, young brides and middle-aged matrons—they all took a share in caring for the poor. They gave of their resources but they also gave their time for this work" (Peterson, *Family, Love, and Work*, 138).

56. [Allen], *Polite Lady*, 274.

57. Chapone, *Improvement of the Mind*, 58.

58. Dr. Gregory's advice to his daughters on the subject of charity (1774) echoes Chapone: "The best effect of your religion will be a diffusive humanity to all in distress.—Set apart a certain proportion of your income as sacred to charitable purposes. But in this, as well as in the practice of every other duty, carefully avoid ostentation" (Gregory, *Father's Legacy*, 20).

59. [Allen], *Polite Lady*, 268–269.

60. Chapone, *Improvement of the Mind*, 88. Richardson's Clarissa does not fail to remember the worthy poor when writing her exact (and exacting) will: "It has always been a rule with me in my little donations, to endeavor to aid and set forward the sober and industrious poor. . . . But it is my express will and direction that let this fund come out to be ever so considerable, it shall be applied only in support of the *temporary exigencies* of the persons I have described; and that no one family or person receive from it, at one time, or in one year, more than the sum of twenty pounds" (quoted in Scheuermann, *Her Bread to Earn*, 76).

61. Blair, *Prostitutes Reclaimed*, 65.

62. Walkowitz comments that participating in charitable institutions is beneficial to the charitable in that the institutions themselves protect the value (and the persons) of the middle class: "As one examines the double-edged strategy of evangelical reform—the rescue of some individual fallen souls while consigning the rest to social and spiritual damnation—it becomes readily apparent that solicitude for prostitutes or even their actual redemption were secondary considerations. The agents of moral reform were the principle beneficiaries of the program: activity in a righteous cause tested their virtue while repressive laws and institutions

of confinement protected them and their sons from unrestrained moral contagion" (Wal-kowitz, *Prostitution in Victorian Society*, 40-41).

63. In *Desire and Domestic Fiction*, Nancy Armstrong brilliantly argues for the "political desire" created by the conduct books that elevates the domestic woman to prominence over the aristocratic woman.

64. *Guardian Society* (1817), 20.

65. Richardson, *Pamela*, 220. All further references to this edition of the first part of *Pamela* are made parenthetically in the text. I refer to the second part of *Pamela* (volumes 3 and 4) in chapter 2.

Chapter 2
"The Matter of Letters"

1. Stallybrass, "Patriarchal Territories," 123.

2. Stallybrass, "Patriarchal Territories," 126–127.

3. Conduct manuals have survived in twentieth-century popular culture in the form of magazines for adolescent girls such as *Seventeen, YM,* and even the more progressive *Sassy,* and in picture books for the young that promote polite behavior. See Aliki's *Manners.*

4. Some examples of the myriad popular seventeenth- and eighteenth-century conduct manual include: [Richard Allestree], *The Whole Duty of Man* (1659) and *The Ladies Calling* (1673); Hester Chapone, *Letters on the Improvement of the Mind* (1773); William Darrell, *The Gentleman Instructed, In the Conduct of a Virtuous and Happy Life. In Three Parts. Written for the Instruction of a Young Nobleman. To Which is added, A Word to the Ladies, by Way of Supplement to the First Part* (1704); James Fordyce, *Sermons to Young Women* (1766); John Gregory, *A Father's Legacy to his Daughters* (1774); Henry Peacham, *The Compleat Gentleman: Fashioning Him absolute in the most Necessary and Commendable Qualities, concerning Mind, or Body, that may be required in a Person of Honor* (1622); Sarah Pennington, *An Unfortunate Mother's Advice to her Absent Daughters* (1761).

Conduct literature has been the focus of many literary studies, including: Nancy Arms-trong, *Desire and Domestic Fiction;* Carol Houlihan Flynn, *Sir Charles Grandison: The Compleat Conduct Book;* Susan Fraiman, *Unbecoming Women: British Women Writers and the Novel of Development;* Mary Poovey, *The Proper Lady and the Woman Writer;* and Ruth Yeazell, *Fictions of Modesty.* For a bibliography of early domestic manuals see Powell, *English Domestic Relations, 1487–1653.*

5. Woolley treats fish in the same manner as small birds. I record it here not only as another example of the conduct discourse of command, but also for its poetics: "For Fish, Chine that Salmon, String the Lamprey, Splat that Pike, Sauce that Plaice, and Sauce that Tench, Splay that Bream, Side that Haddock, Tusk that Barbel, Culpon that Trout, Transon that Eel, Tranch that Sturgeon, Tame that Crab, Barb that Lobster" (Woolley, *Gentlewomans Companion,* 113. All further references to this edition are cited parenthetically in the text.) Although Fraiman asserts that conduct manuals "characteristically contest the dominant narrative as it appears in both their own and other works" (Fraiman, *Unbecoming Women,*

15), I am extrapolating elements from one conduct manual to argue for the general consistency of its discourses of the body.

6. I use "anatomy" generally in its older meaning of "analysis." Appropriately enough for my purposes, the *Oxford English Dictionary* cites Kingesmyll's conduct manual *Godly Advise* (1569): "Make an Anatomie of the suter you have in hand, make no confusion of wealthe, witte, bodie and soule" (*OED*, concise edition, 15). However, in my use of "anatomy" I want also to evoke its common meaning of the practice of dissection of the body.

7. Of corollary interest to my discussion of anatomy and dismemberment in Richardson and conduct discourse is Raymond F. Hilliard's essay "*Clarissa* and Ritual Cannibalism."

8. Woolley also published a volume on fishing—*New and Excellent Experiments and Secrets in the Art of Angling* (1675)—taken from her *Accomplished Ladies Delight*.

9. See Ruth Yeazell's second chapter of *Fictions of Modesty* (12–32) for a discussion of "natural modesty" in the conduct manuals.

10. Alpers, *Art of Describing*, 84. I am grateful to Howard Marchitello for bringing this work to my attention.

11. Stallybrass discusses Renaissance England's need for "extra-corporeal" control over the treacherous female body: "She [the Duchess in Marlowe's *The Massacre at Paris*] is . . . a version of the Renaissance *topos* that presents woman as that treasure which, however locked up, always escapes. She is the gaping mouth, the open window, the body that 'transgresses its own limits' and negates all those boundaries without which property could not be constituted" (Stallybrass, "Patriarchal Territories," 128). Although Woolley here also admits and "uses" the antagonism between the sexes to further her didactic program for girls in the conduct manual, she writes that the only effective way to command a destabilizing (unchaste) sexuality is through self-control. This internalized surveillance and control is the movement from punishment to discipline that Foucault traces in *Discipline and Punish*.

12. See Katherine Hornbeak, "The Complete Letter Writer in English, 1568–1800," for a discussion of Richardson as a letter writer. See also Janet Gurkin Altman, "Political Ideology in the Letter Manual (France, England, New England)" for a brief discussion of Richardson's ideological differences from other English letter writers (Altman, "Political Ideology," 116).

13. Richardson's intention of adopting conduct manual discourse for his new undertaking is clearly evident in a letter he writes to Aaron Hill about this genesis of *Pamela*: "I thought the story, if written in an easy and natural manner, suitable to the simplicity of it, might possibly introduce a new species of writing that might possibly turn young people into a course of reading different from the pomp and parade of romance-writing, and dismissing the improbable and marvellous, with which novels generally abound, might tend to promote the cause of religion and virtue" (Barbauld, *Correspondence*, lxxiii–xxiv).

14. Carroll, *Letters*, 46–47.

15. *Pamela Censured*, 64. All further references to this edition are cited parenthetically in the text.

16. Davis, *Factual Fictions*, 188.

Tassie Gwilliam's discussion of *Pamela Censured*'s "pornographic effect" focuses on Pamela's "auto-scopophilic" fantasies that also involve the reader. Watching Pamela, Richardson and the (male) reader identify with her and thus undergo a pleasurable transvestism: "The excitement generated by this scene [Pamela unconscious on the floor] comes from the representation of Pamela seeing herself as a man would see her through the keyhole, itself perhaps the fantasy of a man imagining himself a woman being watched by a man" (Gwilliam, "Duplicitous Body," 122–123). For a discussion of the publication history and popular reception of *Pamela* and the "anti-Pamelas" see Kreissman, *Pamela-Shamela*. See also Nickel, "*Pamela* as Fetish," and Pickering, " 'Ambiguous Circumstances,'" 153–154.

17. Evans remarks that the only "noteworthy" response to *A Collection* was the issuance of a card game in 1769 advertised as follows: "The New Impenetrable Secret; or, Young Lady and Gentleman's Polite Puzzle. Being an entire new Set of Entertaining Cards . . . Consisting of moral and diverting Sentiments, extracted wholly from the much admired Histories of PAMELA, CLARISSA, and SIR CHARLES GRANDISON. The whole designed, while they amuse & entertain, to establish Principles of Virtue and Morality in the Minds of both Sexes" (Evans, *Moral and Instructive Sentiments,* xx–xxi).

18. In "P/B: *Pamela* as Sexual Fiction," Terry Castle names Pamela "P," evoking Roland Barthes. The psychosexual semiotics she describes in the conclusion of her essay dramatize Pamela's growth to maturity: "Symbolic plot in *Pamela* resolves into a sexual ideogram concealed at the primitive level of the text. P and B are primary signs in the novel's mythic code: the opposition P/B marks off iconographically the basic sexual dialectic of absence/presence, woman/man. Pamela's P, to adapt Roland Barthes, is a "initial of castration." P lacks what B shows; P(amela) reconstitutes, metaphorically, her missing part by becoming (Lady) B" (Castle, "P/B," 487–488).

19. Richardson used Webster's comments as part of his preface to the second edition of *Pamela* (quoted in Gwilliam, "Duplicitous Body," 114).

20. Stuber, "Teaching *Pamela*," 13. Florian Stuber has recorded the impressions that his 1985 composition class at the Fashion Institute of Technology (New York, N.Y.) wrote in response to *Pamela*.

21. Stuber, "Teaching *Pamela*," 16.

22. Stuber, "Teaching *Pamela*," 21.

23. Stuber, "Teaching *Pamela*," 21.

24. This abridgment is sometimes separated into different volumes; the 1795 Cooperstown edition reprints *Clarissa* only. The first American abridgment of *Pamela* was published in 1793 in New York, printed by J. Harrisson for J. Reid, followed in 1794 by an edition from the influential Worcester (Mass.) publisher, Isaiah Thomas. Early American children's literature is largely composed of two strains: the Puritan sermon or tract describing exemplary children's deaths, and reprints of popular British texts, sometimes slightly modified for an American audience. The first Worcester edition of *Pamela* falls into the second category. It is interesting to note that *Pamela; or, Virtue Rewarded,* 5th ed., was the first novel published in America, reprinted and sold by Benjamin Franklin in 1742–43.

For a thorough discussion of nineteenth-century American children's literature, see Anne Scott MacLeod, *A Moral Tale: Children's Fiction and American Culture, 1820–1860.*

25. Pickering, " 'Ambiguous Circumstances,' " 154. Pickering notes that the 1769 edition, which cost a shilling, was popular not only with middle-class children (read "parents"), but with lower-class adults (Pickering, "Ambiguous Circumstances," n169).

26. *Critical Review* 1 (1756), 315.

27. *Monthly Review* 14 (1756), 581. This reviewer is unable to form an opinion on the abridger's ability, however, as that would necessitate the onerous task of reading all of Richardson's novels for comparison: "As to the judgment, skill, or taste, with which this abridgement is made, our readers will not expect that we should, in very explicit terms, inform them; as, in order to do that, we must have made a review of all the twenty or thirty volumes (the Duce knows how many of 'em there are) with which Mr. R has obliged the public: but for this there is no absolute necessity; and we have other employment" (*Monthly Review* 14 [1756], 581).

28. Carroll quotes a letter Richardson wrote to Sophia Westcomb (1746?) as an indication of Richardson's epistolary theory and practice: "I make no scruple to aver, that a correspondence by letters, written on occasions of necessary absence, and which leaves a higher joy still in hope, which presence takes away, give the most desirable opportunities of displaying force of friendship, that can be wished for by a friendly heart. This correspondence is, indeed, the cement of friendship: it is friendship avowed under hand and seal: friendship upon bond as I may say, more pure, yet more ardent, and less broken in upon, than personal conversation can be even amongst the most pure, because of the deliberation it allows from the very preparation to, and act of writing" (Carroll, *Letters,* 31–32).

In the introduction to *The Converse of the Pen,* Redford quotes this letter as an example of "the *cor* of *correspondence* in the eighteenth-century literary familiar letter" (Redford, *Converse of the Pen,* 1). See also Janet Gurkin Altman, *Epistolarity.*

29. Kauffman, *Discourses of Desire,* 26.

30. Altman comments that "this sense of immediacy, of a present that is precarious can only exist in a world where the future is unknown. The present of epistolary discourse is vibrant with future-orientation. Interrogatives, imperatives and future tenses—rarer in other types of narrative—are the vehicles for expression of promises, threats, hopes, apprehensions, anticipation, intention, uncertainty, prediction. Letter writers are bound in a present preoccupied with the future" (Altman, *Epistolarity,* 124).

31. Richardson, *History of Pamela,* 6–7. All further references to this edition are made parenthetically in the text.

32. The abridgment, while downplaying the sexual, maintains—or perhaps highlights— social mobility. Pickering argues that *Pamela* succeeds as a children's book precisely for its class-based ideology: "In early children's books, the vast majority of which were written for and reflected the aspirations of the rapidly growing middle classes, there was little room for an aristocracy. . . . To some extent *Pamela* owed its popularity as a children's book to its being an educational fable for the times. As an aristocrat, Mr. B had not received a proper education; his real education began only when he took Pamela, the middle-class girl as his teacher and her writings as his books" (Pickering, " 'Ambiguous Circumstances,' " 154). It is significant that in the Worcester edition *Pamela*'s middle-class values were held up as examples to the rich: "From the economy [Pamela] proposes to observe in her elevation let even ladies of condition learn, that there are family employments, in which they may and ought to make themselves useful, and give good examples to their inferiors, as well as equals: And that their duty to God, Charity to the poor and sick, and different branches of

household management, ought to take up the most considerable portions of their time" (Pickering, " 'Ambiguous Circumstances,' " 164–165).

33. Pamela reports her discomfort with Mrs. Jewkes' freedoms: "And once she offered to kiss me. But I said, I don't like this sort of carriage, Mrs. Jewkes; it is not like two persons of one sex" (109).

34. We may be reminded here of Lovelace's justification for his desire to ill-treat and enclose Clarissa as originating in his childish acts of trapping birds: "I will illustrate what I have said by the simile of a Bird new-caught, we begin, when Boys, with Birds, and when we grow up, go on to Women; and both, perhaps, in turn, experience our sportive cruelty" (quoted in Kauffman, *Discourses of Desire,* 135).

35. I develop this point more fully in chapter 3.

36. Pickering discusses the important influences *Pamela* had on early children's books in terms of their plots, including *The History of Little Goody Two-Shoes* (1765), *Tales of the Hermitage* (1800), and *The Renowned History of Primrose Prettyface, who by her sweetness of Temper & Love of Learning, was raised from being the daughter of a poor cottager, to great Riches, and the Dignity of Lady of the manner.*

37. For an extended discussion of Pamela's letters on Locke, and B's "misreading" of some of his pedagogical ideas, see Lois A. Chabor, "From Moral Man to Godly Man: 'Mr. Locke' and Mr. B in Part 2 of *Pamela.*"

38. Richardson, *Pamela,* 4:343.

39. Richardson, *Pamela,* 4:345.

Chapter 3
The Value of Virtue

Note to epigraph: Quoted in Goodsell, *Marriage and the Family,* 330.

1. Myers, "Impeccable Governesses," 33.

2. Fielding, *Governess,* 1. All further references to this edition are made parenthetically in the text.

3. Examples of late eighteenth-century books on female education written by women authors include Hannah More, *Strictures on the Modern System of Female Education* (1799); Clara Reeve, *Plans of Education, with Remarks on the Systems of Other Writers* (1792); Catharine Macaulay, *Letters on Education* (1790); Maria Edgeworth (with R. L. Edgeworth), *Practical Education* (1798), for boys and girls; and Mary Wollstonecraft, *Thoughts on the Education of Daughters* (1787).

4. By the end of her days of instruction, Jenny's educational method has been so successful, readers learn, that her "pupils" become celebrated for their intellectual as well as moral development: "In short, Mrs. *Teachum*'s School was always mentioned throughout the Country, as an Example of Peace and harmony: and also by the daily improvement of all her Girls, it plainly appear'd, how early young People might attain great Knowledge, if their Minds were free from foolish Anxieties about Trifles" (125).

5. Myers, "Impeccable Governesses," 49–50.

6. For a description and discussion of the "rise" of the conduct novels, see Joyce Hemlow,

Notes to pages 41–49

174

"Fanny Burney and the Courtesy Books." The terms "conduct novel" and "courtesy book" can be used interchangeably.

7. Poovey, *Proper Lady*, 29.

8. Quoted in Huang, *Transforming the Cinderella Dream*, 19. Medieval practice suggests that a woman's virginity was directly related to her "material worth": "In general, then, the population of the Western Mediterranean in the early Middle Ages, no matter what its ethnic origin, had adopted a system of marital assigns whose chief award was neither the dowry of the ancient world nor the bridepiece of the ancient Germans but a grant that had grown out of *morgengabe,* originally awarded to the wife as the price of her virginity" (Hughes, "From Brideprice to Dowry," 26–27).

9. Blackstone's definition of coverture is well known, but worth repeating here as a chilling reminder of gender inequities in law (which have not been entirely rectified): "By marriage the husband and wife are one person in law: that is, the very being or legal existence of the woman is suspended during the marriage, or at least is incorporated and consolidated into that of the husband; under whose wing, protection, and *cover,* she performs every thing; and is therefore called in our law-french a *feme-covert, femina viro co-operta*; is said to be *covert-baron,* or under the protection and influence of her husband, her *baron,* or lord; and her condition during her marriage is called her *coverture*" (Blackstone, *Laws of England* 1: Bk 1, 355).

10. Blackstone, *Laws of England* 1: Bk 1, 107.

11. Mingay, *English Landed Society,* 35.

12. Blackstone, *Laws of England* 1: Bk 2, 111.

13. Staves, *Married Women's Separate Property,* 60.

14. There are many other examples of this "Cinderella" plot in literature. For example, Jane Eyre is first beloved by Rochester while a governess in his home and, conversely, Rosamond is spurned by St. John Rivers because of her social class and social position. In fact, once an "excessive" virtue is established, actual property can then be revealed without competing with virtue's value. See Huang Mei, *Transforming the Cinderella Dream: From Frances Burney to Charlotte Brontë.*

15. The inverse is true for Burney's virtuous heiress Cecilia (in her novel of the same name), whose fortune is seemingly "cursed," resulting directly or indirectly in duels, madness, violent illness, and suicide. Cecilia can be happily married only after she relinquishes her fortune to a distant relative, her name to obscurity, and her finances to Delvile's control. She is ultimately rewarded for her sacrifice, however, by an unexpected and unencumbered legacy (much smaller than her original fortune) initially intended for her husband.

Dickens's commentary on nineteenth-century "industrial culture" in *Hard Times* remarks the productive and aquisitive "manufacturing aspect" of Louisa's marriage to Bounderby: "Love . . . on all occasions during the period of betrothal, took a manufacturing aspect. Dresses were made, jewellery was made, cakes and gloves were made, settlements were made" (quoted in Michie, *Outside the Pale,* 125).

16. Harth, "Virtue of Love," 134.

17. I am grateful to Claudia Nelson for her insightful comments on an earlier version of this argument.

To every rule there is an exception: a 1793 *Gentleman's Magazine* wedding announcement elaborately celebrated a true love match where the groom's "deficiency" was rectified by the paternal Grace: "At Burlington-house, by the Bishop of Peterborough, Charles Greville, esq. to Lady Charlotte Cavendish Bentinck, eldest daughter of the Duke of Portland. This match, however rare in the fashionable circles, is literally one of affection. The fortune of the former is small; but the liberality of his Grace reconciled all differences. He had made an additional £20,000 to the £10,000 which is the settled portion of a duke's daughter" (*Gentleman's Magazine* 73, [April 1793], 372).

18. Blackstone, *Laws of England* 1: Bk 2, 246.

19. Holmes, *Common Law,* 253.

20. Blackstone, *Laws of England* 1: Bk 2, 239.

The contracts that ensue from marriage—jointure, settlements, portions—use *valuable* consideration, however, in order to give the jointure, for example, greater "teeth" in the case of noncompliance: "Though whenever, at the creation of powers, certain formalities of execution are prescribed, those formalities ought in strictness to be closely pursued; still, if a person, having a power, executes an instrument for valuable consideration, (and marriage is so considered), he is understood, *in equity,* to engage with the person with whom he is dealing, to make the instrument as effectual as he has the power to make it . . . thus, if a jointuring power ought to have been executed by deed, but has been executed by will, the jointure will be supported" (Blackstone, *Laws of England* 1: Bk 2, 109–110 n32).

Staves argues that the common-law understanding of contract ideology as it related to marriage ultimately faltered in the nineteenth century: "Efforts to apply contract ideas to the marital relation in the mid-eighteenth century led to results which were found socially intolerable. Thus, by the end of the period the courts retreated from contract ideology in this field and reimposed what I am going to argue were deeper patriarchal structures" (Staves, *Married Women's Separate Property,* 4).

21. The value of Pamela's "excessive virtue," as I have called it, equals the value of B's estate, which allows the marriage to stand as appropriate within the world of the novel. Ann Louise Kibbie notes, however, that this balancing act is problematic in that the story of the market thus becomes entwined with the story of virtue rewarded: "Yet while the articulation of virtue as a property of the self asserts an equality of persons that would render other kinds of property irrelevant, it also makes both Pamela and her author vulnerable to charges of hypocrisy and crass materialism, as the language of the marketplace and the narrative of currency encroach on the virtuous narrative" (Kibbie, "Sentimental Properties," 562).

22. "Seised in fee" describes what might be called "absolute ownership" over property: there exists no bar or limitation on ownership; the property is controlled completely by the owner and his or her heirs. An estate in fee-tail, by contrast, limits the ownership of the property in terms of determining qualified heirs. These heirs are usually limited to those of the body of the grantee. An "estate in tail male general" indicates that female heirs should never inherit the property (Blackstone, *Laws of England* 1: Bk 2, 90).

23. It is commonplace to state that men and women are treated differently under the law. A seventeenth-century tract on women's legal rights calls the woman "a poor rivulet," and one who "hath lost her stream" (quoted in Greenberg, "Legal Status of the English

Woman," 173). However, the *feme sole*, or single woman, retains some property rights under the common law that the *feme covert* has "given up" through marriage "becauseof [her] association with people presumed to be more capable than [she], namely, [her] husband" (Greenberg, "Legal Status of English Women," 175).

Staves and other social historians have remarked the ideologically gendered implications of laws regulating property dispersal. As Staves succinctly states, "rules concerning married women's property have always functioned to facilitate the transmission of significant property from male to male; entitlements of women have been to provide them with subsistence for themselves and minor children who are dependent upon them" (Staves, *Married Women's Separate Property*, 35). Blackstone justifies the legal difference between sons and daughters as resulting from "the worthiest of blood shall be preferred" (Blackstone, *Laws of England* 1: Bk 2, 171).

One important distinction the laws made between male and female ownership of property (beyond the repressive coverture), was between the right to dower and the man's right of "curtesy" in the event of his wife's death. Curtesy is the husband's right ("by the curtesy of England"), if there were living children at the time of the wife's death, to life tenancy control over his wife's property. The difference in value between dower and curtesy is described (and the ideological difference implied) by Ann Kettle in " 'My Wife Shall Have It': Marriage and Property in the Wills and Testaments of Later Mediaeval England": "The wife could inherit or acquire lands during marriage but the husband controlled those lands while the marriage lasted and, if a child was born of the marriage, 'if a cry was heard within four walls,' the husband who survived his wife was entitled to a life estate in her lands 'by the curtesy of England.' The widower's right of curtesy . . . was thus more generous than the widow's right to one third of her husband's lands" (Kettle, "Marriage and Property," 90).

Stave comments that "Early curtesy is not the husband's entitlement to his wife's lands by a special favor of the law, as later commentators tended to say; instead, curtesy is a continuation of the husband's possession of land already his as the lord's man and tenant, even if the land had earlier come to him as his wife's inheritance. He needs no action to secure such possession and consequently has no writ" (Staves, *Married Women's Separate Property*, 83). See also Lee Holcombe for a clear and concise definition of curtesy and its distinction from dower (Holcombe, *Wives and Property*, 22). For an engaging study of twentieth-century "gendered law," see Zillah Eisenstein, *The Female Body and the Law.*

24. Bonfield, *Marriage Settlements*, 94–95.

25. Briefly, under the strict settlement, "the titular owner of an estate at any one time was only life-tenant: he could lawfully alienate an estate only for the period of his own life; until his first son came of age he could not sell the property outright, at the most he could mortgage it, and then usually only up to specified amounts and for specified purposes" (Mingay, *English Landed Society*, 32). In this way, the family—as a social entity—was forcibly preserved for the future, mitigating the "damage" any one "profligate" heir could inflict.

26. The outcome of Hatchett v. Baddeley determined some restrictions placed on adulterous wives: "Hatchett v. Baddeley contributed to the development of a rule that eloped wives living in adultery without separate maintenance are not to have credit in their own right, nor are their husbands to be responsible for their debts" (Staves, *Married Women's*

Separate Property, 173). See also Staves's article "Money for Honor: Damages for Criminal Conversation."

27. The "rules" was the neighborhood immediately surrounding the prison house, over which the Fleet prison had quasi jurisdiction. See Henry Gally, "Some Considerations upon Clandestine Marriages" (1750). See also Roger Lee Brown, "The Rise and Fall of the Fleet Marriages," and Erica Harth, "The Virtue of Love: Lord Hardwicke's Marriage Act." My thanks to Shawn Maurer for the latter reference.

28. In his discussion of the history of legal understandings of the difference between public and private, Morton J. Horwitz cites the competing interests between two different means of protection—from one another, or from the state: "On the one hand, with the emergence of the nation-state and theories of sovereignty in the sixteenth and seventeenth centuries, ideas of a distinctly public realm began to crystallize. On the other hand, in reaction to the claims of monarchs and, later, parliaments to the unrestrained power to make law, there developed a countervailing effort to stake out distinctly private spheres free from the encroaching power of the state" (Horwitz, "Public/Private Distinction," 1423).

29. Staves, *Married Women's Separate Property,* 49.

30. Staves, *Married Women's Separate Property,* 132.

For a discussion of the function of "movable property" in eighteenth-century colonial America, by contrast, see Ward's essay "Women's Property and Family Continuity in Eighteenth-Century Connecticut." Ward argues that "the same laws that protected the descent of land in the male line, also guaranteed the matrilineal descent of personal property" (Ward, "Women's Property," 83).

31. Harris, "Power, Profit, and Passion," 61.

32. Ezell, *Patriarch's Wife,* 18.

33. Ezell, *Patriarch's Wife,* 18.

Joan Perkin also credits mothers as the matchmakers in their daughters' marriages: "In English upper-class families the mothers were usually the marriage brokers. . . . Mothers with marriageable daughters largely determined in the field of selection, and contrived suitable meetings between the buyers and the sellers in the marriage market" (Perkin, *Women and Marriage,* 64). See also Brophy for an anecdote about a marriage negotiation between Ann Massinberd and Henry Brondbeth that concerned the marriage of her daughter and his son (Brophy, *Women's Lives,* 102–103).

34. Bonfield, *Marriage Settlements,* 103.

In the early modern period, radical pamphleteers advocated the passing of legal limitations on the amounts of bride portions in order to reduce the numbers of marriages made for purely economic reasons: "A number of writers argued during the 1640s and 1650s that the state should intervene to discourage marriages of convenience. The restriction or abolition of the bridal portion—the often substantial cash sum that the bride brought to her new husband—was advocated by Gerrard Winstanley, the leader of the proto-communist Digger community . . . and by the republican theorist, James Harrington. Both argued that such a measure would prevent men marrying solely for money" (Durston, *Family in the English Revolution,* 16).

Even while promoting a conventional view of the virtuous wife, and disparaging fortune hunters, Susanna Jefferson's *A Bargain for Bachelors, or: the Best Wife in the World for a Penny* (1675) rather baldly confronts the practical importance of money even in a so-called love match: "After her qualities, let your next consideration be her portion; for though Riches alone of themselves are not a sufficient ground for a Match (for then it would be not a Marriage, but a Bargain and Sale) yet they are excellent good and comfortable additions; The hottest love being apt to cool and decay, where there is not the fewel of a Competent estate to feed and maintain it" (Jefferson, *Bargain for Bachelors*, 8).

35. As Susan Miller Okin notes, "the common law ruling that the wife's property became the husband's prevailed in all cases [until 1870] in which no settlement made explicit provision to the contrary. This meant that, unless a bride had parents or responsible friends concerned for her interests, she could easily end up married without any protection at all" (Okin, "Patriarchy and Married Women's Property," 129).

36. Quoted in Scheuermann, *Her Bread to Earn*, 242.

37. Scheuermann, *Her Bread to Earn*, 240.

38. Quoted in Scheuermann *Her Bread to Earn*, 242–243.

39. Cannon, *Aristocratic Century*, 73.

Staves illuminates wonderfully the marriage settlement's complex legal maneuvering by describing a potential settlement for Tom Jones and Sophia Western (Staves, *Married Women's Separate Property*, 61–70). For a sample eighteenth-century marriage settlement see Staves, *Married Women's Separate Property*, 136–139.

40. Evelina's more fanciful and vague notice, the novel prompts us, might have been crafted so: "Oct 13 [approximately] Lord Orville,—to a daughter of Sir John Belmont, Bart., late of Paris. £30,000.

41. An exception to this practice occurred in the December 1778 issue where the groom was overshadowed by his learned bride and older brother: the "celebrated historian Mrs. Macauley to the younger brother of Dr. Graham."

42. I am aware of the flaws in my casual "statistical" analysis of the *Gentleman's Magazine*—I do not know if the dowry figures reported were accurate or inflated, or how the information was communicated to the magazine (through gossip or by family members). But the sample, while revealing admittedly limited data, nonetheless allows the reader a glimpse into the past practices of dowry and courtship and the place they held in the eighteenth-century imagination.

43. Kibbie, "Sentimental Properties," 569.

44. Kibbie, "Sentimental Properties," 569.

45. According to Swinburne's treatise on spousals written for "the benefit and Instruction of the meaner Sort" (preface), spousals could be interrupted for "natural" causes and yet still stand as legally contracted: "When the Act is naturally necessary; and therefore to make Water, or to exonerate the Body, or to Dine or Sup, doth not interrupt the continuance of Consent, especially in so favourable a Case as Matrimony" (Swinburne, *Treatise of Spousals*, 160).

There were also instances when spousals were legally dissolvable, for example, if one person was infected with some *"foul Disease,* as *Leprosy,* or the *French-pox,* or to be afflicted with some notable deformity, as the loss of her Nose, or her Eye, &c." (Swinburne, *Treatise of Spousals*, 238). Swinburne assumes that the infected or diseased partner is female. Swinburne also comments, however, that if the male "dowry," his sexual "debt," was unpaid [if the groom "be unable to pay his due"] then the marriage could be nullified as well (Swinburne, *Treatise of Spousals*, 49).

46. Wiltshire, *Jane Austen and the Body*, 79.

47. Von Mücke, *Virtue*, 77.

48. Von Mücke, *Virtue*, 76.

49. Von Mücke, *Virtue*, 76.

50. Von Mücke, *Virtue*, 76.

51. Von Mücke, *Virtue*, 76. See also John Zomchick's analysis of *Clarissa* and "family contracts" in *Family and the Law in Eighteenth-Century Fiction*, 58–80. Mona Scheuermann also discusses *Clarissa* and finance in *Her Bread to Earn*, 60–95.

52. Mary Poovey discusses a similarly public display of the knowledge of female sexuality communicated by Evelina's blush: "As a proper young lady [Evelina] is theoretically ignorant of sexuality, but as a fully developed young woman she clearly *is* a sexual being. When she blushes she unwittingly signals not only her modesty but also her consciousness of her innocence. . . . The dilemma for Evelina is that, in a knowing world, a woman can*not* be truly innocent, for she will always unintentionally betray the sexuality that virtue exists to protect" (Poovey, *Proper Lady*, 26).

53. Of course, the epistolary novel itself enacts a kind of public disclosure of private events by "publishing" intimate letter and journal entries, especially in the case of conduct novels like Richardson's and Burney's that function simultaneously within both literary and didactic genres. Sheila Conboy considers *Pamela* in this vein of public discourse in "Fabric and Fabrication in Richardson's *Pamela*." Gina Campbell makes similar observations in "How To Read Like a Gentleman: Burney's Instructions to Her Critics in *Evelina*," 561.

54. From my informal survey of the *Gentleman's Magazine*, it would seem that Harriet's ultimate fortune—between £25,000 and £26,000 (with the promise of additional income)—is very respectable indeed.

55. Richardson, *Grandison* 6:34–35. All further references to this edition are made parenthetically in the text.

56. This point is made by the inverted argument put forth in *The Beggar's Opera*, where Peachum's aspirations for Polly's marriage can be realized only if she mirrors the values of the upper classes:

Peach: And had you not the common view of a gentlewoman in your marriage, Polly?
Polly: I don't know what you mean, sir.
Peach: Of a jointure, and of being a widow.
Polly: But I love him, sir: how could I have thoughts of parting with him?
Peach: Parting with him! why that is the whole scheme and intention of all marriage articles. The comfortable estate of widowhood is the only hope that keeps up a wife's spirits. (Gay, *The Beggar's Opera*, act I, scene 10)

57. Harriet's reluctance to name the nuptial day is so developed that she is pointedly reminded by Grandison himself that in the matter of expected marriage, "punctilio has no determinate end: Punctilio begets punctilio" (6:128). She is also put "on trial" by three "judges" (her grandmother, aunt, and cousin Lucy) who "recommend . . . Harriet, in consideration of the merits of the requester [Grandison] . . . to fix as early a day as in prudence she can" (6:131).

58. Burney, *Evelina,* 347. All further references to this work are made parenthetically in the text.

59. Sir John Belmont refused this "opportunity" in his own marriage to Evelina's mother. For lack of an expected dowry, Belmont had burned the marriage certificate that was Caroline Evelyn's only legal proof of her marriage. Once Evelina reached puberty, however, his bloodline is clearly legible through her physical resemblance to his dead wife.

60. Hughes, "Brideprice to Dowry," 39.

61. Evelina's lineage is "troubled," of course, as a result of her maternal grandfather's marriage to a tavern maid and her father's profligacy. Madame Duval and her relations, the Snow-Hill Branghtons, cause Evelina much social embarrassment, but once Evalina is owned (literally and figuratively) by her father, Sir John Belmont, and chosen by Lord Orville, her poor relations fade in their social significance. Orville signifies his limited class largesse by magnanimously inviting Macartney and his intended bride, the recently "divested" imposter Miss Belmont, to visit his home after their respective marriages (382).

62. Richetti, "Voice and Gender in Eighteenth-Century Fiction," 270.

63. Campbell reads Evelina's silence at the love-moment between hero and heroine differently: as clarifying Burney's difficulties in attempting to narrate a love between equals without denying either the importance of modest behavior or the heroine's volition: "While Burney recognizes that the silence the feminine ideal of modesty imposes on women can be a tool for reducing women to sexual objects, her unwillingness to renounce chastity means that in representing desire between equals she emasculates the hero, obliterates the heroine's body, and fails to report any passion. The proposal scene thus reasserts the silence of modesty that Burney combats in her account of Evelina's textualization" (Campbell, "Read Like a Gentleman," 581). I return to this scene in chapter 4.

64. Any estate that Belmont owned in fee simple could be transferred through his will, in common law, to any person he devises. Orville is referring to the counterfeit Miss Belmont's "illegal" yet just claims to Sir John's affections (she is not related to him by blood in any way).

The only real "protection" from being taken advantage of in the negotiation of marriage settlements, Staves comments, is no different than the girl/woman ever has—her right of saying "no" to the marriage itself. Once spousals have been contracted, however, she is at the mercy of her father (or whatever relative or guardian helps to contract the articles) and her intended husband (and relations): "The woman's real protection is not the refusal of jointure for dower but the refusal of the offer of marriage with the individual man. As Justice Wilmot says, 'This is a kind of Condition annexed by the Husband to the disposal of himself. If she takes him, she ought in justice to abide by the terms on which she accepted him; she ought not to retain the benefit of the Contract, and then reject the Condition upon which the Husband entered into it.' . . . The absence of dower in practice transforms jointure from a simple substitution for dower or even a benefit secured under contract in exchange for valuable consideration, transforms it almost magically, into the husband's private, individual gift" (Staves, *Married Women's Separate Property,* 129–130).

Chapter 4

1. Of course, to call the home "private" does not mean that this ideal was not discussed or negotiated in public. Indeed, such public discussions were predicated precisely upon both the valorization of the home as a place apart and the related desire to construct "privacy" as a category.

2. Thompson, *English Working Class,* 56–57.

3. Cutt, *Ministering Angels,* 16.

4. The ideology behind this "literacy movement" was based on the belief in the spiritual equality of the soul. See Thomas Laqueur, *Religion and Respectability: Sunday Schools and Working-Class Culture.*

5. J. S. Bratton marks the unconscious nature of the authors of Sunday school fiction: "Often, however, the author is not aware of the extent of the reader, has not perhaps explored his own assumptions and values. These are often naive writers, as well as naive readers; their interaction is mediated by a literary object, a story told according to established patterns and conventions, which is sometimes more powerful in itself than either of them understands" (Bratton, *Victorian Children's Fiction,* 25).

See Kimberley Reynolds's *Girls Only? Popular Children's Fiction in Britain, 1880–1910,* for a discussion of the image of the child and the child reader in late Victorian and Edwardian fiction, 30–48.

6. See Jacqueline Rose's discussion of the relationship between the "desiring" adult and the "fantasized" child created by children's literature in *The Case of Peter Pan or the Impossibility of Children's Fiction,* 1–11. In the introduction to *The Impact of Victorian Children's Fiction,* Bratton discusses the differences between the relationship of a novelist and his or her reader and that of a Sunday school prize book author and his or her "very precisely defined reader": "By the people who wrote these books the novelist's desire to explore and convey his or her own perception of the world was felt rather as an explicitly didactic intention to teach certain moral and social attitudes, which were not even necessarily general truths, but which were specific to the age, sex and social standing of a very precisely defined reader. The intended reader had therefore none of the freedom of choice which constitutes the novel and reader's influence upon the adult fiction which is written and published, but could only accept whatever books were offered to him, complete with the lessons they taught" (Bratton, *Victorian Children's Fiction,* 20).

7. For simplicity's sake, I am grouping these two religious writers together. There are, however, doctrinal differences in their beliefs; most notably, Barbauld would not term herself an Evangelical, but belongs rather to the similar tradition of Dissent. Yet both women believed in religious enthusiasm and reform. See Vineta Colby, *Yesterday's Woman,* 145–149.

8. The strategy of the exemplar has a long history in children's fiction, originating from

both the emblem (John Bunyan's *Book for Boys and Girls* [1686] later known as *Divine Emblems, or Temporal Things Spiritualized,* for instance) and from narratives of the deaths of pious children, one of the earliest examples of literature written specifically for children (for example, James Janeway, *A Token for Children* [1671]). See Summerfield, *Fantasy and Reason,* for a brief discussion of the influence of the emblem on didactic fiction, 233.

9. In a discussion of late eighteenth-century female educators, Mitzi Myers describes the practical realities and domestic triumphs illuminated in their works for girls. This attention to life's detail is also found in More's *Tracts*. While written for a purpose somewhat modified by class-consciousness and religious zeal, both the tracts and female moralists/educators attempted to revise contemporary literature available for children in similar ways: "Opposing the debilitating unrealities of sentimental narrative writing for girls, [educators such as Maria Edgeworth] subtly redefine the reality they purport to describe. It is *this* that matters, they say: this is the real, this small daily heroism, these small domestic details" (Myers, "A Taste for Truths," 122).

For further discussion of the place and role of women in the reform movement see Myers, "Reform or Ruin." For an alternative view of Hannah More and the reform movements, see Kowaleski-Wallace, "Hannah and Her Sister: Women and Evangelicalism in Early Nineteenth-Century England."

10. Kowaleski-Wallace offers a divergent and provocative understanding of the More sisters' charitable enterprise. She describes the Mores' activities with the poor as informed by their "embodied" class anxieties: "They [Hannah and Patty] displace an anxiety about the 'grotesque body' with its volatile potential, its very possibilities of rebelling against and resisting containment, onto the body of the working-class 'Other' " (Kowaleski-Wallace, "Hannah and Her Sister," 72).

11. See especially the introduction to *The Origins of the English Novel, 1600–1740,* for McKeon's discussion of dialectical genre theory.

12. See Bratton for a detailed discussion of the Religious Tract Society and the Society of the Propagation of Christian Knowledge, institutions that shared the Cheap Repository Tracts' goals of "Christian literacy" (Bratton, *Victorian Children's Fiction,* 31–52).

13. Barbauld, *Hymns,* 33–34. All further references to this edition are made parenthetically in the text.

14. See Myers, "Hannah More's Tracts for the Times" (275). Many critics have noted the close relationship between More and eighteenth-century conduct manual authors such as Reverend Thomas Gisborne (*An Enquiry into the Duties of the Female Sex,* 1797): see, for example, Litvak, "The Infection of Acting: Theatricals and Theatricality in *Mansfield Park*"; Sulloway, *Jane Austen and the Province of Womanhood*; Fowler, "The Courtesy-book heroine of *Mansfield Park*"; and Tanner, *Jane Austen.*

15. Hopkins, *Hannah More and Her Circle,* 135.

Kirkham adds a corollary to the narrative of this famous outburst by arguing that More ultimately read *Vindication* and was influenced by it in terms of her work on female education (Kirkham, *Jane Austen,* 11).

16. See also Myers' discussion of the importance of female conduct in Mary Wollstonecraft's fiction in "Impeccable Governesses."

17. Myers, "Tracts for the Times," 271.

18. Myers, "Tracts for the Times," 268.

19. More, *Works*, 250. All further references to this edition are made parenthetically in the text. For a discussion of More's four antislavery *Tracts*, see Moira Ferguson, *Subject to Others: British Women Writers and Colonial Slavery, 1670–1834*, 214–228.

20. Bratton notes that Betty's "industry is conspicuously more important than her piety" (Bratton, *Victorian Children's Fiction*, 48).

21. For a discussion of the theme of seduction as it is confronted in children's literature, see Avery, *Childhood's Pattern*, 68. See also Mary Sherwood's cautionary tale warning working-class girls against sexual temptations, *The History of Susan Gray* (1801).

Sarah Trimmer's *Sunday Scholar's Manual*, a series of lectures published as working-class children's Sunday reading (which included lectures on topics like "On Stealing and Its Consequences" and "On Capital Punishment"), cautions girls against the dangers and miseries of prostitution in the strongly worded lecture entitled "On Chastity": "The want of chastity is a crime which destroys thousands and thousands.—It is that which fills the streets of London and other places with shameless females who disgrace their sex. . . . When these girls [who have not been taught the importance of chastity] grow up they easily fall prey to the delusions of artful men, who soon desert and leave them. . . . —If [the unchaste girl] wants a service she is refused by reputable families, and in consequence of this is often reduced to great straits, so as to be in danger of starving; add to this that her mind is continually unhappy; and very frequently she gives herself up to the most wretched of all professions, that of a *street-walker*, and her condition becomes completely miserable; the horrors of this course of life are great beyond description; and every woman who parts with her chastity has reason to think she may be reduced to follow it for a livelihood" (Trimmer, *Sunday Scholar's Manual*, 239–240).

22. Hopkins, *Hannah More and her Circle*, 140.

23. Myers, "Taste for Truths," 122.

24. Hopkins comments on the remarkable number of tracts sold: "In one year over two million were bought by the well-to-do and distributed among the poor, some through hawkers, others in prisons, in the army and navy, and in schools" (Hopkins, *Hannah More and Her Circle*, 212). For further detail on the particulars of Sunday school education, and for statistics on the effectiveness of the Sunday schools in improving the reading and writing abilities of working-class children, see Laqueur, *Religion and Respectability*, 119–123. For a discussion of the "religious phase" of eighteenth- and early nineteenth-century English education, see J. M. Goldstrom, *Social Content of Education*, 8–25.

Hollis indicates that although the tracts were universally distributed, they were not widely read: "Street sellers who found it difficult to sell the *Penny Magazine*, found that religious tracts were so much waste paper. A young London pickpocket, interviewed by Mayhew in the late 1840s told him that tracts were brought to the lodging house where they were used to light pipes. 'Tracts won't fill your belly. Tracts is no good, except to a person that has a home; at the lodging houses they're laughed at' " (Hollis, *Pauper Press*, 142). The belief in the effectiveness of More's tracts in particular vary from those who feel that their influence on the political and moral makeup of society was minimal, to the thought that More's writing checked "disaffection and infidelity," as well as "a very formidable riot" (Jones, *Hannah More,* 147). For a detailed discussion of progressive religious movements and their influence on the working classes and the Industrial Revolution, see Wearmouth, *Some Working-Class Movements,* 298–321, and Thomis, *Town Labourer,* 165–183. Whatever the degree of support for More's *Tracts* as influential political and social propaganda, there is widespread belief that the Evangelical Movement and its writings helped to create literary and social history. Cutt asserts that Evangelicalism "had a formidable effect upon nineteenth-century writing for children, and its influence extended well into the present century, not only in Britain, but in America, in the dominions, and in Europe, where the works of many English Evangelical tract writers were well known in translation" (Cutt, *Ministering Angels,* 183–184). Jones comments on the historical value of the descriptions of the living conditions of the poor, the attitudes of the wealthy toward the needy, and the depiction of the various occupations common in late eighteenth-century life (Jones, *Hannah More,* 145–146).

25. For detailed insight into many of the particulars of Evangelical culture informed by diaries, letters, and periodicals of the late eighteenth and early nineteenth centuries, see Rosman, *Evangelicals and Culture.* Chapter 4, "Faith and Family Life" (97–118), for example, describes Evangelical family life and the "underlying happiness of many evangelical homes" (115).

26. Sherwood, *Fairchild Family,* 53. All further references to this edition are made parenthetically in the text.

27. Sara Keith reminds contemporary readers of *The Fairchild Family* that in 1818 "crime, punishment, and morality were just that stark" [as the corpse hanging upon the gibbet]. She also notes that in the 1876 reprint of *The Fairchild Family,* Sherwood's sense of Old Testament justice and morality was downplayed. The quarrel between the girls was revised to "pinching and slapping instead of biting and scratching and culminated in 'I do not love you, you naughty girl!' " (Keith, "Gruesome Examples," 184). Subsequent twentieth-century editions of the book go so far as to omit the original's graphic deathbed scenes and myriad corpses, as well as the prayers and hymns, lightening the violence *and* the religion in the book. A 1931 edition of the first and second parts of *The Fairchild Family* tells the story of three very obedient children who are rarely seen at prayer and whose fortunes rise when their father inherits his brother's wealthy estate.

Yet Bratton agrees that Sherwood's original stern morality served a serious and sincere literary purpose: "In her obviously different framework, Mrs. Sherwood took childhood experience as seriously as Wordsworth did, and did not seek to deny the importance of moral acts simply on the grounds of the youth of the participants. Within the unfailingly supportive, and clearly ordered, moral world of their parents, the Fairchild children are taken entirely seriously as moral beings. Such scenes [of the corpse on the gibbet] were part of the appeal of the book for children, as many memoirs suggest: even those who most strongly disclaim any influence from or even understanding of the religious implications of the book were conscious of its powerful situations and sensational action" (Bratton, *Victorian Children's Fiction,* 56).

28. In conduct novels for older readers, the fear of this disjunction relates specifically to the perceived threat created by unrestrained female sexuality. Because female desire and

reproduction are so "mysterious"—the mark of the father on his child must be taken largely on faith—the good girl or woman must not participate in any kind of disguise or masquerade.

Bawdy Restoration dramas were largely condemned in the later eighteenth century because their corrupt female characters were often paraded as innocent. See, for example, the debate over Congreve's *Love for Love* in *Evelina* that gives rise both to Lovel's insult of Evelina's character (that while she appears all naive country manners, she is actually knowing), and the discussion of natural complexion.

29. Paula Marantz Cohen uses "family systems theory" to illuminate these issues in *Mansfield Park* and to argue that the obsessive insularity of the Bertram family at the novel's end reflects the ideals and anxieties of the nineteenth century generally, as well as its literary productions: "[Austen's] closing vision of the Bertram family as sealed and immutable is what the nuclear family, insofar as it defines itself as a closed system, aspires to be. The history of the nineteenth-century family and of the nineteenth-century novel is, I believe, a struggle to achieve this equilibrium and, ultimately, to come to terms with its impossibility" (Cohen, "Family System," 670).

30. The Evangelical Alliance was formed at an international conference on Evangelical Protestantism held in London in 1846. The Alliance pledged to uphold the doctrines of Evangelicalism throughout the world.

31. Armstrong and Tennenhouse, "Literature of Conduct," 10.

32. Armstrong, "Domestic Woman," 100.

33. Stephen Derry has noted that Austen's early (unfinished) juvenile story "Catharine," in which the character Camilla Stanley is a "silly and affected girl" (Derry, "Jane Austen," 20), might be a comment on More's *Coelebs*. In a letter to her sister, Cassandra, that mentions More's novel, Austen reports, "I do not like the Evangelicals" (quoted in Sulloway, *Province of Womanhood*, 84). While this evidence might seem to dissociate Fanny Price from Lucilla Stanley, the moral values each author espouses in her fiction are largely similar. Tony Tanner writes, "Jane Austen's *ideal* of what a young woman should be—and what the most important qualities in a woman were—comes close to Hannah More's prescriptions" (Tanner, *Jane Austen*, 34).

34. Armstrong, "Domestic Woman," 116.

35. Jane Nardin's discussion of the role of leisure in Austen also credits the combined effects of Evangelicalism, capitalism, and the French Revolution in the creation of Fanny Price (Nardin, "Problem of Leisure," 130). For a discussion of Austen in the context of the French Revolution, see Roberts, *Jane Austen and the French Revolution*, and Kelly, "Jane Austen and the English Novel of the 1790s."

For a different view of *Mansfield Park*'s participation in political/social fantasy, see Ann Banfield, "Influence of Place": "*Mansfield Park*, then, is the first great English novel to confront the new society created by capitalism, with its deepening class divisions, its alterations of the social as well as natural landscape, its growing ports and cities. . . . The place [Fanny] longs for across the gulf of class differences is the utopia of Tory reform where the classes are united through an enlargening of sympathy brought by social consciousness" (44).

36. Jan Fergus notes that the public nature of courtship is determined by "all available eighteenth-century records—journals, letters, sermons, conduct books, essays, and novels"

(Fergus, "Sex and Social Life," 68). She argues, however, that Austen, while censuring Jane Fairfax's secret engagement in *Emma,* is essentially free from the constraints of the didactic writers. I would argue that although Austen, like Wollstonecraft, adapts didactic ideology in her own fictive worlds, she is never free from it.

37. See chapters 2 and 3. Hannah More was among these "novel nay-sayers": "As Hannah's absorption in religion grew stronger and stronger, her interest in literature lessened, until she came to fear that most literature was an evil influence on The Young Person. *Coelebs* contains the melancholy story of a girl who was ruined by reading poetry to excess" (Hopkins, *Hannah More and Her Circle,* 230). See also Myers's "A Taste for Truths."

38. Quoted in Jones, "Ideas and Innovations," 9. Hopkins, *Hannah More and Her Circle,* 229.

39. More, *Coelebs,* viii. All further references to this edition are cited parenthetically in the text.

40. The character of Charles (the name "Coelebs" indicates a bachelor) is said to be based on a friend of More's—John Scandreth Harford. Hopkins notes that the actual courtship techniques of Thomas Day (author of the popular children's novel *Sanford and Merton,* 3 vols., 1783–89) were similar to Charles's protracted apprenticeship as a suitor. Day had unsuccessfully attempted to woo Maria Edgeworth's sister and the two Sneyd sisters (each of whom, in turn, married Maria's father, Richard Lovell Edgeworth). Finally, Day adopted two girls in the hopes that one of them would eventually prove to be a satisfactory wife. (Neither did.) Day was eventually happily married to Elizabeth Milnes (Hopkins, *Hannah More and Her Circle,* 229).

41. Although the Sunday School Movement was in some senses a radical educational venture in its separation of child and home, for More, as for many other moral "activists," home was the appropriate arena of reform. The Evangelically educated child was to function for the family as an inoculation: in this case religious values would spread through the "body" (again, the house of the poor) to guard against the diseases of "ignorance," godlessness, and class unrest.

Certainly George Eliot's ascetic and enthusiastic Dorothea Brooke, although compared to Saint Theresa, in her original preoccupation with building tenant cottages reflects the tenets of home-focused Evangelical reformists. This obsession ultimately becomes subsumed under her devotion to one husband's concerns after another's. The declaration to Will Ladislaw that she will marry him, live in London, and "learn what everything costs," restrains Dorothea's social sphere—but perhaps not her social impact—to the home: "Her finely-touched spirit had still its fine issues, though they were not widely visible. . . . But the effect of her being on those around her was incalculably diffusive: for the growing good of the world is partly dependent on unhistoric acts; and that things are not so ill with you and me as they might have been, is half owing to the number who lived faithfully a hidden life, and rest in unvisited tombs" (Eliot, *Middlemarch,* 896). Eliot concludes this novel of the mid-Victorian period with the vigorously Victorian ideology of female influence.

42. More's ideology of influence is conventional in the sense that it reflects conduct book discourse as well as Rousseauist principles. The "angel in the house's" loss of influence was

an argument used to refute the demands made by female reformers of the later nineteenth century in the suffrage movement, for example.

43. One can't help but be reminded here of Alcott's *Little Women* and the scene of the "fallen" young Meg Brooke's inability to face "a man to dinner" after her jam debacle. Marmee, speaking in the voice of patriarchal authority, however, sets Meg to rights on her duties to her husband (see chapter 5).

44. Fielding's Jenny Peace is a good example of the desirable female transparency communicated to girl readers: "To give any Description of her Eyes beyond the Colour and Size, which was perfectly the Medium, would be impossible; except by saying they were expressive of every-thing that was amiable and good: For thro' them might be read every single Thought of the Mind; from whence they had such a Brightness and Chearfulness, as seemed to cast a Lustre over her whole Face" (13). This transparency of thought and motive is sometimes described as a male virtue. In *A Simple Story*, Inchbald's hero, Dorriforth (while he is yet consistent and virtuous), is also described as transparent: "On his countenance you beheld the feelings of his heart—saw all its inmost workings—the quick pulses that beat with hope and fear, or the placid ones that were stationary with patient resignation" (Inchbald, *Simple Story*, 8).

45. Lucilla considers that Eve's remorse at leaving paradise might be directly connected to her love of gardening. More feared this fault in herself, and wrote it into Lucilla's character. Hopkins comments, "When Hannah wrote *Coelebs* she had the heroine hang her watch on a tree lest she spend too much time working in the vegetable garden. Hannah herself worried lest she do wrong in loving her garden too well" (*Hannah More and Her Circle*, 113).

46. The insightful reading of Fanny's blush in John Wiltshire's excellent book *Jane Austen and the Body* can be compared with Lucilla's (and Evelina's) somatic response to the proposal: "[Fanny's] blushing manifests her desire to the reader (and her shame) but being confined to a signal on the envelope of her body, desire remains mute, inoperative, passive" (Wiltshire, *Jane Austen and the Body*, 83). See chapter 2, " 'Eloquent Blood': The coming out of Fanny Price" (62–109), for a provocative discussion of Fanny's blush that concludes with the evocation of the critic's own coloring: "Of course this is another selective reading: I have made the heroine 'my Fanny' too. One might wonder, in turn, about the motives of this (male) critic in reconstructing the figure, and the novel, in these apparently nonpolitical, nonromantic terms. What reply shall he give—but to blush?" (Wiltshire, *Jane Austen and the Body*, 109). John Mullan concurs with this reading of "body language": "The body's visible fluctuations are symptomatic of the sensibility which cannot be disguised, but which is supposed not to be spoken. It is a corpus of irrepressible signs" (Mullan, *Sentiment and Sociability*, 113).

47. Hopkins quotes one of More's friends: "Dr. Johnson who was sometimes more observant of these matters than would have been supposed, once gave it as a test that [Mrs. Garrick] was a very good dresser, that people did not remark what she had on, meaning that everything was in such good keeping as to prevent any part of her attire from being too prominent" (Hopkins, *Hannah More and Her Circle*, 68).

48. For contemporary reviews of *Coelebs* see *Edinburgh Review* 14 (April 1809): 145–151, and *The Monthly Magazine* 27 (1809, supp. July 30): 663–665. In an ironic twist on

Evangelical notions of display, the reviewer for *The Monthly Magazine* finds the religious discussions in *Coelebs* to be indecorous.

49. "Coelebs," *Edinburgh Review* 14: 146, 147.

50. Colby, *Fiction With a Purpose*, 80. By contrast, Austen's contemporary audience was small. Her novels tended not to go into many printings (the three for *Pride and Prejudice* was the most). Each edition averaged about 1,000 copies. By 1833 there were five editions of Mary Brunton's *Self-Control* and ten of Amelia Opie's *The Father and Daughter*. See Ann H. Jones, *Ideas and Innovations: Best Sellers of Jane Austen's Age*. In the manner of *Pamela*, there were numerous responses to *Coelebs*, including *Coelebs Married*, and a spurious parody, *Coelebs in Search of a Mistress* (Colby, *Fiction With a Purpose*, 280).

51. Jones, *Hannah More*, 217.

52. Cohen discusses the shrinking family at Mansfield Park as a kind of "relational eugenics that focuses on the quality of the blood line" (Cohen, "Family System," 678).

53. Brunton's hero Maitland reminds us of Austen's Knightley: the December 1815 *Monthly Review* questioned Maitland's heroic qualities, commenting that Maitland is not conventionally handsome and thus "We fear that he will not excite interest, although he may command approbation" (*Monthly Review* [1815], 398). Quoting Ellen Moers, Marylea Meyersohn notes that Austen was so impressed by Brunton's *Self-Control* that she was consciously trying to imitate and outdo it in *Mansfield Park*: "Ellen Moers reports that before the writing of *Mansfield Park*, Austen was reading a little-known (to us) novel, Mary Brunton's *Self-Control*, of which she says in a letter to her sister that she means to write ' . . . a close imitation. . . . I will improve upon it'" (Meyersohn, "What Fanny Knew," 224).

Ann Jones remarks that Brunton was inspired by More's *Coelebs* to write her first novel, *Self-Control*, which was so popular that the first edition was sold out in one month (Jones, *Ideas and Innovations*, 80). For a brief biographical sketch of Brunton, see Mary McKerrow, "Joanna Baillie and Mary Brunton."

54. Jones, *Ideas and Innovations*, 79.

55. Quoted in Jones, *Ideas and Innovations*, 105.

56. Brunton, *Discipline*, 1–2. All further references to this edition are made parenthetically in the text.

57. See Terry Castle, *Masquerade and Civilization*. While this study of the masquerade in English literature and culture does not consider Brunton, Castle's discussion of the masquerade as the "realm of women" in Inchbald and Burney, especially, illuminates similar themes in *Discipline* (Castle, *Masquerade and Civilization*, 253).

58. In Inchbald's *Simple Story*, the beautiful yet unchaste Miss Milner and pious yet unattractive Miss Woodley are "combined" in the second generation to create the "perfected" Miss Matilda.

59. Another of Maitland's Evangelical characteristics is his ardent work for the abolitionist cause.

60. Ellen is not allowed to convert to "just any" sect of Christianity. There is a short span of time in the novel when Ellen is enthralled by the enthusiasm of the Methodist service, before Miss Mortimer reveals the "folly" of such misplaced zeal.

61. Any discussion of *Mansfield Park* must attempt to come to terms with Fanny Price,

whose character is so disturbing that she has excited both energetic admiration and positive disgust. For many critics, Fanny's submissive nature and selflessness indicates her deficiencies in comparison with Austen's other female characters, her charmlessness for the reader and even her egoism. For a discussion of Fanny as a deficient character see Joseph M. Duffy, Jr., "Moral Integrity and Moral Anarchy in *Mansfield Park*." For discussions of Fanny as an unlikable heroine, see Jan Fergus, *Jane Austen and the Didactic Novel*, and Nina Auerbach, "Feeling as One Ought About Fanny Price." John Wiltshire locates some of the unease about Fanny Price in her frail body and the inability of some readers to "flirt with her" (Wiltshire, *Jane Austen and the Body,* 61). Fanny as an egotistical character is discussed in chapter 4 of Laura G. Mooneyham, *Romance, Language, and Education in Jane Austen's Novels*, and David Monaghan, "Jane Austen and the Position of Women." Criticism on *Mansfield Park* has argued that Fanny is the "victim" of familial oppression from incest or child abuse (see Johanna Smith and Joan K. Ray) that results in "agoraphobia" (see Sulloway). Hudson understands the incestuous relationships in *Mansfield Park* to be more successful than non-incestuous relationships due to the former's insularity and "roots" in domestic rather than sexual love (Hudson, *Sibling Love and Incest,* 25).

My view of Fanny in this chapter is that she represents part of Austen's Evangelical inheritance. For readings sympathetic to this view see Avrom Fleischman, *A Reading of "Mansfield Park,"* and Warren Roberts, *Jane Austen and theFrench Revolution*. See also Joseph Wiesenfarth, *The Errand of Form: An Assay of Jane Austen's Art*, and Robert A. Colby, *Fiction With a Purpose: Major and Minor Nineteenth-Century Novels*.

The nature of religion in Austen's fiction has also been the subject of a lively critical debate. Some critics find Austen to be a highly religious author, her firm moral vision indicating a general (rather than sectarian) religious influence. See Gene Koppel, *The Religious Dimension of Jane Austen's Novels* for a lengthy discussion of this view. See also Lesley Willis, "Religion in Jane Austen's *Mansfield Park*." Others argue for a specifically Evangelical outlook in *Mansfield Park*: see Marilyn Butler, "History, Politics, Religion."

Another critical stance taken on the issue of religion in Austen maintains that Austen is not influenced by Evangelicalism in any significant way. See David Monaghan, "*Mansfield Park* and Evangelicalism: A Reassessment." My understanding of Austen and Evangelicalism in *Mansfield Park* is that she could hardly avoid the influence of the Evangelical fervor that was having such a profound effect upon national identity, economic practices, social mores, as well as her own family. In the creation of a heroine whose dominant feature was the exercise of moral standards within a literary milieu emphasizing the early nineteenth-century equivalent of "safe sex," Austen participated in an Evangelistic program for moral reform.

Discussions of Austen and Evangelicalism are best informed by considerations of Austen's social context. For an interesting and readable look at the minutiae of Austen's world, see W. A. Craik, *Jane Austen in Her Time*. For a discussion of the "misinterpretations" of Austen's social context, see historian David Spring's "Interpreters of Jane Austen's Social World: Literary Critics and Historians."

62. Kirkham, "Feminist Irony," 118.

63. Butler, "History, Politics, and Religion," 206.

64. Patricia Meyer Spacks writes that Fanny's "youthful discernment" does not indicate

ideological construction on Austen's part, but I would argue that, nevertheless, like the conduct books themselves, Austen participates in the formation of ideology. Armstrong succinctly describes this movement: "Because they [conduct books] appeared to have no political bias, these rules took on the power of natural law, and as a result, they presented— in actuality, still present—readers with ideology in its most powerful form" (Armstrong, "Domestic Woman," 97). See Patricia Meyer Spacks, "Muted Discord: Generational Conflict in Jane Austen," 159–179.

65. See Fowler for a thorough discussion of Fanny's courtesy-book heroinism. Mary Poovey, in *The Proper Lady and the Woman Writer*, calls Fanny a "textbook Proper Lady," 212.

66. Austen, *Mansfield Park*, 44. All further references to this edition are made paren- thetically in the text.

67. In "*Mansfield Park*: The Revolt of the 'Feminine Woman,'" Leroy W. Smith reveals a basic misunderstanding of Fanny's powers as a watchful and sentient moral exemplar despite her submissiveness when he writes that Fanny "receives as little preparation as her cousins and Mary Crawford to act as a free and responsible individual" (147).

68. Nearly a century before *Mansfield Park*'s publication, a correspondent to the *Gentle- man's Magazine* (1745) also discussed the unnerving habit of "social presumption" found in women (here the bride) who have recently changed their status: "I must therefore desire you in the first place to be very slow in changing the modest behaviour of a virgin: It is usual in young wives, before they have been many weeks married, to assume a bold, forward look, and manner of talking; as if they intended to signify in all companies, that they were no longer girls, and consequently that their whole demeanor before they got a husband, was a constraint upon their nature" (*Gentleman's Magazine* [Sept. 1745], 473). As, of course, it was.

69. Hudson "ennobles" Austen's fictional incestuous relationships by describing them as stabilizing forces within a tumultuous, commercial world: "Incest in Austen's novels cre- ates a loving and enclosed family circle; by drawing the bonds of the family tighter and tighter, the household is strengthened and reconsecrated" (Hudson, *Sibling Love*, 35).

70. Staging a play in private is in itself a "risky business," as was the case for Hannah More's early "Search for Happiness"; however, the right choice of text can sometimes excuse the relatively immodest action of displaying oneself in costume, upon a stage, for applause. In addition to the immodesty of acting generally, "Lovers' Vows" is hardly an Evangelical or decorous play. Fanny is horrified at the play's impropriety: "Her curiosity was all awake, and she ran through it with an eagerness which was suspended only by intervals of aston- ishment, that it could be proposed and accepted in a private Theatre! Agatha and Amelia appeared to her in their different ways so totally improper for home representation—the situation of one, and the language of the other, so unfit to be expressed by any woman of modesty, that she could hardly suppose her cousins could be aware of what they were engaging in; and longed to have them roused as soon as possible by the remonstrance which Edmund would certainly make" (161). David Marshall discusses Fanny's "[opposition] to the dangerous impersonation of the theater" (Marshall, "True Acting," 87).

This is not to argue, however, that Fanny is not tempted by acting (on stage, or improperly). Readers must come to terms with Fanny's temptation and her threatening ductility (in her softening toward the theatrical as well as toward Henry Crawford). D. A. Miller argues that part of Austen's strength as a writer comes from her ability to narrate "outside" the realm of her ideology of manners: "Jane Austen's moral negation permits her to bring into language what otherwise, according to a strict construction of her ideology, could never properly be mentioned. Her novels can bring forward a fascinated delight with unsettled states of deferral and ambiguity, provided that they also, gently or firmly, repudiate them as not belonging (so to speak) to their real selves" (Miller, *Narrative and Its Discontents*, 66).

71. Quoted in Fowler, "Courtesy-book Heroine," 42.

72. Quoted in Colby, *Fiction With a Purpose*, 85.

73. Yeazell, *Fictions of Modesty*, 161. I discuss the relationship between the dirty and the clean within the domestic science movement and institutional reform in nineteenth-century America in chapter 6.

74. Wiltshire, *Jane Austen and the Body*, 22.

Chapter 5
The Daughters of the New Republic

1. Litvak, *Caught in the Act*, xi.

2. Blake, *Play, Games, and Sport*, 109. See James R. Kincaid's discussion of play and Alice in *Child-Loving: The Erotic Child and Victorian Culture*, 288–295.

3. I agree with Kathleen Blake that the Caucus-race "includes the notion of competition and winning," but only in order to turn those ideas on their head, not to designate the race as a social form (Blake, *Play, Games, and Sport*, 114).

4. Carroll, *Annotated Alice*, 49. All further references to this edition are made parenthetically in the text.

5. Linda Hughes discusses girls' play in contemporary American society in " 'You Have To Do It With Style': Girls' Games and Girls' Gaming." Her observations made about a group of girls who regularly played four-square dovetails with my "play fair" argument: "[Getting someone out of the game] was, in their view, not '*really*' mean, because it was only the unintended, unfortunate, and incidental side-effect of the desire, and, indeed, the obligation, to 'be nice' to their 'friends' " (Hughes, " 'You Have to Do It With Style,' " 140).

6. Alger, *Ragged Dick*, 131.

7. Sedgwick, *Live and Let Live*, 54.

8. Following Carroll's advice about canaries, of course, is Beth March's only failing: Beth's little canary Pip is a "casualty" of the girls' experiment in laziness and selfishness.

9. Walker, "Wit," 6.

10. Quoted in Armstrong, "Here Little," 459. We are reminded of Alcott's sentiments convincing herself to give up acting on a large stage in her last novel, *Jo's Boys*, when the ardent amateur actress Josie Brooke is persuaded by a "real" actress to modify and diminish her dramatic aspirations. Karen Halttunen notes that "in obeying her stage idol, Josie unconsciously fits 'herself to play her part well on whatever stage the great Manager might prepare for her' " (Halttunen, "Domestic Drama," 248).

11. MacLeod, *Moral Tale,* 21.

12. See Mary Lystad, *From Dr. Mather to Dr. Seuss: 200 Years of American Books for Children,* for a complete history of American children's literature. For a study of early American children's books see Monica Kiefer, *American Children Through Their Books, 1700–1835.* See also Gillian Avery, "Children's Books and Social History," for a discussion of the differences between nineteenth-century American and English children's literature, as well as a good general discussion of children's literature and culture.

13. MacLeod, *Moral Tale,* 31. See Gillian Avery for a discussion of American Evangelicalism. See also Mary Lystad, especially chapters 2 and 3.

14. See MacLeod, *American Childhood,* 88.

15. MacLeod, "Children's Literature," 21.

16. Cogan, *All-American Girl,* 16.

17. For a description of the ideal of True Womanhood, see Cogan, *All-American Girl,* 5–6. Significantly, the ideals of womanhood True and Real were predicated on the assumption that the women in question were white Protestants.

18. Cogan, *All-American Girl,* 4.

19. Baym, *Woman's Fiction,* 27.

20. Hygiene is one aspect of physical health directly addressed by some of the advice book writers. In *The Young Lady's Friend,* for example, Eliza Farrar tackles the problems of unpleasant body odors and unhealthy skin in her discussion of the importance of daily bathing (Farrar, *Young Lady's Friend,* 160–163).

21. In *Means and Ends; or, Self-Training* (1839), Catharine Maria Sedgwick rather harshly states, "Diseases are the consequences of the violation of God's laws" (Sedgwick, *Means and Ends,* 41). In *Morals of Manners; or, Hints for Our Young People* (1846) she writes: "The civilization of different countries is measured by the amount of soap they consume" (Sedgwick, *Morals of Manners,* 10–11).

22. Alcott, *Letters to a Sister,* 49.

23. Cogan, *All-American Girl,* 47.

24. Lewis, *Our Girls,* 22–23. Lewis devotes an entire chapter of *Our Girls* to a discussion of body size: "Large Women vs. Small Women? Why Are Women so Small?" Lewis has a decided preference for big women (whom he defines as weighing between 140 and 160 pounds), because he believes that they are generally more intelligent than smaller women (Lewis, *Our Girls,* 88–90).

See Carroll Smith-Rosenberg, *Disorderly Conduct: Visions of Gender in Victorian America,* for a discussion of medical theories of adolescence and puberty (182–191).

25. See chapter 1 of Cogan for a detailed discussion of the importance and duties of health and exercise in establishing the "real" ideal, 29–61. Elizabeth Stuart Phelps, author of numerous books for adults and juveniles—including the Gypsy series discussed later in this chapter—wrote an essay about women's health and clothing entitled "What to Wear" (1873) in which she argues against oppressive fashions such as corsets. My thanks to Pamela Matthews for this reference.

26. *Young Girl's Book,* 3.

27. Child, *Frugal Housewife,* 3. Domestic economy not only saves work, it transforms

the home into a utopian state. Sedgwick's narrator in *Live and Let Live* asserts: "It has been well said, that, when domestic economy was perfected, there would be no need of political economy. We would venture further, and say, that when our family communities are perfectly organized the Millennium will have come" (Sedgwick, *Live and Let Live,* 120).

28. Child, *Frugal Housewife,* 12. She goes on to admonish parents, " 'in early childhood, you lay the foundation of poverty or riches, in the habits you give your children,' she cautioned. 'Teach them to save everything . . . ' In the next breath she added, 'not for their *own* use, for that would make them selfish—but for *some* use' " 1(quoted in Boydston, *Home and Work,* 128).

29. Cogan discusses Catharine Beecher and her domestic manuals (Cogan, *All-American Girl,* 85–87). See also Gillian Brown, *Domestic Individualism: Imagining Self in Nineteenth-Century America,* 18–25. I refer to Beecher's *Treatise on Domestic Economy* in chapter 6.

30. Beecher, *American Woman's Home,* 43–48. All further references to this edition are made parenthetically in the text.

31. I discuss this extension of domestic duty to the world outside of the home—most notably in "homelike" institutions such as the National Florence Crittenton Mission for unwed mothers—in chapter 6.

32. Burnap, *Sphere and Duty of Women,* ix.

33. Burnap, *Sphere and Duties of Women,* 71, 82.

34. Sedgwick, *Morals of Manners,* 40. In this volume Sedgwick also complains about spitting tobacco juice, America's "vulgarity in national manners" (Sedgwick, *Morals of Manners,* 29).

35. Sedgwick, *Morals of Manners,* 61.

36. Sedgwick, *Means and Ends,* 108–109.

37. Sigourney, *Letters to Young Ladies,* 35, 31.

38. There are echoes of Mary Wollstonecraft's thoughts throughout American advice books for girls. Augusta Larned, much like Maria in *Maria: or, The Wrongs of Woman,* dramatically cries: "Dear Girl, if I could blazon the walls of every school-house in the land with but one sentence, I would write as with a pencil of living light: IN CHRIST'S DEAR NAME, BE TRUE TO YOURSELVES" (Larned, *Talks with Girls,* 245).

39. Sedgwick, *Means and Ends,* 19.

40. Sedgwick, *Means and Ends,* 30.

41. Sedgwick, *Means and Ends,* 111. Similarly, in her fictional meditation on these same principles of domestic management and female duty in her novel *Live and Let Live,* Sedgwick's narrator rather stiffly states that "it is as consummate a folly to permit an *American* girl to grow up ignorant of household affairs, as it would be to omit mathematics in the education of an astronomer, or the use of a needle in the training of a milliner" (Sedgwick, *Live and Let Live,* 182).

42. The cautionary aspect to Dodge's work resembles the American evangelical tracts that were particularly prominent children's literature earlier in the century and which, like More's *Cheap Repository Tracts,* typically assumed that poor girls erred easily or needed greater guidance than upper-class girls.

43. Dodge, *Letters to Busy Girls,* 29.

44. Phelps, *Gypsy Breynton* (1895), preface.

45. Patricia Marks suggests in *Bicycles, Bangs, and Bloomers: The New Woman in the Popular Press* that the New Woman, the Progressive Era's adult version of the tomboy, though a figure of fun to the American press, was generally not an object of biting ridicule. "In many cases, the American press seems more to be laughing *with* the New Woman than *at* her, an attitude that demonstrates a degree of acceptance, at least of the myth, if not of the New Woman's substance" (Marks, *Bicycles,* 22).

46. Elbert, *Hunger for Home,* 233.

47. "Sanctioned rebel" is Judith Fetterley's term for Tom Sawyer. See her article "The Sanctioned Rebel."

48. Habegger, *Gender, Fantasy, and Realism,* 171.

49. Habegger, *Gender, Fantasy, and Realism,* 172–183.

50. Little, *Comedy and the Woman Writer,* 3.

51. Little, *Comedy and the Woman Writer,* 2.

52. The theatrical girl can also be an erotic, powerful figure. Auerbach notes that Carroll's love of the theater, little girls (including the child actress Ellen Terry), and photography culminate in his staged portraits: "[Carroll's] infusion of theatricality even into his photographs of nonactresses—all suggest that the mobile self-definition of acting crystallized the potential power he found in the little girl" (Auerbach, *Romantic Imprisonment,* 157).

53. Indeed, we may recall the first book of *Little Women* where Alcott self-consciously invokes the theater and its audience at the novel's conclusion. The principal actors are posed in positions on the parlour "set" that reveal their important relationships or interests (father and mother sit together, Amy draws, Meg and John Brooke are absorbed in each other, Laurie smiles at Jo in a mirror, etc.); the narrator implies that she is waiting for the reading public's applause for the production so far: "So grouped the curtain falls upon Meg, Jo, Beth and Amy. Whether it ever rises again, depends upon the reception given to the first act of the domestic drama, called 'Little Women' " (235).

54. Earnest, *American Eve,* 66.

55. Martin, *Triumph of Wit,* 5. Donald Gray, however, offers an opposing view of Victorian humorists, arguing that they comforted their readers with the creation of an organized environment where people could safely laugh (Gray, "Uses of Victorian Laughter," 176).

56. In *Jo's Boys,* the narrator reports that it was "impossible for the humble historian of the March family to write a story without theatricals in it" (quoted in Halttunen, "Domestic Drama," 234). See Alan Gribben's essay " 'I Did Wish Tom Sawyer Was There': Boy-Book Elements in *Tom Sawyer* and *Huckleberry Finn*" for an extended discussion of the relationship between Aldrich and Twain. See also MacLeod, *American Childhood,* 69–76.

57. Eve Kornfeld and Susan Jackson, in "The Female Bildungsroman in Nineteenth-Century America: Parameters of a Vision," describe much fiction for adolescent girls as fitting the *bildungsroman* model. The eighteenth century saw the publication of popular works for boys like Rousseau's *Emile and Sophie* (1762) (although she shares the title, Sophia barely figures in the story) and Thomas Day's *Sandford and Merton* (1783–89), a Rousseauesque novel about the education of two boys. As I have discussed in earlier chapters, girls were also treated to stories of schooling, in, for example, Sarah Fielding, *The Governess; or, Little*

Female Academy (1749), and Mary Wollstonecraft, *Original Stories from Real Life* (1788). The premier adventure story for boys was *Robinson Crusoe* (1719); to my knowledge there are no equivalent eighteenth-century girls' adventure stories. Peter Parley (Samuel Goodrich) and Horatio Alger wrote many books for boys detailing rags-to-riches success stories, and Oliver Optic (William Taylor Adams) wrote series of adventure and travel books for boys.

58. Habegger, "Nineteenth-Century American Humor," 884. For a psychological/statistical study on the differences of sex role standards in the use of humor in male and female children, see Paul E. McGhee, "The Role of Laughter and Humor in Growing Up Female."

59. Habegger, "Nineteenth-Century American Humor," 885. Habegger expands this thesis in his book *Gender, Fantasy, and Realism in American Literature*.

60. Cox, *Mark Twain*, 151.

61. Twain, *Tom Sawyer*, 12. All further references to this edition are made parenthetically in the text.

62. Alger's tales of fortunes made, however, while aided in nearly every instance by chance, are built upon an unswerving dedication to capitalism and the gradual accumulation of wealth. Tom and Huck also deserve their reward, yet it is a serendipitous prize for their defense of the innocent Muff Potter, rather than Alger-ian recompense for dogged labor.

63. As John W. Crowley writes about the March girls: "Even as a child, each is expected to wrestle her 'bosom enemy' (her characteristic vice) into submission. A girl's character is conceived to be far from static and determined; it is alterable and, for salvation's sake, it must be altered" (Crowley, "*Little Women* and the Boy-Book," 387).

64. See especially Nancy Walker, "Wit, Sentimentality and the Image of Women in the Nineteenth Century."

65. Sedgwick, *Means and Ends*, 234.

66. Quoted in Utter and Needham, *Pamela's Daughters*, 384.

67. Huizinga, *Homo Ludens*, 10.

68. Huizinga, *Homo Ludens*, 10.

69. In *Caught in the Act* Joseph Litvak makes a similar argument about theatricality and subversion in the works of Charlotte Brontë and Jane Austen.

70. Karen Halttunen discusses the importance of home theatricals to Alcott and her family (especially in her relationship to Bronson Alcott) in "The Domestic Drama of Louisa May Alcott." She argues that in Alcott's own melodramatic plays she not only distanced herself from the allegorical fables Bronson Alcott favored, also but subverted them (Halttunen, "Domestic Drama," 238).

71. Keyser, "Alcott's Portraits," 446. Halttunen finds Jo's dual role to indicate Alcott's own struggle: "Jo enacts Louisa May Alcott's internal struggle: as Hugo, she fully vents her deep-seated anger against affected little Amy, but as Roderigo, she sets aside that anger and marries her sister in the finale" (Halttunen, "Domestic Drama," 244–245).

72. Showalter, *Sister's Choice*, 50.

73. Louisa Tuthill's *Young Lady's Home* (1848) includes instructions for creating mnemonica to help in training the memory (25–26). She also devotes a chapter to "memory, glorious treasure-house of mind!" (22–34).

The anxiety over playacting and the desire to vindicate it was not unfounded. In fact,

Alcott's publisher, Thomas Niles, reported to her that Sunday school librarians had objected to the "The Witch's Curse" chapter, although he felt that they were some of the best scenes of the book (Showalter, *Sister's Choice,* 53).

74. Martin, *Triumph of Wit,* 65–66.

75. Farrar, *Young Lady's Friend,* 17.

76. Masculine foibles are also exploited for humorous purpose in *The Story of a Bad Boy* when Tom Bailey becomes a Byronic "blighted being" for the unrequited love of an older cousin. His comic pose is short-lived, however, and leaves no lasting marks, unlike the internalized scars that the Alcott, Phelps, and Coolidge characters endure.

77. Gaard, "Self-Denial," 5–6.

78. Hair, of course, is a mythic symbol of power, virility, or feminine beauty, and its loss—through sacrifice or weakness—reveals the self within. Samson suffers from his haircut because he has first been weakened by his irrational love for Delilah; the mermaid sisters in Hans Christian Andersen's "Little Mermaid" sacrifice their hair to the sea witch in order to save their sister's life. The "misuse" of hair also leads to punishment: in Ovid's *Metamorphoses* Medusa transforms her beautiful hair into snakes as vengeance for her rape by Neptune, and Scylla, Nisus' daughter, steals his lock of purple hair where his power lay, only to deliver it to her beloved, the Cretan king Minos, and suffer repudiation in return. In *Little Women,* Meg's loss of hair exposes her vanity, while Jo's sacrifice of her "one beauty" inwardly "feminizes" her nature while outwardly "masculinizing" her appearance. L. T. Meade's *World of Girls,* shows the faulty but courageous Annie Forest shearing her beautiful curly hair in "rough fashion" in order to disguise herself as a gipsy and rescue a kidnapped child (Meade, *World of Girls,* 132). My thanks to Laureen Tedesco for reminding me of this incident.

Hair removal can also function as a subversive action when girls choose to be shorn as acts of defiance against prevailing expectations of female beauty. In Catherine Sinclair's *Holiday House* (1839), for example, Laura Graham cuts off all of her curls to avoid the torment of nightly curl papers. Independent Maggie Tulliver in George Eliot's *Mill on the Floss* cuts her hair to be rid of its care and the "teasing" she receives about it from her relatives. The New Woman of the late nineteenth and early twentieth century, to the amusement of the popular press, persisted in "banging" her hair to create her own style (Marks, *Bicycles,* 156–157). As I have noted in chapter 1, headshaving was a means of punishment for disobedient inmates of the Magdalen House.

79. In his "Short Sermon About Matrimony" (in *Our Girls*), Dio Lewis claims that the reason men do not propose marriage to women is that the women appear to lack common-sense and have expensive tastes. However, he writes: "Let [men] see you are industrious, economical, with habits that secure health and strength, that your life is earnest and real, that you are willing to begin at the beginning in life with the man you would consent to marry, then marriage will become the rule, and not as now, among certain classes, the exception" (Lewis, *Our Girls,* 196).

80. Gribben, "Boy-Book Elements," 151.

81. Huizinga, *Homo Ludens,* 13.

82. Phelps, *Gypsy* (1895), 55.

83. Phelps, *Gypsy* (1866), 65. All further references to this edition will be made parenthetically in the text.

84. Castle, *Masquerade and Civilization*, 4–5. Pamela, for example, is never so pleased with her appearances as when she "tricks" herself up in country garb in preparation for her return to her parents and certain poverty. Like Gypsy, she goes on searching for applause— "I went down to look for Mrs. Jervis, to see how she liked me" (51)—and is delighted when the other servants fail to recognize her. Just as the teacher comes down hard on the school-child Gypsy, Pamela the waiting maid is disciplined for *her* playacting by her master's authority: "He kissed me for all I could do; and said, Impossible! you are a lovelier girl by half than Pamela; and sure I may be innocently free with *you*, though I would not do her so much favour" (53).

85. Interestingly, subsequent editions of *Gypsy Breynton* downplay Gypsy's punishment by reducing her humiliation in the classroom. An 1895 edition of the novel abbreviates this scene thus: "Miss Melville motioned [Gypsy] to her seat, but took no further notice of her" (Phelps, *Gypsy Breynton* [1895], 61).

86. "Good acting" sometimes occurs in girls' books as "ladylike" behavior. The rewards of acting "like" a lady are revealed after Amy convinces Jo to accompany her on a round of obligatory social visits. From a sheer love of perversity and antic tricks, Jo acts "inappropriately" at each stop (which sometimes means that she mocks ladylike behavior), only to lose, in the end, her cherished trip to Europe. Ultimately, Jo refuses to act as anyone other than her naturally bold and straightforward self. The lesson is not "be true to your self" but Amy's "nice sort of morality" that serves others as they would like to be served. Impressed by Amy's manners and style, the aunts award her the coveted trip. Greta Gaard makes a similar point (Gaard, "Self-Denial," 8–9).

87. Even the indomitable, lively, and undomesticated Gypsy, who is generally left by her parents to run wild, is severely reproved after she runs away from her snooty Boston relations to return home. Her mother soberly reminds Gypsy that "in every one of these little thoughtless words and acts God sees a *sin*" (Phelps, *Gypsy Breynton* [1895], 258). Though Aunt Polly certainly reminds Tom of his heavenly prospects, the tone, unlike *Gypsy Breynton*, is comic, for both character and reader.

88. It is only in melodrama that Alcott's vision of acting can truly resemble Twain's where the stakes are high, and the female's ability to mask resembles male freedom. Jean Muir, the heroine of Alcott's "Behind a Mask," acts the part of an innocent and modest governess disguising her true identity (an angry thirty-year-old actress). Her motives are "diabolical": she means to gain economic power, social status, and security for herself by marrying her employer. Jean is a negative character, yet her disguises and stratagems are ingenious and effective, as are Huck's. There is a price paid for the female impersonator that the male is not expected to pay, however: universal hatred and disgust. Greta Gaard's essay was the inspiration for making this point (Gaard, "Self-Denial," 17–18). (I am also indebted to Pamela Matthews for sharing her thoughts on *Huckleberry Finn* with me).

89. Robinson, "Social Play and Bad Faith," 15.

90. Aldrich, *Story of a Bad Boy*, 65.

91. Aldrich, *Story of a Bad Boy*, 66.

92. Another function of humor in girls' novels is to highlight the "domestic disaster" that leads the character to a better understanding of, and appreciation for, domestic management. In *Little Women,* for example, Jo undertakes a dinner party without any help as the finale of an "experimental" week of leisure. The results are highly comical: she buys "a very young lobster, some very old asparagus, and two boxes of acid strawberries" (114), and, among other catastrophes, salts the berries swimming in soured cream. The presence of the ubiquitous Laurie helps to secure the event as a useful "standing joke"—a reminder to the girls that work (read "housework") is a necessary ingredient for a happy home. (Nancy Walker discusses the traditional satire of domestic situations in nineteenth-century women's writing in *A Very Serious Thing.*) It is clear that the only "advice book" or conduct manual the March girls need is the maternal gift of *Pilgrim's Progress.* Marmee is a model of successful True Womanhood for her girls, and teaches them the importance of work and domestic management.

When motherless Katy Carr tries her hand at housekeeping after her aunt's death, she also makes some funny mistakes that the family must endure: "Katy got hold of a book upon 'The Stomach,' and was seized with a rage for wholesome food. She entreated Clover and the other children to give up sugar, and butter, and gravy, and pudding-sauce, and buckwheat cakes, and pies, and almost everything else that they particularly liked. Boiled rice seemed to her the most sensible dessert, and she kept the family on it until finally John and Dorry started a rebellion, and Dr. Carr was forced to interfere" (Coolidge, *What Katy Did,* 232–233). American advice books in general promoted plain, bland food and discouraged cooking or eating sweets, pies, or rich foods both for their detrimental bodily effects and the excessive time it took to make them. See Cogan, *All-American Girl,* 52–53.

93. Elizabeth Stuart Phelps wrote four Gypsy novels: *Gypsy Breynton* (1866), *Gypsy's Sowing and Reaping* (1866), *Gypsy's Cousin Joy* (1866), and *Gypsy's Year at the Golden Crescent* (1867). Susan Coolidge (the pen name of Sarah Chauncey Woolsey) published five Katy novels: *What Katy Did* (1872), *What Katy Did At School* (1874), *What Katy Did Next* (1886), *Clover* (1888), and *In the High Valley* (1890).

In the sequels to *The Adventures of Tom Sawyer—Tom Sawyer Abroad* and *Tom Sawyer Detective*—Tom's escapades become even more elaborate. Aldrich's autobiographical story ends as Tom Bailey is transformed into an Alger-ian character and goes off to employment in a counting house after his hopes for a college education are dashed by his father's loss of fortune in a bank failure.

94. Compare with Charlotte Yonge's *Daisy Chain* (1856), wherein the mysterious paralysis suffered by eldest sister Margaret results in her slow decline and death after several years of suffering. Gypsy Breynton, too, is "gentled" by the softening influence of a long-suffering, crippled teenager, Pease Maythorne, who is slowly dying from a back injury that resulted when a group of frolicsome girls accidentally pushed her downstairs. Alcott's lively heroine Jill from *Jack and Jill* (1880) is injured in a sledding accident and must lie in bed patiently. She eventually emerges from her recuperation a "tamed" and meek girl. MacLeod relates *Jack and Jill* to *What Katy Did* in *American Childhood,* 20–22.

95. Coolidge, *What Katy Did,* v–vi.

96. Auerbach, *Private Theatricals,* 81.

97. Mrs. Abell's "chapter for young girls," in *Woman in her Various Relations: Containing Practical Rules for American Females* (1851) reminds us of Sarah Fielding's theories of female behavior. Like Fielding, Abell describes the symbiotic relationship between submission/self-lessness and happiness: "There is really nothing more important to the happiness than the early learning to yield your own will to that of *others*. It will save you in after life from much trouble, as no one can get on peacefully through the world without it" (Abell, *Woman in Her Various Relations*, 162).

98. Auerbach, *Private Theatricals*, 27.

99. In "*Little Women*: Alcott's Civil War," Judith Fetterley notes that "Little women must not be angry because they cannot afford it. Marmee's description of John is frightening for the veiled threat it contains—men's love is contingent: be careful, very careful not to lose it, for then where will you be?" (Fetterley, "*Little Women*," 376).

Sarah Elbert offers a more positive interpretation than does Fetterley of the title or term "little women" when she describes Alcott's use of it as Dickensian: "*Little Women* portrays just such a complex overlapping of stages from childhood to elder child, little woman to young woman, that appears in *Bleak House*. Like Esther, each of Alcott's heroines has a scarring experience that jars her into painful awareness of vanished childhood innocence and the inescapable woman problem" (Elbert, *Hunger for Home*, 196). Frances Armstrong's essay " 'Here Little, and Hereafter Bliss': *Little Women* and the Deferral of Greatness" discusses in detail littleness choices of self-effacement or caution made by Alcott in her life and in her fiction, and yet, she ultimately argues that if Alcott and her characters are "little women," the "strength of their aspirations confers on them a greatness of spirit, if not of achievement" (Armstrong, "Here Little," 472).

100. Crowley, "Boy-Book," 385.

101. Cox, *Mark Twain*, 131. Cox explains the parodic nature of *Tom Sawyer*: "The relationship between Tom and Becky burlesques romantic conventions; the conversions of Tom and Huck, after the graveyard murder, parody religious conversions; lamentations of the village over Tom's apparent death mock funeral rituals and conventional language of grief" (Cox, *Mark Twain*, 132).

102. Although it is not written specifically about children's texts, *Last Laughs: Perspectives on Women and Comedy,* edited by Regina Barreca, discusses the "anarchic" nature of women's subversive humor. A useful analysis of women's comedy from the nineteenth century to the present is offered by Nancy Walker in *A Very Serious Thing: Women's Humor and American Culture*. See also Neil Schmitz, *Of Huck and Alice: Humorous Writing in American Literature*, for a lively discussion of the history of humor in "high" and "low" art (Schmitz, *Huck and Alice*, 3–29).

103. Henkle, *Comedy and Culture*, 205.

104. I am referring here, of course, to Hélène Cixous's important essay "The Laugh of the Medusa" wherein she celebrates and encourages women's writing—"the rhythm that laughs you" as a joyful and fulfilling aspect of feminine destiny (Cixous, "Laugh of the Medusa," 252).

105. Deleuze, "The Schizophrenic and Language," 280.

106. Elbert, *Hunger for Home*, 219.

Chapter 6

1. Yeazell, *Fictions of Modesty,* 161.

2. Barrett, *Conduct of a Rescue Home,* 76. All further references to this edition are made parenthetically in the text. Kunzel notes that by 1909 there were 78 Florence Crittenton Homes in operation across the country. The organization was incorporated as the National Florence Crittenton Mission in 1918 and granted a national charter by Congress—the first charitable institution to receive this consideration (Kunzel, *Fallen Women, Problem Girls,* 14).

3. Gillian Brown makes a related argument about the sanctity of domestic placement in Harriet Beecher Stowe's writing: "The glory of sentimental things emerges in their domestic placement; the organization of drawers and cupboards and closets matters in Stowe's abolitionism because the coherence of these domestic compartments constitutes the extra-market condition of a stable individualism" (Brown, *Domestic Individualism,* 45).

4. Charles Dickens's open letter to fallen women (1846) describes the Home that a "great lady" (Angela Burdett Coutts) has established for the redemption and succor of prostitutes: She "has resolved to open at her own expense a place of refuge near London for a small number of females, who without such help are lost for ever, and to make a HOME for them. In this home they will be taught all household work that would be useful to them in a home of their own and enable them to make it comfortable and happy. In this home, which stands in a pleasant country lane and where each may have her little flower-garden if she pleases, they will be treated with the greatest kindness: will lead an active, cheerful, healthy life: will learn many things it is profitable and good to know" (quoted in Flint, *Victorian Novelist,* 235). Dickens's description of the cozy home is persuasive for its one-two punch: not only does it tempt by way of conjuring up the future home a reformed prostitute might have if sufficiently repentant, it also harkens back to the memories of a home that she should have had as a child—even if she didn't.

Dickens managed Coutts's Urania Cottage from 1846 to 1858. See Amanda Anderson's discussion of Urania Cottage in *Tainted Souls and Painted Faces,* 68–79. Unlike most refuges for fallen women, Urania Cottage functioned as a kind of "clearinghouse" for penitents: every woman admitted was to be sent abroad to Australia (Anderson, *Tainted Souls,* 69).

5. In *Their Sisters' Keepers,* Estelle Freedman discusses Anthony's theory of "Social Purity": "Anthony distinguished between the causes of crime in men and women, claiming that the former acted from 'love of vice,' while the latter acted 'from absolute want of the necessaries of life'" (Freedman, *Their Sister's Keepers,* 41). See also Ginzberg's *Women and the Work of Benevolence* for an extended discussion of the history of women's participation in the reform movements and campaigns of the nineteenth century.

The "celebration" of difference offered by many female reformers of the nineteenth century accentuated the moral "superiority" of women over men; in fact, men were often viewed as impediments to the creation of a new moral society: "[Moral reform] could not be entrusted to man, as . . . he is often the worst enemy of the other sex, and generally has not virtue sufficient to qualify him for the trust" (quoted in Ginzberg, *Women and the Work of Benevolence,* 20).

6. Later leaders of the domestic science movement, which was eventually referred to as home economics, included the chemists Ellen Swallow Richards and Isabel Bevier, who were among the first university-level instructors of home economics.

7. Sklar, *Catharine Beecher,* 156.

8. For an interesting discussion of the economic implications of "women's work" (its changing treatments in census terminology and classification in Britain and the United States) see Nancy Folbre, "The Unproductive Housewife: Her Evolution in Nineteenth-Century Economic Thought." See Nell Du Vall, *Domestic Technology: A Chronology of Developments,* for descriptions of domesticity's technological advances, as opposed to socio-moral practices. See also Jeanne Boydston, *Home and Work: Housework, Wages, and the Ideology of Labor in the Early Republic.*

9. Boydston, *Home and Work,* 114.

10. Sklar, *Catharine Beecher,* 156. *A Treatise on Domestic Economy* was reprinted nearly every year until 1856. The enlarged and revised version was published in 1869 under the title *The American Woman's Home,* with Harriet Beecher Stowe listed as co-author. *Principles of Domestic Science; As Applied to the Duties and Pleasures of the Home: A Text Book for the Use of Young Ladies, in Schools, Seminaries, and Colleges* (1870) was another of the domestic science manuals for girls Beecher jointly produced with Stowe (Sklar, *Catharine Beecher,* 306).

For a discussion of the Beecher sisters (Harriet Beecher Stowe, Catharine Beecher, and Isabella Beecher Hooker) and their writings, personal and professional, see Boydston, Kelley, and Margolis.

11. Sklar, *Catharine Beecher,* 144.

12. Although we cannot describe a politically viable and institutionalized domestic science movement until nearer the turn of the century, we may nevertheless characterize its emergent midcentury form as a movement on the level of ideology, if not fully on the level of the social. The first four-year domestic science curricula were established about 1875 in the state colleges of Illinois, Iowa, and Kansas. By 1899–1910, 39 colleges had departments of domestic science. Although ultimately changed to "home economics," domestic science continued to be used as a descriptive term (East, *Home Economics,* 20–24). Emma S. Weigley's article provides a brief but detailed history of the home economics movement.

13. There are two levels to Beecher's understanding of the practical need for a (middle-class) girl to gain domestic knowledge: the first is that she needs this knowledge in order to execute her female role with dignity and skill, and the second is that the lack of "suitable" domestics for hire will force her to undertake some of their jobs (whether in their "proper" training or to make up their absence). In the second chapter, "Difficulties Peculiar to American Women," which succinctly reveals her racism and xenophobia, Beecher cites the scarcity of female domestics as a difficulty most housewives would face: "There is such a disproportion between those who wish to hire, and those who are willing to go to domestic service, that, in the non-slaveholding states, were it not for the supply of poverty-stricken foreigners, there would not be one domestic for each family who demands one. And this resort to foreigners, poor as it is, scarcely meets the demand; while the disproportion must every year increase, especially if our prosperity increases" (Beecher, *Domestic Economy,* 17).

14. Beecher, *Domestic Economy,* 46. All further references to this edition are made par-

enthetically in the text. Lucy Larcom considers the "difficulties of modern housekeepers" in her autobiography for girls, and connects them to the opening of the Lowell factories and the freedom from domestic work it brought to its employees. (Larcom worked at Lowell as a factory hand during its start-up period, 1835–45.) "Country girls were naturally independent, and the feeling that at this new work the few hours they had of every-day leisure were entirely their own was a satisfaction to them. They preferred it to going out as a 'hired help.' It was like a young man's pleasure in entering upon business for himself" (Larcom, *New England Girlhood*, 199–200).

15. The beliefs of Beecher's major predecessors (Theodore Dwight, Heman Humphrey, Thomas Alcott, and Lydia Maria Child), in contrast to her own, included an assumption of "male control of the domestic environment" (Sklar, *Catharine Beecher*, 153).

16. Sklar, *Catharine Beecher*, 156. Consult *Gender, Class, Race, and Reform in the Progressive Era* for essays that focus upon the very relationships that Beecher dismisses between gender, class, and race in the nineteenth century.

17. An example of Beecher's organization of household tasks is the breakdown of the week into units of domestic labor: Monday is "devoted to preparing the labors of the week," Tuesday is washing, Wednesday is ironing, and so on (149).

18. Stowe, *Minister's Wooing*, 16.

19. Stowe, *Minister's Wooing*, 2–3.

Boydston describes one result of the "pastorilization of housework" found in Stowe's writing, for example: "As romantic narrative played against lived experience, the labor and economic value of housework ceased to exist in the culture of the antebellum Northeast. It becomes work's opposite: a new form of leisure" (Boydston, *Home and Work*, 46). See Walter Buehr's *Home Sweet Home in the Nineteenth Century* for illustrations and brief commentary on nineteenth-century gadgets and labor-saving devices for the household. One interesting example of a labor-combining invention that could enable a "literary" housewife to read and complete other tasks at the same time was a portable bookrest which a woman strapped around her waist and shoulders, freeing her hands and arms (Buehr, *Home Sweet Home*, 56–58).

20. Sklar, *Catharine Beecher*, 154.

21. David J. Rothman links the "rise" of the asylum in nineteenth-century America with the abundance of domestic tracts such as Beecher's (Rothman, *The Discovery of the Asylum*, 216).

22. In *Women and the Work of Benevolence*, Lori D. Ginzberg quotes an admiring comment made about reformer Paulina Wright Davis's head (1853): "Her strongest moral organ is Benevolence" (Ginsberg, *Women*, 11).

23. Quoted in Freedman, *Their Sister's Keepers*, 23.

24. A good general discussion of prostitution and reform in America can be found in Barbara Meil Hobson, *Uneasy Virtue: The Politics of Prostitution and the American Reform Tradition*.

There were institutions for good girls as well: the Shelter for Respectable Girls was established in New York City in 1874. The Girls' Friendly Society was modeled on the English Society and established in 1877 by female reformers of the Episcopal church in order to help girls in "the most exposed and trying period of their lives" (Edson, "Girls' Friendly Society," 45). The latter two organizations were distinctly separatist in membership, attempting to aid those young female workers who had not (yet) fallen. "No one who had not borne a virtuous character" could be a member of the Girls' Friendly Society (Donovan, *A Different Call,* 85).

25. Mahood, *Magdalenes,* 62. Under Barrett's direction, the National Florence Crittenton Mission shifted the focus of its reformative program from rescuing prostitutes to sheltering unwed teenaged mothers. In his history of the institution, Wilson writes: "In the public mind the name of Florence Crittenton is no doubt rightly associated with any kind of help to the victims of sexual irregularity, but first and foremost it stands for help to the erring girl in her first mistake" (60).

Like the Home for Deserted Mothers (established in Britain in 1873), which restricted admission to "first time fallen" girls only, the Crittenton Mission was much less forgiving of girls who returned to the Mission again pregnant. Although Barrett writes that the matron and board could decide to readmit a girl who had had one child under Christian influence yet returned pregnant out of wedlock, such a readmission would have been rare indeed (Barrett, *Conduct of a Rescue Home,* 88).

26. In its most reduced and polemical form, the gender-based ideology of women's prisons, juvenile reformatories for girls, rescue homes, *and* the domestic science movement (as well as women's suffrage, if one ignores race) privileged gender over class within the reform movement. As Freedman writes about prison reform: "The use of sisterhood to describe the relationship of women prisoners and reformers suggests the influence of the ideology of women's separate sphere. Reformers attempted to dismiss class difference and emphasized the common bond of an innate womanly spirit. Moreover, case histories in their annual reports stressed the leveling influence of the home. In 1849, for example, an upper-class woman and an Irish servant, both seduced and abandoned by upper-class men, were given shelter. The former was 'placed on an equal footing' with other inmates, all of whom achieved redemption through penitence and docility" (Freedman, *Their Sister's Keepers,* 33).

27. In a general essay on the National Florence Crittenton Mission's work written before *Conduct of a Rescue Home,* Barrett addresses the deleterious effects, for both worker and inmate, of the girls' stories of street life: "Particularly we should avoid having our minds poisoned by listening to the nauseating details of lives of sin that often girls from houses of vice are so willing to pour in our ears. . . . I have seen girls that have gone back into sin just because they never permitted themselves to forget the past; they were constantly lolling it under their tongues as a sweet morsel" (Barrett, *Fourteen Years' Work,* 26).

Although disapproving, Barrett recognized the seductive pleasure of the act of telling these stories and listening to them. She could not, in good conscience, legislate against such pleasure, but she could warn others to guard against it. In practice, however, Kunzel comments, these injunctions were generally disregarded by the girls and, ironically, the "homes designed to inhibit unmarried mothers' sexuality became virtual clearing houses of sexual information" (Kunzel, *Fallen Women, Problem Girls,* 80–81).

Another issue of privacy was similarly raised during the question-and-answer period of the first general convention of the NFCM held at Mountain Lake Park, Maryland, in July

1897 (the speeches, discussions, prayers, and songs of the conference were reported in *Fourteen Years' Work*). One participant asked whether a matron had the right to open letters. One home's solution was to have the girl open the letter and hand it over to the matron for the first reading. This sequence of events obviously did not sit well with some of the listeners, but "Mrs. Barrett thought the girl gave her consent to the rules of the home by being in it" (Barrett, *Fourteen Years' Work,* 136). Obviously, it was felt that one could retain one's rights to privacy even while relinquishing them. Although it may seem that the NFCM's relationship to the rights of the inmates was ill-informed at best, the leaders and workers in the movement knew what questions to ponder seriously, even while they dodged the repressive implications of their decisions.

28. The British model of assigning two separate identities for the illicitly sexual woman of the nineteenth century as either seduced or fallen is described by Sally Mitchell in *The Fallen Angel.* The fallen woman, unlike the seduced one, was thought to be "capable of sin and therefore responsible for her own destiny" (Mitchell, *Fallen Angel,* x). One of the goals of the Crittenton organization was to enable the figure of the victim to overshadow that of the sexual "criminal." The "Hints and Suggestions" column of *Fourteen Years' Work With "Erring Girls"* proposes that matrons and workers could prevent the victimization of unsuspecting girls by making the rounds of various stores, alerting the clerks to their charity, and asking to be notified if they noticed any girls "being led off." Interestingly, shoe stores were singled out as the most likely setting for such abductions (Barrett, *Fourteen Years' Work,* 203).

Although the newly professionalized social worker of the Progressive Era understood unmarried mothers as " 'social units' in need of 'adjustment,' " rather than "erring daughters," Kunzel argues that "the multiple and changing understandings of the unmarried mother— as innocent victim, sex delinquent, unadjusted neurotic—suggest that evangelical women and social workers inscribed their own anxieties and those of their time and place in the narratives of out-of-wedlock pregnancy they popularized and promoted" (Kunzel, *Fallen Women, Problem Girls,* 5).

29. Wilson, *Fifty Years' Work,* 179.

30. [Green], *Mental Improvement,* 61.

31. Quoted in Freedman, *Their Sister's Keepers,* 34.

32. The higher-class inmate of the Magdalen Hospital was treated to better food, for example. Stanley Nash's history of the Magdalen Hospital notes that by the 1780s many of the admitted women were not prostitutes but seduced and abandoned women. Until 1817 the inmates were classified by "birth, education and behavior" and the seduced women were housed in separate wards. After 1817, however, this policy was abandoned—because of "jealousy" amongst the penitents—in favor of sending every inmate to the probationary ward (Nash, "Prostitution and Charity," 619).

Regina Kunzel makes a similar observation about the familial nature of NFCM maternity work, and contrasts this ideology with the later twentieth-century view of maternity homes as "places of treatment." The preferred relationship between worker and unmarried mother became " 'professional' to 'client,' " rather than sister to sister or mother to daughter (Kunzel,

"Professionalization of Benevolence," 30). She expands her analysis of women's reform efforts and professionalism in *Fallen Women, Problem Girls*.

33. Just as nineteenth-century Progressive Era female reformers attempted to conflate the institution with the home, they also agitated for a separation between the factory and the home. Many female reformers like Mary Simkhovitch testified against the practice of tenement homework: "I speak of [tenement homework] as a business rather than a home because we know very well these homes have the form but not the substance of home" (quoted in Boris, "Reconstructing the Family," 75). Home ideology was critical, as well, to the Women's Christian Temperance Union (WCTU), whose slogan was "Home Protection" (Ginzberg, *Women and the Work of Benevolence*, 203).

34. Kunzel, *Fallen Women, Problem Girls*, 33.

35. Levy, *Other Women*, 47. Levy also examines the system of "moral management" in lunatic asylums of early nineteenth-century England (Levy, *Other Women*, 100–106).

36. Bell, *Literature and Crime in Augustan England*, 150.

37. In fact, women's prisons contained domestic science equipment and training similar to that provided in colleges. Nicole Hahn Rafter describes the well-equipped domestic science department of the women's reformatory in Albion, New York, noting that "from [1912] inmates received instruction in: manufacture and source of food supplies, relative cost, and nutritive values; the care of the kitchen, pantry, and dining room; construction and care of the sinks, stoves (both gas and coal) and refrigerators; table etiquette; the planning and serving of meals; and waitress' duties" (Rafter, "Chastizing the Unchaste," 296).

In their discussion of Progressive Era juvenile reformatories, Steven Schlossman and Stephanie Wallach cite evidence that the domestic science element in juvenile institutions for girls was used primarily as "propaganda" in the service of its reform ideology rather than as a field of knowledge: "To increase public regard for the vocational training programs, reformatory superintendents described them as if they were part of the larger home-economics movement that swept the country in the Progressive Era. Actually, the training rarely went beyond the chores necessary for personal hygiene and cottage upkeep, with a cooking class or two added for good measure" (Schlossman, "Crime of Precocious Sexuality," 77).

See also Barbara Brenzel's *Daughters of the State* for an excellent discussion of the first "family-style" reformatory for girls, established in Lancaster, Massachusetts, in 1856.

38. Cohen, *Visions of Social Control*, 32–33. Michael Ignatieff notes the insistent nature of humanistic prison reform meant to be persuasive to the objects of reform: "The persistent ideal of prison reform was a kind of punishment at once so humane and so just that it would convince the offender of the moral legitimacy of the law and its custodians. The penitentiary was designed to embody this reconciliation of the imperatives of discipline with the imperatives of humanity" (Ignatieff, "State, Civil Society, and Total Institutions," 87–88).

39. The female inmates of the Western House of Refuge (Albion, New York) were minor public-order offenders, but it was permitted (by the "commitment law") to keep inmates for five years. After an 1899 amendment the length of incarceration was lowered to three years (Rafter, "Chastizing the Unchaste," 290).

See Hobson for a discussion of W. I. Thomas's *The Unadjusted Girl* (1923), a book about female juvenile delinquency as seen through the lens of the Roaring Twenties (Hobson, *Uneasy Virtue*, 184–189). See also Schlossman and Wallach for a discussion of sexual discrimination in juvenile delinquency theory in the Progressive Era. Chapter 8 of Rothman's *Conscience and Convenience* offers a discussion of the failures of reform ideology in juvenile institutions in the Progressive Era (Rothman, *Conscience and Convenience,* 261–289).

40. Freedman, *Their Sister's Keepers,* 84–85. See Brenzel for a detailed discussion of stubbornness as a "catchall" complaint used to incarcerate girls with behavioral problems (Brenzel, *Daughters of the State,* 123–128). "Stubbornness" often masked the real complaints against the girls which might be wantonness, lewdness, disobedience, or "in need of a home." See also Ruth M. Alexander's " 'The Only Thing I Wanted Was Freedom': Wayward Girls in New York, 1900–1930."

41. Wilson, *Fifty Years' Work,* 88–89.

42. Freedman describes the two primary aims of female prison reform as practiced by Hodder and Davis: "First, [Hodder and Davis] attempted to transcend the physical limitations of women's prisons by emphasizing the cottage system, parole, outdoor work, and recreation. Secondly, they pressed against the less-tangible boundaries of domesticity by expanding training to include academic and industrial classes and non-traditional women's work" (Freedman, *Their Sister's Keepers,* 131). See Freedman for an extended discussion of Davis and Hodder, as well as other female prison reform leaders.

There remains a women's prison in Bedford Hills, New York, today; it is the only maximum-security prison for women in the state. A recent *New York Times Magazine* article by Jean Harris offers an insider's view of the Parenting Center at Bedford Hills where child-care and parenting classes are taught to pregnant inmates. Harris notes that only New York State allows mothers and infants to stay together in the prison (until the child turns one year old; if the mother will be paroled within 18 months, the child can stay in the prison until the mother leaves). Harris laments the as-yet pervasive penology that requires the separation of mother and infant in prison: "Bedford sets an important example, but in the other 49 states the impulse to punish the mother takes precedence over the good that can be done both mother and infant if they can be together" (Harris, "Babies of Bedford," 26). It is to her credit that Kate Waller Barrett, among others, took the conventional belief in "motherhood as a means to regeneration" (Barrett's phrase) and applied it to those women and girls who, by their actions, were considered by most to be unfit mothers. Using a rather awkward metaphor to describe children born in prison, Barrett defends the maternity home from its potential detractors: "Next to an incubator-hatched chicken, I think an institution-reared child seems most abnormal, and deserves the sympathy of those who know what it is to have a home" (Barrett, *Fourteen Years' Work,* 56).

43. Freedman, *Their Sister's Keepers,* 133.

44. Admission into the Magdalen charity, by contrast, was offered only to the "cream," to use Andrew's word, of the prostitutes. As I mention in chapter 1, the admission policies were strict and rigorous: "Each applicant for admission had to face an examination by a board of governors who questioned and scrutinized her in an attempt to discover how deep and genuine her contrition was. This was an important process—it was essential to distin-

guish those women who were truly penitent from those who only wanted a temporary vacation from all labor" (Andrew, *Philanthropy and Police*, 124–125).

It is important to note that the Crittenton Mission also desired the "best" of the fallen to help promote and sustain their charitable enterprise that required philanthropic support from a generally disapproving society simply in order to survive. A telling example of the mission's conservative policies even in the face of great social need was the conflict in the late nineteenth century between a Crittenton Mission in Kansas City and an association of Free Methodists that sought to open a rescue home in the same area. Both sides agreed that two such institutions would be in competition with each other for funds and community support, so they agreed to unite their forces. This idea proved difficult to enact, as "Mother" Lee (a Free Methodist rescue worker) describes in *Mother Lee's Experience in Fifteen Years' in Rescue Work,* for doctrinal as well as ideological differences between the two groups: the Free Methodists felt that the Crittenton Mission was not strict enough in enforcing particular religious principles, and the Crittenton association disagreed with the others in their admission policies. The conflict was resolved by the superintendence of the home by the Methodists with the agreed provisos—mandated by the Florence Crittenton Mission—that the home would remain part of their organization (with the Crittenton name) and that entrance could never be denied any white girl, whereas permission for black girls had to be obtained from the Mission's president (Lee, *Mother Lee's Experience,* 103). In fact, while president of NFCM, Robert Barrett claimed that "the real field of work of protecting and claiming unfortunate women and girls lies with the white race" (quoted in Kunzel, *Fallen Women, Problem Girls,* 71).

Similarly, "Mother Benedict's" break with the WCTU's sponsored rescue home ("Benedict House") in 1886 was a result, she states, of the WCTU's greed for the $5,000 set aside for the Benedict House by the Iowa legislature. However, the Union again reported the cause of the separation as the result of a difference of opinion over admission policies. Benedict wanted to minister to any repentant, fallen girl, while the WCTU made clear in a letter to its members that they could not support such standards for many reasons, among them, "Mrs. Benedict desires to have the doors of the Home open to all classes of women who have strayed from the paths of virtue, viz: abandoned women whose undisciplined lives and drinking habits make voluntary subjection to the discipline of the Home almost impossible, they really needing mild prison discipline, which we are not authorized to enforce" (Benedict, *Woman's Work for Woman,* 167).

For a discussion of domesticity, social work and the WCTU, see Barbara Leslie Epstein, *The Politics of Domesticity: Women, Evangelism, and Temperance in Nineteenth-Century America.*

45. Stowe's Katy Scudder, when a girl, could perform feats of physical as well as domestic strength—each seeming to take the same degree of courage and skill, and all without harming her status as a lady: "Katy could harness a chaise, or row a boat; she could saddle and ride any horse in the neighborhood; she could cut any garment that ever was seen or thought of, make cake, jelly, and wine, from her earliest years, in most precocious style;—all without seeming to derange a sort of trim, well-kept air of ladyhood that sat jauntily on her" (Stowe, *Minister's Wooing,* 3–4).

46. Mahood, *Magdalenes,* 84.

47. In her discussion of the conflict over maternity work that arose between the female social workers and the Evangelical reformers (after 1915), Regina Kunzel notes that the social workers disagreed with the belief in domestic redemption for many practical reasons: many "fallen" girls fell while working as domestics, the work could not hold the interest of the girls, the work was too demanding for young women with small children. Social workers also disagreed with the central tenet of the NFCM—that mother and child should stay together in practically every instance. Caseworkers wanted to advise each girl on a case to case basis, but generally advocating, Kunzel argues, adoption for the infant (Kunzel, "Professionalization of Benevolence," 34).

48. Evangelical reformers of the National Florence Crittenton Mission were at odds with social workers over the question of what to do with the illegitimate child each inmate of the home produced. The National Florence Crittenton Mission, as we have seen, strenuously believed in the importance of keeping mother and child together, whereas social workers advocated placing the children in adoptive families, or in some cases (for "feeble-minded" women), sterilization, as a means to prevent future children. This difference of opinion indicates one ideological split between the two groups: "Whereas evangelical women's belief in the redemptive power of motherhood led them to endorse the potentially radical notion of a fatherless family, social workers informed more by an ideology of family and motivated by a concern about 'family breakdown' tended to see unmarried mothers as 'mothers in name only,' unfit to raise their own children" (Kunzel, *Fallen Women, Problem Girls,* 130). Kunzel notes that although the National Florence Crittenton Mission maintained its policy of keeping mother and child together, they also reluctantly began to place children in adoptive homes when the mothers requested it (Kunzel, *Fallen Women, Problem Girls,* 89).

49. Philips, "Just Measure of Crime," 61.

50. Freedman, *Their Sister's Keepers,* 198, n35.

51. Elsewhere Barrett seems to equivocate on this issue (see note 27 above).

52. Jerusha Abbott, the foundling heroine of Jean Webster's novel *Daddy-Long-Legs* (1912), abhors blue gingham for the memories it arouses of her childhood in the John Grier Home (Webster, *Daddy-Long-Legs,* 24). I return to *Daddy-Long-Legs* in the afterword.

53. In this way the rescue home resembles a hospital where the caretakers—nurses—are identified and "crowned" by their white caps. My thanks to Claudia Nelson for this observation.

Barrett earned her medical degree from the Medical College of Georgia in 1892. Although she was never a practicing physician, her knowledge of medicine and status as a doctor "legitimized" her work with the fallen.

54. The visions of many female reformers—and therefore the practices of their institutions—had to be altered from this belief in the redemptive family-atmosphere to the acceptance of old-style punishment. Freedman describes the "failure" of the new penology in women's prisons: "Despite the founders' self-conscious differentiation of women's prisons from other nineteenth-century institutions, the feminine experiments eventually resembled traditional prisons in many respects. Like other efforts to humanize institutional care, such as the 'soft-line' in juvenile reformatories or 'moral therapy' in insane asylums, women's prisons increasingly relied on traditional methods of discipline. . . . In both skill training and

character building the tension between domesticity and discipline pervaded the internal life of the women's prisons" (Freedman, *Their Sister's Keepers,* 90).

Afterword

1. Shakespeare, *Hamlet* (II, ii, 399), note on 476. In a similar story found in the German folktale "The Girl Without Hands," the daughter's sacrifice allows for her greater redemption by God symbolized in the healing of her mutilated body and the reward of an aristocratic marriage. The father in this tale, who is greedy for money rather than glory, agrees to give the devil what is standing behind his mill in return for riches. It is the daughter, of course. She has three years, not the three months given to Jeptha's daughter, to wait for the enactment of the promise. When the devil returns for his prize, he is thwarted again and again by the daughter's purity (she bathes her hands with her tears) until he finally orders the father to chop off her hands so that he can take her away. This daughter answers, as Jeptha's daughter had, "Do what you will with me. I am your child" (*Grimms' Tales for Young and Old,* 114). Although the dutiful daughter's hands are sacrificed, she is able to wash the stumps clean with her tears so that the devil has no power over her and gives up the struggle. The daughter then leaves her father's house to wander in poverty and neglect. The folktale, unlike the ballad, however, has a happy ending: a king meets the daughter and is moved by her piety (she is watched by an angel) and her beauty. He marries her and has silver hands made for her. Of course, true happiness is not finally achieved by the new family until further suffering is endured: the king goes off to war leaving the daughter unprotected, and the devil returns. He forges letters to the king telling him that his newborn child is a changeling and to the queen mother informing her that the daughter and the baby must be killed. These orders are ostensibly carried out, but the daughter is sent from the kingdom with the child on her back to hide somewhere in the world. When the king returns he wanders for many years, taking neither food nor drink, searching for his wife and child. When he finally finds them, he discovers that God had allowed new hands to grow from her stumps, and that his son, Sorrowful, is seven years old. The family rejoices and celebrates their reunion with another wedding. Similarly, in Marie le Prince de Beaumont's version of "Beauty and the Beast," Beauty willingly sacrifices herself to the Beast in exchange for the rose that her father had picked. The ending of her story, too—a companionate marriage—is the result of this "fortuitous" bargain.

2. Shakespeare, *Hamlet* (III, i), 283.

3. Webster, *Daddy-Long-Legs,* 1. All further references to this edition are made parenthetically in the text.

4. Appropriately enough, *Dear Enemy* (1915), the sequel to *Daddy-Long-Legs,* is the story of the reformation of the John Grier Home into a model institution that uses the cottage system. In contrast to the rescue home, the blue gingham clothing, and "orphan-asylum attitude toward life"—"soul-crushing unreasoning obedience"—are done away with in the course of the novel.

5. Clark, "Fairy Godmothers," 172.

6. Gilligan et al., *Making Connections,* 25, 19.

Bibliography

Abell, Mrs. L. G. *Woman in Her Various Relations: Containing Practical Rules for American Females*. New York, 1851.

Acton, William. *Prostitution*. 1857. Macgibbon and Kee, 1968.

Alcott, Louisa May. *Little Women*. 1868–69. New York: Penguin, 1989.

Alcott, William A. *Letters to a Sister; or, Woman's Mission*. Buffalo, 1850.

Aldrich, Thomas Bailey. *The Story of a Bad Boy*. 1870. New York: Garland, 1976.

Alexander, Ruth M. " 'The Only Thing I Wanted Was Freedom': Wayward Girls in New York, 1900–1930." In *Small Worlds: Children and Adolescents in America, 1850–1950*, ed. Elliott West and Paula Petrik, 275–295. Lawrence: University Press of Kansas, 1992.

Alger, Horatio, Jr. *Ragged Dick and Struggling Upward*. 1868. New York: Penguin, 1985.

[Allen, Charles]. *The Polite Lady*. London, 1760.

[Allestree, Richard]. *The Whole Duty of Man*. London, 1659.

——. *The Ladies Calling*. Oxford, 1673.

Alpers, Svetlana. *The Art of Describing: Dutch Art in the Seventeenth Century*. Chicago: University of Chicago Press, 1983.

Altman, Janet Gurkin. *Epistolarity: Approaches to a Form*. Columbus: Ohio State University Press, 1983.

——. "Political Ideology in the Letter Manual (France, England, New England)." *Studies in Eighteenth-Century Culture* 18 (1988): 105–122.

Anderson, Amanda. *Tainted Souls and Painted Faces: The Rhetoric of Fallenness in Victorian Culture*. Ithaca: Cornell University Press, 1993.

Andrew, Donna T. *Philanthropy and Police: London Charity in the Eighteenth Century*. Princeton: Princeton University Press, 1989.

Ape-Gentle-Woman, or The Character of an Exchange-Wench. London, 1675.

Armstrong, Frances. " 'Here Little, and Hereafter Bliss': *Little Women* and the Deferral of Greatness." *American Literature* 64 (1992): 453–474.

Armstrong, Nancy. *Desire and Domestic Fiction: A Political History of the Novel*. Oxford: Oxford University Press, 1987.

——. "The rise of the domestic woman." In *The Ideology of Conduct*, ed. Nancy Armstrong and Leonard Tennenhouse, 96–141. London: Methuen, 1987.

Armstrong, Nancy, and Leonard Tennenhouse. "The literature of conduct, the conduct of literature, and the politics of desire." In *The Ideology of Conduct*, ed. Nancy Armstrong and Leonard Tennenhouse, 1–24. London: Methuen, 1987.

Auerbach, Nina. "Feeling as One Ought About Fanny Price." In *Jane Austen's* Mansfield Park, ed. Harold Bloom, 103–116. New York: Chelsea House, 1987.

——. *Private Theatricals: The Lives of the Victorians*. Cambridge: Harvard University Press, 1990.

——. *Romantic Imprisonment: Women and Other Glorified Outcasts*. New York: Columbia University Press, 1986.

——. *Woman and the Demon: The Life of A Victorian Myth*. Cambridge: Harvard University Press, 1982.

Austen, Jane. *Mansfield Park*. 1814. Penguin Classics, 1988.

Avery, Gillian. "Children's Books and Social History." In *Research About Nineteenth-Century Children and Books*, ed. Selma K. Richardson, 23–40. University of Illinois Graduate School of Library Science no. 17, 1980.

——. *Childhood's Pattern: A Study of the Heroes and Heroines of Children's Fiction, 1770–1950*. Leicester: Hodder and Stoughton, 1975.

Banfield, Ann. "The Influence of Place: Jane Austen and the Novel of Social Consciousness." In *Jane Austen in a Social Context*, ed. David Monaghan, 128–48. Totowa, N.J.: Barnes and Noble,1981.

Barbauld, Anna Laetitia. *Hymns in Prose for Children*. 1781. New York: Garland, 1977.

——. *The Correspondence of Samuel Richardson*. 6 vols. 1804. New York: AMS Press, 1966.

Barreca, Regina, ed. *Last Laughs: Perspectives on Women and Comedy*. Studies in Gender and Culture, vol 2. New York: Gordon and Breach, 1988.

Barrett, Kate Waller. *Some Practical Suggestions on the Conduct of a Rescue Home*. 1903. New York: Arno, 1974.

——. *Fourteen Years' Work With "Erring" Girls*. Washington, D.C., 1897.

Barrie, J. M. *Peter Pan*. 1911. New York: Puffin, 1986.

Baym, Nina. *Woman's Fiction: A Guide to Novels By and About Women in America, 1820–1870*. Ithaca: Cornell University Press, 1978.

Beecher, Catharine E. *A Treatise on Domestic Economy*. 1841. New York: Source Book Press, 1970.

Beecher, Catharine E., and Harriet Beecher Stowe. *The American Woman's Home*. 1869. Hartford: Stowe-Day Foundation, 1985.

Bell, Ian A. *Literature and Crime in Augustan England*. New York: Routledge, 1991.

Bender, John. *Imagining the Penitentiary*. Chicago: University of Chicago Press, 1987.

Benedict, Lovina B. *Woman's Work for Woman*. Des Moines: Iowa Printing, 1892.

Blackstone, William. *Commentaries on the Laws of England*. 2 vols. (1765–69). New York: W. E. Dean, 1849.

Blair, William. *Prostitutes Reclaimed and Penitents Protected*. London, 1809.

Blake, Kathleen. *Play, Games, and Sport: The Literary Works of Lewis Carroll*. Ithaca: Cornell University Press, 1974.

Blondel, Madeleine. "A Minor Eighteenth-Century Novel Brought to Light: *The Life and Adventures of a Reformed Magdalen*." *Notes & Queries* 31 (229) (1984): 36–37.

Bonfield, Lloyd. *Marriage Settlements, 1601–1740*. Cambridge: Cambridge University Press, 1983.

Boris, Eileen. "Reconstructing the 'Family': Women, Progressive Reform and the Problem of Social Control." In *Gender, Class, Race, and Reform in the Progressive Era*, ed. Noralee Frankel and Nancy S. Dye, 73–86. Lexington: University of Kentucky Press, 1991.

Boydston, Jeanne. *Home and Work: Housework, Wages, and the Ideology of Labor in the Early Republic*. New York: Oxford University Press, 1990.

Boydston, Jeanne, Mary Kelley, and Anne Margolis. *The Limits of Sisterhood: The Beecher Sisters on Women's Rights and Women's Sphere*. Chapel Hill: University of North Carolina Press, 1988.

[Brandenberg], Aliki. *Manners*. New York: Greenwillow, 1990.

Bratton, J. S. *The Impact of Victorian Children's Fiction*. Totowa, N.J.: Barnes and Noble, 1981.

Brenzel, Barbara M. *Daughters of the State: A Social Portrait of the First Reform School for Girls in North America, 1856–1905*. Cambridge: MIT Press, 1983.

———. "Domestication as Reform: A Study of the Socialization of Wayward Girls, 1856–1905." *Harvard Educational Review* 50 (1980): 196–213.

Brophy, Elizabeth Bergen. *Women's Lives and the Eighteenth-Century English Novel*. Tampa: University of South Florida Press, 1991.

Brown, Gillian. *Domestic Individualism: Imagining Self in Nineteenth-Century America*. Berkeley: University of California Press, 1990.

Brown, Roger Lee. "The Rise and Fall of the Fleet Marriages." In *Marriage and Society: Studies in the Social History of Marriage*, ed. R. B. Outhwaite, 117–136. New York: St. Martin's Press, 1981.

Brunton, Mary. *Discipline*. 1815. London and New York: Pandora, 1986.

———. *Self-Control*. 1810–11. London and New York: Pandora, 1986.

Buehr, Walter. *Home Sweet Home in the Nineteenth Century*. New York: Crowell, 1965.

Burnap, George Washington. *Lectures on the Sphere and Duties of Women, and Other Subjects*. Baltimore, 1841.

Burney, Frances. *Evelina*. 1778. Oxford University Press, 1982.

Butler, Marilyn. "History, Politics, and Religion." In *The Jane Austen Companion*, ed. J. David Grey, 190–208. New York: Macmillan, 1986.

"By-Laws and Regulations of the Magdalen Hospital." London, 1802.

Campbell, Gina. "How to Read Like a Gentleman: Burney's Instructions to Her Critics in *Evelina*." *English Literary History* 57 (1990): 557–584.

Cannon, John. *Aristocratic Century: The Peerage of Eighteenth-Century England*. Cambridge: Cambridge University Press, 1984.

Carroll, John. *Selected Letters of Samuel Richardson*. Oxford: Clarendon Press, 1964.

Carroll, Lewis. *The Annotated Alice*. Ed. Martin Gardner. New York: Meridian, 1960.

———. *The Complete Works of Lewis Carroll*. New York: Vintage, 1976.

Castle, Terry. *Masquerade and Civilization: The Carnivalesque in Eighteenth-Century English Culture and Fiction*. Stanford: Stanford University Press, 1986.

———. "P/B: *Pamela* as Sexual Fiction." *Studies in English Literature* 22 (1982): 469–489.

Chabor, Lois A. "From Moral Man to Godly Man: 'Mr. Locke' and Mr. B in Part 2 of *Pamela*." *Studies in Eighteenth-Century Culture* 18 (1988): 213–216.

Chapone, Hester. *Letters on the Improvement of the Mind*. 2 vols. 1773. 3d. ed. London, 1774.

"Charity as a Portion of the Public Vocation of Women." *The English Woman's Journal* 3 (1859): 193–196.

Child, Lydia Maria. *The Frugal Housewife*. Boston, 1829.

Cixous, Hélène. "The Laugh of the Medusa." In *New French Feminisms*, ed. Elaine Marks and Isabella de Courtivron, 245–264. New York: Schocken Books, 1981.

Clark, Beverly Lyon. "Fairy Godmothers or Wicked Stepmothers? The Uneasy Relationship of Feminist Theory and Children's Criticism." *Children's Literature Association Quarterly* 18 (1993–94): 171–176.

———. "Thirteen Ways of Thumbing Your Nose at Children's Literature." *Lion and the Unicorn* 16 (1992): 240–244.

"*Coelebs in Search of a Wife*." Review. *Edinburgh Review* 14 (1809 supp. July 1930): 663–665.

Cogan, Frances B. *All-American Girl: The Ideal of Real Womanhood in Mid-Nineteenth-Century America*. Athens: University of Georgia Press, 1989.

Cohen, Paula Marantz. "Stabilizing the Family System at Mansfield Park." *English Literary History* 54.3 (1987): 669–693.

Cohen, Sherrill. *The Evolution of Women's Asylums Since 1500: From Refuges for Ex-Prostitutes to Shelters for Battered Women*. Oxford: Oxford University Press, 1992.

Cohen, Stanley. *Visions of Social Control: Crime, Punishment and Classification*. Oxford: Polity, 1985.

Cohen, Stanley, and Andrew Scull, eds. *Social Control and the State*. New York: St. Martin's, 1983.

Colby, Robert A. *Fiction With a Purpose: Major and Minor Nineteenth-Century Novels*. Bloomington: Indiana University Press, 1967.

Colby, Vineta. *Yesterday's Woman*. Princeton: Princeton University Press, 1974.

Conboy, Sheila C. "Fabric and Fabrication in Richardson's *Pamela*." *English Literary History* 54 (1987): 81–96.

Coolidge, Susan [Sarah Chauncey Woolsey]. *What Katy Did*. 1872. New York: Garland, 1976.

Cox, James M. *Mark Twain: The Fate of Humor*. Princeton: Princeton University Press, 1966.

Craik, W. A. *Jane Austen in Her Time*. London: Thomas Nelson, 1969.

Crowley, John W. "*Little Women* and the Boy-Book." *New England Quarterly* 58 (1985): 384–399.

Cutt, Margaret Nancy. *Ministering Angels: A Study of Nineteenth-Century Evangelical Writing for Children*. London: Five Owls Press, 1979.

Darrell, William. *The Gentleman Instructed, In the Conduct of a Virtuous and Happy Life. In Three Parts. Written for the Instruction of a Young Nobleman. To Which is added, A Word to the Ladies, by Way of Supplement to the First Part.* London, 1704.

Davis, Lennard J. *Factual Fictions: The Origins of the English Novel.* New York: Columbia University Press, 1983.

Deleuze, Gilles. "The Schizophrenic and Language: Surface and Depth in Lewis Carroll and Antonin Artaud." In *Textual Strategies: Perspectives in Post-Structuralist Criticism,* ed. Josu V. Harari, 277–295. Ithaca: Cornell University Press, 1979.

Derry, Stephen. "Jane Austen's Reference to Hannah More in 'Catharine.' " *Notes and Queries* 37 (235) (1990): 20.

"Discipline." Review. *Monthly Review* n.s. 78 (Dec. 1815): 397–400.

Dodd, William. *Advice to the Magdalens.* 1776. In *Prostitution Reform,* ed. Randolf Trumbach. New York: Garland, 1985.

———. "Some Account of the Magdalen Hospital." *Gentlemen's Magazine* 29 (June 1759): 279–280.

Dodge, Grace H. *A Bundle of Letters to Busy Girls on Practical Matters.* 1887. Women in America From Colonial Times to the 20th Century. New York: Arno, 1974.

Donovan, Mary Sudman. *A Different Call: Women's Ministries in the Episcopal Church, 1850–1920.* Wilton, Conn.: Morehouse-Barlow, 1986.

Duffy, Joseph M., Jr. "Moral Integrity and Moral Anarchy in *Mansfield Park.*" *English Literary History* 23.1 (1956): 71–91.

Durston, Christopher. *The Family in the English Revolution.* Oxford: Basil Blackwell, 1989.

Du Vall, Nell. *Domestic Technology: A Chronology of Developments.* Boston: Hall, 1988.

Dyhouse, Carol. *Girls Growing Up in Late Victorian and Edwardian England.* London: Routledge and Kegan Paul, 1981.

Earnest, Ernest. *The American Eve in Fact and Fiction, 1775–1914.* Urbana: University of Illinois Press, 1974.

East, Marjorie. *Home Economics: Past, Present, and Future.* Boston: Allyn and Bacon, 1980.

Edgeworth, Maria, and R. L. Edgeworth. *Practical Education.* 2 vols. (1798) New York: Garland, 1974.

Edson, E. M. "The Girls' Friendly Society." *Church Work* 1 (1885–86): 45–48.

Eisenstein, Zillah R. *The Female Body and the Law.* Berkeley: University of California Press, 1988.

Elbert, Sarah. *A Hunger for Home: Louisa May Alcott's Place in American Culture.* New Brunswick: Rutgers University Press, 1987.

Eliot, George. *Middlemarch.* 1871–72. New York: Penguin, 1983.

Epstein, Barbara Leslie. *The Politics of Domesticity: Women, Evangelism and Temperance in Nineteenth-Century America.* Middleton, Conn.: Wesleyan University Press, 1981.

Evans, Hilary. *Harlots, Whores and Hookers: A History of Prostitution.* New York: Taplinger, 1979.

Evans, James E. Introduction to *A Collection of the Moral and Instructive Sentiments* by Samuel Richardson. Delmar, N.Y.: Scholars' Facsimiles & Reprints 357, 1980.

Ezell, Margaret J. M. *The Patriarch's Wife: Literary Evidence and the History of the Family.* Chapel Hill: University of North Carolina Press, 1987.

Farrar, Eliza W. R. *The Young Lady's Friend,* 1836. Women in America From Colonial Times to the 20th Century. New York: Arno, 1974.

"Feminine Humour." *Saturday Review* 32 (15 July 1871): 75–76.

Fergus, Jan S. *Jane Austen and the Didactic Novel.* London: Macmillan, 1983.

——. "Sex and Social Life in Jane Austen's Novels." In *Jane Austen in a Social Context,* ed. David Monaghan, 66–85. Totowa, N.J.: Barnes and Noble, 1981.

Ferguson, Moira. *Subject to Others: British Women Writers and Colonial Slavery, 1670–1834.* New York: Routledge, 1992.

Fetterley, Judith. "*Little Women*: Alcott's Civil War." *Feminist Studies* 5 (1979): 369–383.

——. "The Sanctioned Rebel." In *Critical Essays on* The Adventures of Tom Sawyer, ed. Gary Scharnhorst, 119–129. New York: G. K. Hall, 1993.

Fielding, John. "A Plan for preserving those deserted girls in this Town, who become Prostitutes from Necessity." London, 1758. *Prostitution Reform,* ed. Randolf Trumbach. New York: Garland, 1985.

Fielding, Sarah. *The Governess; or, Little Female Academy.* 1749. New York: Pandora, 1987.

Fleischman, Avrom. *A Reading of* Mansfield Park. Minneapolis: University of Minnesota Press, 1967.

Flint, Kate. *The Victorian Novelist: Social Problems and Social Change.* New York: Croom Helm, 1987.

——. *The Woman Reader, 1837–1914.* Oxford: Clarendon, 1993.

The Florence Crittenton League of Compassion: Story of a Great Philanthropy. N.p., n.d.

Folbre, Nancy. "The Unproductive Housewife: Her Evolution in Nineteenth-Century Economic Thought." *Signs: Journal of Women in Culture and Society* 16 (1991): 463–484.

Fordyce, James. *Sermons to Young Women.* 2 vols. London, 1766.

Foucault, Michel. *Discipline and Punish: The Birth of the Prison,* trans. Alan Sheridan. New York: Vintage, 1979.

Fowler, Marian E. "The Courtesy-book Heroine of *Mansfield Park.*" *University of Toronto Quarterly* 44.1 (1974): 31–46.

Fraiman, Susan. *Unbecoming Women: British Women Writers and the Novel of Development.* New York: Columbia University Press, 1993.

Frankel, Noralee, and Nancy S. Dye, eds. *Gender, Class, Race, and Reform in the Progressive Era.* Lexington: University of Kentucky Press, 1991.

Freedman, Estelle B. *Their Sister's Keepers: Women's Prison Reform in America, 1830–1930.* Ann Arbor: University of Michigan Press, 1981.

Fried, Albert, and Elman, Richard M. *Charles Booth's London.* New York: Pantheon, 1968.

Gaard, Greta. " 'Self-Denial was All the Fashion': Repressing Anger in *Little Women.*" *Papers on Language and Literature* 27 (1991): 3–19.

Gally, Henry. "Some Considerations Upon Clandestine Marriages." 1750. *The Marriage Act of 1753: Four Tracts.* New York: Garland, 1984.

Gay, John. *The Beggar's Opera.* In *The Beggar's Opera and Other Eighteenth Century Plays,* ed. John Hampden, 106–159. New York: Dutton, 1975.

Gentleman's Magazine. 1731–1914. London.

Gilligan, Carol, Nona P. Lyons, and Trudy J. Hanmer. *Making Connections: The Relational Worlds of Adolescent Girls at Emma Willard School.* Cambridge: Harvard University Press, 1990.

Ginzberg, Lori D. *Women and the Work of Benevolence: Morality, Politics, and Class in the Nineteenth-Century United States.* New Haven: Yale University Press, 1990.

Goldstrom, J. M. *The Social Content of Education, 1808–1870: A Study of the Working Class Reader in England and Ireland.* Shannon, Ireland: Irish University Press, 1972.

Goodsell, Willystine. *A History of Marriage and the Family.* 1934. New York: AMS Press, 1974.

Gorham, Deborah. *The Victorian Girl and the Feminine Ideal.* Bloomington: Indiana University Press, 1982.

Gouge, Thomas. *The Surest and Safest Way of Thriving.* London, 1676.

Gray, Donald J. "The Uses of Victorian Laughter." *Victorian Studies* 10 (1966): 147–176.

[Green, Sarah]. *Mental Improvement for a Young Lady, on Her Entrance into the World.* London, 1796.

Greenberg, Janelle. "The Legal Status of the English Woman in Early Eighteenth-Century Common Law and Equity." *Studies in Eighteenth-Century Culture* 4 (1975): 171–181.

Gregory, John. *A Father's Legacy to His Daughters.* 1774. New York: Garland, 1974.

Gribben, Alan. " 'I Did Wish Tom Sawyer Were There': Boy-Book Elements in *Tom Sawyer* and *Huckleberry Finn.*" *One Hundred Years of* Huckleberry Finn: *The Boy, His Book, and American Culture,* ed. Robert Sattelmeyer and J. Donald Crowley, 149–170. Columbia: University of Missouri Press, 1985.

Gwilliam, Tassie. "*Pamela* and the Duplicitous Body of Femininity." *Representations* 34 (1991): 104–133.

Habegger, Alfred. *Gender, Fantasy and Realism in American Literature.* New York: Columbia University Press, 1982.

———. "Nineteenth-Century American Humor: Easygoing Males, Anxious Ladies, and Penelope Lapham." *PMLA* 91 (1976): 884–899.

Halttunen, Karen. "The Domestic Drama of Louisa May Alcott." *Feminist Studies* 10 (1984): 233–254.

Harris, Barbara J. "Power, Profit, and Passion: Mary Tudor, Charles Brandon, and the Arranged Marriage in Early Tudor England." *Feminist Studies* 15 (1989): 59–88.

Harris, Jean. "The Babies of Bedford." *New York Times Magazine,* March 28, 1993.

Harth, Erica. "The Virtue of Love: Lord Hardwicke's Marriage Act." *Cultural Critique* 9 (1988): 123–154.

Haywood, Eliza. *The History of Miss Betsy Thoughtless.* 1751. London and New York: Pandora, 1986.

Head, Richard. *The Miss Display'd.* London, 1675.

Hemlow, Joyce. "Fanny Burney and the Courtesy Books." *PMLA* 65 (1950): 732–761.

Henkle, Roger B. *Comedy and Culture: England 1820–1900.* Princeton: Princeton University Press, 1980.

Hill, Bridget. *Eighteenth-Century Women: An Anthology.* London: Allen and Unwin, 1984.

Hilliard, Raymond F. "*Clarissa* and Ritual Cannibalism." *PMLA* 105 (1990): 1083–1097.

Hobson, Barbara Meil. *Uneasy Virtue: The Politics of Prostitution and the American Reform Tradition*. New York: Basic Books, 1987.

Holcombe, Lee. *Wives and Property: Reform of the Married Women's Property Law in Nineteenth-Century England*. Toronto: University of Toronto Press, 1983.

Hollis, Patricia. *The Pauper Press: A Study in Working-Class Radicalism of the 1830s*. Oxford: Oxford University Press, 1970.

Holmes, Oliver Wendell, Jr. *The Common Law*. 1881. Boston: Little, Brown, 1923.

Hopkins, Mary Alden. *Hannah More and Her Circle*. London: Longmans, 1974.

Hornbeak, Katherine. "The Complete Letter Writer in English, 1568–1800." *Smith College Studies in Modern Languages* 15.3–4 (1934): 1–148.

——. "Richardson's *Familiar Letters* and the Domestic Conduct Books: Richardson's Aesop." *Smith College Studies in Modern Languages* 19 (1939): 1–50.

Horne, Melville. *A Sermon Preached Before the Governors of the London Female Penitentiary*. 2d. ed. London, 1811.

Horwitz, Morton J. "The History of the Public/Private Distinction." *University of Pennsylvania Law Review* 130 (1982): 1423–1428.

Huang, Mei. *Transforming the Cinderella Dream: From Frances Burney to Charlotte Brontë*. New Brunswick: Rutgers University Press, 1990.

Hudson, Glenda A. *Sibling Love and Incest in Jane Austen's Fiction*. New York: St. Martin's, 1992.

Hughes, Diane Owen. "From Brideprice to Dowry in Medieval Europe." In *The Marriage Bargain: Women and Dowries in European History*, ed. Marion A. Kaplan. *Women and History* 10 (1985): 13–58.

Hughes, Linda A. " 'You Have To Do It With Style:' Girls' Games and Girls' Gaming." In *Feminist Theory and the Study of Folklore*, ed. Susan Tower Hollis, Linda Pershing, and M. Jane Young, 130–148. Urbana: University of Illinois Press, 1993.

Huizinga, Johan. *Homo Ludens: A Study of the Play-Element in Culture*. 1944. London: Routledge and Kegan Paul, 1980.

Hunter, J. Paul. " 'The Young, the Ignorant, and the Idle': Some Notes on Readers and the Beginnings of the English Novel." In *Anticipations of the Enlightenment in England, France, and Germany*, ed. Alan Charles Kors and Paul J. Korshin, 259–282. Philadelphia: University of Pennsylvania Press, 1987.

Ignatieff, Michael. "State, Civil Society and Total Institutions: A Critique of Recent Social Histories of Punishment." In *Social Control and the State*, ed. Stanley Cohen and Andrew Scull, 75–105. New York: St. Martin's, 1983.

Inchbald, Elizabeth. *A Simple Story*. 1791. Oxford: Oxford University Press, 1988.

Jefferson, Susanna. *A Bargain for Bachelors, or: the Best Wife in the World for a Penny*. 1675.

Jones, Ann H. *Ideas and Innovations: Best Sellers of Jane Austen's Age*. New York: Fordham University Press, 1967.

Jones, M. G. *Hannah More*. Cambridge: Cambridge University Press, 1952.

Jordan, W. K. *Philanthropy in England, 1480–1660*. London: Allen and Unwin, 1959.

——. *The Charities of London, 1480–1660*. London: Allen and Unwin, 1960.

Kauffman, Linda S. *Discourses of Desire: Gender, Genre, and Epistolary Fictions.* Ithaca: Cornell University Press, 1986.

Keith, Sarah. "Gruesome Examples for Children: The Real Purpose of Mr. Fairchild." *Notes and Queries* 12 (1965): 184–85.

Kelly, Gary. "Jane Austen and the English Novel of the 1790s." In *Fetter'd or Free? British Women Novelists, 1670–1815,* ed. Mary Anne Schofield and Cecilia Macheski, 285–306. Athens: Ohio University Press, 1986.

Kent, Countess of. *A Choice Manuall, Rare and Select Secrets in Physick and Chyrurgery.* 2d. ed. London, 1653.

Kettle, Ann. " 'My Wife Shall Have It': Marriage and Property in the Wills and Testaments of Later Mediaeval England." In *Marriage and Property,* ed. Elizabeth M. Craik, 89–103. Aberdeen: Aberdeen University Press, 1984.

Keyser, Elizabeth Lennox. "Alcott's Portraits of the Artist as Little Woman." *International Journal of Women's Studies* 5 (1982): 435–444.

Kibbie, Ann Louise. "Sentimental Properties: *Pamela* and Memoirs of a Woman of Pleasure." *English Literary History* 58 (1991): 561–577.

Kiefer, Monica. *American Children Through Their Books: 1700–1835.* Philadelphia: University of Pennsylvania Press, 1948.

Kincaid, James R. *Child-Loving: The Erotic Child and Victorian Culture.* New York: Routledge, 1992.

Kirkham, Margaret. "Feminist Irony and the Priceless Heroine of *Mansfield Park.*" In *Jane Austen's* Mansfield Park, ed. Harold Bloom, 117–133. New York: Chelsea House, 1987.

———. *Jane Austen: Feminism and Fiction.* Totowa, N.J.: Barnes and Noble, 1983.

Koppel, Gene. *The Religious Dimension of Jane Austen's Novels.* Ann Arbor: UMI Research Press, 1988.

Kornfeld, Eve, and Susan Jackson. "The Female Bildungsroman in Nineteenth-Century America: Parameters of a Vision." *Journal of American Culture* 10 (1987): 69–75.

Kowaleski-Wallace, Beth. "Hannah and Her Sister: Women and Evangelicalism in Early Nineteenth Century England." *Nineteenth Century Contexts* 12 (Fall 1988): 29–51.

———. *Their Father's Daughters: Hannah More, Maria Edgeworth and Patriarchal Complicity.* New York: Oxford University Press, 1991.

Kreissman, Bernard. *Pamela-Shamela. University of Nebraska Studies* 22 (1960): 1–98.

Kunzel, Regina G. *Fallen Women, Problem Girls: Unmarried Mothers and the Professionalization of Social Work, 1890–1945.* New Haven: Yale University Press, 1993.

———. "The Professionalization of Benevolence: Evangelicals and Social Workers in the Florence Crittenton Homes, 1915–1945." *Journal of Social History* 22 (1988): 21–43.

Laqueur, Thomas Walter. *Religion and Respectability: Sunday Schools and Working-Class Culture, 1780–1850.* New Haven: Yale University Press, 1976.

Larcom, Lucy. *A New England Girlhood.* 1889. Boston: Northeastern University Press, 1986.

Larned, Augusta. *Talks With Girls.* New York, 1874.

Lee, Martha A. *Mother Lee's Experience in Fifteen Years' Rescue Work.* Omaha, 1906.

"A Letter to a Young Lady on Her Marriage." *Gentleman's Magazine* 15 (September 1745): 473–476.

Levy, Anita. *Other Women: The Writing of Class, Race, and Gender, 1832–1898.* Princeton: Princeton University Press, 1991.

Lewis, Dio. *Our Girls.* 1871. Women in America From Colonial Times to the 20th Century. New York: Arno, 1974.

Lewis, Jane. *Women and Social Action in Victorian and Edwardian England.* Stanford: Stanford University Press, 1991.

Little, Judy. *Comedy and the Woman Writer: Woolf, Spark and Feminism.* Lincoln: University of Nebraska Press, 1983.

Litvak, Joseph. *Caught in the Act: Theatricality in the Nineteenth-Century English Novel.* Berkeley: University of California Press, 1992.

——. "The Infection of Acting, Theatricals, and Theatricality in *Mansfield Park.*" *English Literary History* 53 (1986): 331–355.

Lystad, Mary. *From Dr. Mather to Dr. Seuss: 200 Years of American Books for Children.* Cambridge, Mass: Schenkman, 1980.

Macaulay, Catharine. *Letters on Education.* 1790. New York: Garland, 1974.

MacLeod, Anne Scott. *American Childhood: Essays on Children's Literature of the Nineteenth and Twentieth Centuries.* Athens: University of Georgia Press, 1994.

——. *A Moral Tale: Children's Fiction and American Culture, 1820–1860.* Hamden, Conn.: Archon, 1975.

——. "Children's Literature and American Literature and American Culture 1820–1860." In *Society and Children's Literature,* ed. James H. Fraser, 13–31. New York: David Godine in association with the American Library Association, 1978.

Mahood, Linda. *The Magdalenes: Prostitution in the Nineteenth Century.* New York: Routledge, 1990.

Malvern, Marjorie M. *Venus in Sackcloth: The Magdalen's Origins and Metamorphoses.* Carbondale: South Illinois University Press, 1975.

Mandler, Peter, ed. *The Uses of Charity: The Poor on Relief in the Nineteenth-Century Metropolis.* Philadelphia: University of Pennsylvania Press, 1990.

Marcus, Steven. *The Other Victorians.* New York: Basic Books, 1966.

Marks, Patricia. *Bicycles, Bangs, and Bloomers: The New Woman in the Popular Press.* Lexington: University Press of Kentucky, 1990.

Marks, Sylvia Kasey. *Sir Charles Grandison: The Compleat Conduct Book.* Lewisburg, Pa.: Bucknell University Press, 1986.

Marshall, David. "True Acting and the Language of Real Feeling: *Mansfield Park.*" *Yale Journal of Criticism* 3 (1989): 87–106.

Martin, Robert Bernard. *The Triumph of Wit: A Study of Victorian Comic Theory.* Oxford: Clarendon, 1974.

Mayhew, Henry. *London Labour and the London Poor.* vol. 4. 1861–62. London: Cass, 1967.

McGhee, Paul E. "The Role of Laughter and Humor in Growing Up Female." In *Becoming Female: Perspectives on Development,* ed. Claire B. Kopp, 183–206. New York: Plenum, 1979.

McKeon, Michael. *The Origins of the English Novel, 1600–1740.* Baltimore: Johns Hopkins University Press, 1987.

McKerrow, Mary. "Joanna Baillie and Mary Brunton: Women of the Manse." *Living By the Pen: Early British Women Writers*, ed. Dale Spender, 160–174. New York: Teachers College Press, 1992.

Meade, L. T. *A World of Girls*. 1886. Chicago: M. A. Donohue, n.d.

The Metropolitan Charities. London, 1844.

Meyersohn, Marylea. "What Fanny Knew: A Quiet Auditor of the Whole." In *Jane Austen: New Perspectives. Women and Literature* 3. ed. Janet Todd. New York: Holmes and Meier, 1983: 224–230.

Michie, Elsie B. *Outside the Pale: Cultural Exclusion, Gender Difference, and the Victorian Woman Writer*. Ithaca: Cornell University Press, 1993.

Michie, Helena. *The Flesh Made Word: Female Figures and Women's Bodies*. Oxford: Oxford University Press, 1987.

Miller, D. A. *Narrative and Its Discontents: Problems of Closure in the Traditional Novel*. Princeton: Princeton University Press, 1981.

Mingay, G. E. *English Landed Society in the Eighteenth Century*. London: Routledge and Kegan Paul, 1963.

Mitchell, Sally. *The Fallen Angel: Chastity, Class and Women's Reading, 1835–1880*. Bowling Green: Bowling Green University Popular Press, 1981.

Monaghan, David. "Jane Austen and the Position of Women." In *Jane Austen in a Social Context*, ed. David Monaghan, 105–121. Totowa, N.J.: Barnes and Noble, 1981.

——. "*Mansfield Park* and Evangelicalism: A Reassessment." *Nineteenth-Century Fiction* 33 (1978–79): 215–230.

Mooneyham, Laura G. *Romance, Language and Education in Jane Austen's Novels*. New York: Macmillan, 1988.

More, Hannah. *Coelebs in Search of a Wife*. 2 vols. London: 1809.

——. *Strictures on the Modern System of Female Education*. 2 vols. 1799. New York: Garland, 1974.

——. *Works of Hannah More*. 2 vols. New York: Harper, 1840.

Mort, Frank. *Dangerous Sexualities: Medico-moral Politics in England Since 1830*. London: Routledge and Kegan Paul, 1987.

Mullan, John. *Sentiment and Sociability: The Language of Feeling in the Eighteenth Century*. Oxford: Clarendon, 1988.

Myers, Mitzi. "Hannah More's Tracts for the Times: Social Fiction and Female Ideology." In *Fetter'd or Free? British Women Novelists, 1670–1815*, ed. Mary Anne Schofield and Cecilia Macheski, 264–284. Athens: Ohio University Press, 1986.

——. "Impeccable Governesses, Rational Dames and Moral Mothers: Mary Wollstonecraft and the Female Tradition in Georgian Children's Books." *Children's Literature* 14 (1986): 31–59.

——. "Reform or Ruin: 'A Revolution in Female Manners.'" *Studies in Eighteenth-Century Culture* 11 (1982): 199–216.

——. "Romancing the Moral Tale: Maria Edgeworth and the Problematics of Pedagogy." In *Romanticism and Children's Literature in Nineteenth-Century England*, ed. James Holt McGavran, Jr., 96–128. Athens: University of Georgia Press, 1991.

——. " 'A Taste for Truths and Realities': Early Advice to Mothers on Books for Girls." *Children's Literature Association Quarterly* 12.3 (1987): 118–124.

Nardin, Jane. "Jane Austen and the Problem of Leisure." In *Jane Austen in a Social Context*, ed. David Monaghan, 122–141. Totowa, N.J.: Barnes and Noble, 1981.

Nash, Stanley. "Prostitution and Charity: The Magdalen Hospital, A Case Study." *Journal of Social History* 17 (1984): 617–628.

Nelson, Claudia. *Boys Will Be Girls: The Feminine Ethic and British Children's Fiction, 1857–1917*. New Brunswick: Rutgers University Press, 1991.

Nelson, Claudia, and Lynne Vallone. *The Girls' Own: Cultural Histories of the Anglo-American Girl, 1830–1915*. Athens: University of Georgia Press, 1994.

Nicholson, William. *How To Be A Lady*. London, c. 1850.

Nickel, Terri. "*Pamela* as Fetish: Masculine Anxiety in Henry Fielding's *Shamela* and James Parry's *The True Anti-Pamela*." *Studies in Eighteenth-Century Culture* 22 (1992): 37–49.

Okin, Susan Miller. "Patriarchy and Married Women's Property in England: Questions on Some Current Views." *Eighteenth-Century Studies* 17 (1983–4): 121–138.

Pamela Censured. London, 1741.

"*The Paths of Virtue Delineated*." Review. *Critical Review* 1 (May 1756): 315–336.

"*The Paths of Virtue Delineated*." Review. *Monthly Review* 14 (1756): 581–582.

Peacham, Henry. *The Compleat Gentleman: Fashioning Him Absolute in the most Necessary and Commandable Qualities Concerning Mind or Body, that May be Required in a Person of Honor*. London, 1622.

Pelling, Edward. *A Practical Discourse Upon Charity*. London, 1693.

Pennington, Sarah. *An Unfortunate Mother's Advice to her Absent Daughters*. London, 1761.

Perkin, Joan. *Women and Marriage in Nineteenth-Century England*. Chicago: Lyceum, 1989.

Peterson, M. Jeanne. *Family, Love, and Work in the Lives of Victorian Gentlewomen*. Bloomington: Indiana University Press, 1989.

Phelps, Elizabeth Stuart [Ward]. *Gypsy Breynton*. 1866. New York: Dodd, Mead, 1894.

——. *Gypsy Breynton*. 1866. New York: Dodd, Mead, 1895.

Philips, David. " 'A Just Measure of Crime, Authority, Hunters and Blue Locusts': The 'Revisionist' Social History of Crime in Britain, 1780–1850." In *Social Control and the State*, ed. Stanley Cohen and Andrew Scull, 50–74. New York: St. Martin's, 1983.

Pickering, Samuel, Jr. "The 'Ambiguous Circumstances of a *Pamela*': Early Children's Books and the Attitude Towards *Pamela*." *Journal of Narrative Technique* 14 (1984): 153–171.

Poovey, Mary. *The Proper Lady and the Woman Writer: Ideology as Style in the Works of Mary Wollstonecraft, Mary Shelley, and Jane Austen*. Chicago: University of Chicago Press, 1984.

Povey, Charles. *The Virgin in Eden: or, The State of Innocency*. London, 1741.

Powell, Chilton Lapham. *English Domestic Relations, 1487–1653*. New York: Columbia University Press, 1917.

Prochaska, F. K. *Women and Philanthropy in Nineteenth-Century England*. Oxford: Clarendon, 1980.

Quarterly Review 83 (June and September 1848): 359–376.

Rafter, Nicole Hahn. "Chastizing the Unchaste: Social Control Functions of a Woman's Reformatory, 1894–1931." In *Social Control and the State*, ed. Stanley Cohen and Andrew Scull, 288–311. New York: St. Martin's, 1983.

Ray, Joan Klingel. "Jane Austen's Case Study of Child Abuse: Fanny Price." *Persuasions: Journal of the Jane Austen Society of America* 13 (December 1991): 16–26.

Redford, Bruce. *The Converse of the Pen: Acts of Intimacy in the Eighteenth-Century Familiar Letter.* Chicago: University of Chicago Press, 1986.

Reeve, Clara. *Plans of Education: With Remarks on the Systems of Other Writers.* 1792. New York: Garland, 1974.

Remedies for The Wrongs of Women. 3d. ed. London, 1844.

Report of the Provisional Committee of the Guardian Society. London, 1816.

Report of the Provisional Committee of the Guardian Society. London, 1817.

Reynolds, Kimberley. *Girls Only? Gender and Popular Children's Fiction in Britain, 1880–1910.* Philadelphia: Temple University Press, 1990.

Richardson, Samuel. *A Collection of the Moral and Instructive Sentiments.* Delmar, N.Y.: Scholars' Facsimiles & Reprints 357, 1980.

——. *The History of Pamela, or, Virtue Rewarded.* Abridged from the works of Samuel Richardson, esq. Worcester, 1794.

——. *Pamela; or, Virtue Rewarded.* vols. 1–2. 1740. Norton, 1958.

——. *Pamela; or, Virtue Rewarded.* vols. 3–4. 1741. Shakespeare Head Press, 1929.

——. *Sir Charles Grandison.* 1753–54. Oxford: Oxford University Press, 1986.

Richetti, John J. "Voice and Gender in Eighteenth-Century Fiction: Haywood to Burney." *Studies in the Novel* 19 (1987): 263–272.

Roberts, Warren. *Jane Austen and the French Revolution.* New York: St. Martin's, 1979.

Robinson, Forrest G. "Social Play and Bad Faith in *The Adventures of Tom Sawyer.*" *Nineteenth-Century Fiction* 39 (1984): 1–24.

Rose, Jacqueline. *The Case of Peter Pan or, The Impossibility of Children's Fiction.* London: Macmillan, 1984.

Rosman, Doreen M. *Evangelicals and Culture.* London: Croom Helm, 1984.

Rothman, David J. *Conscience and Convenience: The Asylum and Its Alternatives in Progressive America.* Boston: Little, Brown, 1980.

——. *The Discovery of the Asylum: Social Order and Disorder in the New Republic.* Boston: Little, Brown, 1971.

Rowbotham, Judith. *Good Girls Make Good Wives: Guidance for Girls in Victorian Fiction.* Oxford: Basil Blackwell, 1989.

Schaberg, Jane. "How Mary Magdalene Became a Whore." *Bible Review* 8 (1992): 31–52.

Scheuermann, Mona. *Her Bread To Earn: Women, Money, and Society from Defoe to Austen.* Lexington: University Press of Kentucky, 1993.

Schlossman, Steven, and Stephanie Wallach. "The Crime of Precocious Sexuality: Female Delinquency in the Progressive Era." *Harvard Educational Review* 48 (1978): 65–94.

Schmitz, Neil. *Of Huck and Alice: Humorous Writing in American Literature.* Minneapolis: University of Minnesota Press, 1983.

Sedgwick, Catharine Maria. *Live and Let Live; or, Domestic Service Illustrated.* New York: Harper, 1840.

——. *Means and Ends; or, Self-Training.* Boston, 1839.

——. *Morals of Manners; or, Hints for Our Young People.* New York, 1846.

Sherwood, Mary. *The History of the Fairchild Family, Part One.* 1818. New York: Garland, 1977.

——. *The History of Susan Gray.* 1801. Houlston and Wright, 1869.

Showalter, Elaine. *Sister's Choice: Tradition and Change in American Women's Writing.* Oxford: Clarendon, 1991.

Sigourney, Lydia Howard [Huntley]. *Letters to Young Ladies.* Hartford, 1833.

Sklar, Kathryn Kish. *Catharine Beecher.* New Haven: Yale University Press, 1973.

Smith, Johanna M. " 'My Only Sister Now': Incest in *Mansfield Park.*" *Studies in the Novel* 19 (1987): 1–15.

Smith, Leroy W. "*Mansfield Park*: The Revolt of the 'Feminine Woman.'" In *Jane Austen in a Social Context*, ed. David Monaghan, 143–158. Totowa, N.J.: Barnes and Noble, 1981.

Smith-Rosenberg, Carroll. *Disorderly Conduct: Visions of Gender in Victorian America.* New York: Knopf, 1985.

Spacks, Patricia Meyer. "Muted Discord: Generational Conflict in Jane Austen." In *Jane Austen in a Social Context*, ed. David Monaghan, 1159–179. Totowa, N.J.: Barnes and Noble, 1981.

Spring, David. "Interpreters of Jane Austen's Social World: Literary Critics and Historians." In *Jane Austen: New Perspectives. Women and Literature* 3. ed. Janet Todd, 353–72. New York: Holmes and Meier, 1983.

Stallybrass, Peter. "Patriarchal Territories: The Body Enclosed." In *Rewriting the Renaissance: Discourses of Sexual Difference in Early Modern Europe*, ed. Margaret W. Ferguson, Maureen Quilligan, and Nancy J. Vickers, 123–142. Chicago: University of Chicago Press, 1986.

Staves, Susan. *Married Women's Separate Property in England, 1660–1833.* Cambridge: Harvard University Press, 1990.

——. "Money for Honor: Damages for Criminal Conversation." *Studies in Eighteenth-Century Culture* 11 (1982): 279–297.

Stowe, Harriet Beecher. *The Minister's Wooing.* 1859. Hartford: Stowe-Day Foundation, 1978.

Stuber, Florian. "Teaching *Pamela.*" In *Samuel Richardson: Tercentenary Essays*, ed. Peter Sabor and Margaret Anne Doody, 8–22. Cambridge: Cambridge University Press, 1989.

Sulloway, Alison. *Jane Austen and the Province of Womanhood.* Philadelphia: University of Pennsylvania Press, 1989.

Summerfield, Geoffrey. *Fantasy and Reason: Children's Literature in the Eighteenth Century.* Athens: University of Georgia Press, 1984.

Swinburne, Henry. *A Treatise of Spousals, or Matrimonial Contracts.* 1686. New York: Garland, 1985.

Tanner, Tony. *Jane Austen.* Cambridge: Harvard University Press, 1986.

Tenison, Thomas. *A Sermon Concerning Discretion in Giving Alms.* London, 1681.

Thomis, Malcolm I. *The Town Labourer and the Industrial Revolution.* London: B. T. Batsford, 1974.

Thompson, E. P. *The Making of the English Working Class.* 1963. New York: Vintage, 1966.

Trimmer, Sarah. *The Sunday Scholar's Manual.* Part One. London: T. Longman, G. G. J. and
    J. Robinson, and J. Johnson, 1788.

Tuthill, Louisa C. *The Young Lady's Home.* Philadelphia, 1848.

Twain, Mark. *The Adventures of Tom Sawyer.* 1876. New York: New American Library, 1980.

Utter, Robert Palfrey, and Gwendolyn Bridges Needham. *Pamela's Daughters.* New York:
    Macmillan, 1936.

Vallone, Lynne. "The Crisis of Education: Eighteenth-Century Novels for Girls." *Children's
    Literature Association Quarterly* 14 (1989): 63–67.

——. " 'A humble Spirit Under Correction': Tracts, Hymns, and the Ideology of Evangelical
    Fiction for Children, 1780–1820." *The Lion and the Unicorn* 15 (1991): 72–95.

——. "In the Image of Young America: Girls of the New Republic." *The Image of the Child:
    Proceedings of the 1991 International Conference of the Children's Literature Association.*
    Battle Creek, Mich., Children's Literature Association (1991): 300–306.

——. "Laughing With the Boys and Learning With the Girls: Humor in Nineteenth-Century
    American Juvenile Novels." *Children's Literature Association Quarterly* 15 (1990): 127–
    130.

Van Sant, Ann Jessie. *Eighteenth-Century Sensibility and the Novel: The Senses in Social Context.*
    Cambridge: Cambridge University Press, 1993.

Von Mücke, Dorothea E. *Virtue and the Veil of Illusion: Generic Innovation and the Pedagogical
    Project in Eighteenth-Century Literature.* Stanford: Stanford University Press, 1991.

Walker, Nancy A. *A Very Serious Thing: Women's Humor and American Culture.* Minneapolis:
    University of Minnesota Press, 1988.

——. "Wit, Sentimentality and the Image of Women in the Nineteenth Century." *American
    Studies* 22 (1981): 5–22.

Walkowitz, Judith R. *Prostitution and Victorian Society.* Cambridge: Cambridge University
    Press, 1980.

Ward, Barbara McLean. "Women's Property and Family Continuity in Eighteenth-Century
    Connecticut." In *Early American Probate Inventories: The Dublin Seminar for New England
    Folklife,* ed. Peter Benes, 74–85. Boston: Boston University Scholarly Publications, 1989.

Wearmouth, Robert F. *Some Working-Class Movements of the Nineteenth Century.* London:
    Epworth, 1963.

Webster, Jean. *Daddy-Long-Legs.* 1912. Mahwah, N.J.: Watermill, 1988.

——. *Dear Enemy.* 1915. Century Company, n.d.

Weigley, Emma S. "It Might Have Been Euthenics: The Lake Placid Conferences and the
    Home Economics Movement." *American Quarterly* 26 (1974): 79–96.

Weldon, Fay. *Letters to Alice on First Reading Jane Austen.* New York: Taplinger, 1985.

White, Eliza. *Gertrude; or, Thoughtlessness and Inattention Corrected.* London, 1823.

Wiesenfarth, Joseph. *The Errand of Form: An Assay of Jane Austen's Art.* New York: Fordham
    University Press, 1967.

Williams, Anna. "Verses to Mr. Richardson on his History of Sir Charles Grandison." *Gen-
    tleman's Magazine* 24 (Jan. 1754): 40.

Willis, Lesley. "Religion in Jane Austen's *Mansfield Park.*" *English Studies in Canada* 13 (1987):
    65–78.

Wilson, Otto. *Fifty Years' Work With Girls, 1883–1933*. 1933. New York: Arno, 1974.

Wiltshire, John. *Jane Austen and the Body: "The Picture of Health."* Cambridge: Cambridge University Press, 1992.

Wollstonecraft, Mary. *Original Stories from Real Life*. 1788. New York: Garland, 1977.

——. *Thoughts on the Education of Daughters with Reflections on Female Conduct, in the More Important Duties of Life*. 1787. New York: Garland, 1974.

Woolley, Hannah. *The Gentlewomans Companion*. London, 1675.

——. *The Ladies Directory*. 1662. London, 1670.

——. *New and Excellent Experiments and Secrets in the Art of Angling*. London, 1675.

Yeazell, Ruth Bernard. *Fictions of Modesty: Women and Courtship in the English Novel*. Chicago: University of Chicago Press, 1991.

The Young Girl's Book of Healthful Amusements and Exercises. New York, 1840.

Zomchick, John P. *Family and the Law in Eighteenth-Century Fiction: The Public Conscience in the Private Sphere*. Cambridge: Cambridge University Press, 1993.

Index